ALEXANDER THE GREAT'S CAMPAIGNS

A guide to Ancient political and military wargaming

Companion volumes

Napoleon's Campaigns in Miniature
A wargamers' guide to the Napoleonic Wars
1796–1815
by Bruce Quarrie

Air Battles in Miniature
A wargamers' guide to aerial combat 1939–1945
by Mike Spick

In preparation

The Crusades in Miniature
A wargamers' guide to Crusading warfare 1096–1291
by Ian Heath

ALEXANDER THE GREAT'S CAMPAIGNS

A guide to Ancient political and military wargaming

PHIL BARKER

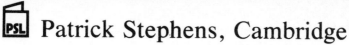 Patrick Stephens, Cambridge

© Phil Barker 1979

Dedication: To Tony Bath, Master
of Hyboria, who started the whole thing off.

First published 1979

British Library Cataloguing in Publication Data

Barker, Phil
    Alexander the Great's campaigns.
    1. War games 2. Macedonia – Armed forces
    3. Macedonia – History – To 168 B.C.
    I. Title
    938'.07   DF234.2

ISBN 0 85059 325 5

Photoset in 10 on 11pt Times Roman. Printed in
Great Britain on Vol 18 90 gsm Supreme Book Wove
by The Garden City Press Limited, Letchworth, and
bound by J. M. Dent & Sons (Letchworth) Limited,
for the publishers, Patrick Stephens Limited, Bar
Hill, Cambridge, CB3 8EL, England.

Contents

Introduction

The story of Alexander the Great is of a young man who took control of what its neighbours thought of as a backward nation, used an army of a radically new kind invented by his father to impose unity on the highly civilised but bitterly quarrelling states of Greece, and then turned east as the champion of civilisation.

His strategic and tactical genius quickly crushed the huge Persian empire, the most feared military power of his day. Continuing east, he imposed his rule on nations beyond the boundaries of the then-known world, battling against armies relying on huge and terrifying unknown beasts.

Returning, he consolidated politically with a new theory of government based on equality of races, only to be struck down by disease while still in his youth as he turned west to complete the conquest of the world. His talented subordinates then fought each other to a draw and split the short-lived empire between the survivors.

This story has been told many times. This retelling differs by treating it as a story that could have had a number of different endings, analysing the personalities and military, geographical, economic and political factors in such a way that the reader and his friends can play it over again as a wargames campaign, each taking the part of a historical character and doing his utmost within the constraints to achieve that character's aims.

Wargames campaigning grew out of the more usual table game played with miniature soldier figures and model terrain according to a set of formal rules. Some players wished to bring the strategic aspects in as well as the purely tactical ones, and evolved a system of map movement which could be transferred to the table when the armies came into contact. Battles might then be fought with unequal forces, attacks made by detachments on flanks or rear, and relentlessness in pursuit or skill in extricating an overmatched army to fight again on better terms be rewarded.

The next factors to be incorporated were supply and weather, then the raising and paying of troops. In periods such as Moderns and Napoleonic, wargames campaigning techniques stopped there. Not so for Ancient wargamers, who had to take into account economic and political factors to an enormously greater extent. In the fully developed Ancient campaign such as Tony Bath's famous Hyborian epic or Bruce Douglas' Known World campaign, an umpire sits like an evilly gloating spider at the centre of a web of postal communication, doling out true, questionable or false information to possibly a dozen or so players who struggle with all the problems facing independent rulers or over-ambitious subordinates.

Intrigue and double dealing tend to be the order of the day, but an occasional honest character creates confusion because no one credits it. There are thus marked parallels with the rise of Macedonia under Alexander and his father Philip, making its story an excellent introduction to Ancient campaigning. The first two chapters set the scene with brief accounts of Macedonian expansion, from the accession of his father to Alexander's birth, and from then until he inherited his murdered father's throne. This is an essential part of the story. Without it, Alexander appears a mere rash cavalryman charging at the head of greatly superior troops against ill-led demoralised hordes to inevitable victory. With it he becomes a cool and calculating balancer of odds, allocating exactly the right proportion of his resources to controlling rebellious allies, consolidating gains and conquering new ones, and keeping his promises.

Events are described from a Macedonian viewpoint. The geography of new areas is therefore described as it starts to influence Macedonian plans. Similarly, the coverage given to foreign politics and wars varies according to their impact on Macedonia. I have sometimes simplified the facts, and there is much conjecture, not always identified as such. Much of the information has either been lost by the passage of nearly 23 centuries or is known only to those more specialised than I. To these scholars I apologise in advance. Other readers wishing to know more of a fascinating era are referred to the bibliography at the back. This is by no means an exhaustive list, I read more myself, but these are the books I personally found most useful.

Most of the names of people and places are quoted in their Greek form, rather than the latinised versions that rather strangely have become usual, and are pronounced exactly as they are spelled. The few exceptions are where I have had to use modern forms to avoid confusion. One example is that our hero is referred to as Alexander, son of Philip, of Macedonia, not as Alexandros Philippou of Makedonia. In some other cases, well-known place names are shown on maps in their modern versions with the Greek name in brackets.

Chapter 1

Macedonia and its neighbours before Alexander

Alexander, to be known to future generations as 'the Great', was born in 356 BC, son of Philip, the King of Macedonia, and his wife Olympias, an Epirot princess.

Macedonia proper consisted of a fairly fertile plain spreading inward from the eastern shore of the Aegean Sea and bounded on all other sides by foothills rising into high mountains. The lowlands grew corn better than most of Greece and provided adequate winter grazing for animals, making the country self-sufficient in food. The highlands included upland valleys in which corn could be grown, forests providing good timber and such game as deer, wild boar, wolves and bear, and grassy slopes on which sheep could graze in summer. However, figs and olives did not grow well, and had to be imported from the south. The climate was warmer than the rest of Greece in summer and colder in winter.

The population split into two distinct groups. The men who farmed the lowlands were descended from immigrants who had followed an exiled king from the south long before. They spoke Greek, although with a strange harsh accent ridiculed by Athenians and other southerners, and had a largely Greek culture. One Greek cultural trait that they did not stress was democracy. The king was absolute monarch in the plains, although with a few constraints reminiscent of the Scottish highlands, being regarded more as a family head whom everyone had both a legal and moral obligation to obey than as the more normal kind of ruler. One of these constraints was that the king could not in theory execute anyone without obtaining the consent of the army, although in practice a strong ruler could often get away with it. Another was that the eldest son did not necessarily succeed to the throne. Instead, a new king had to be elected by the army, although the closest descendant was usually favoured unless barred by extreme youth or disability.

The king had no such authority in the highlands. These split into a number of tribal areas, the four most important being Lynkos, Orestis, Elimiotis and Pelagonia. These each had their own ruling family, and the most that they were prepared to concede to the king was a general overlordship. Sometimes they would not even concede that, and military action would then have to be taken to reduce them to a proper frame of mind, or the matter tactfully shelved until the king felt strong enough. Their culture had much in common with the neighbouring Illyrians, and their dialect mingled so many barbarous words with the Greek as to be largely unintelligible to southerners.

There were, however, a number of unifying factors. The highlanders needed lowland winter grazing for their sheep if they were to get the most value from their summer pastures. Conversely, the lowlanders needed free passage through the mountains if they were to trade with the neighbouring countries. Both were big strong peoples who got plenty to eat including meat and tended to look down on southerners such as the Athenians who were often under-nourished and rarely saw meat. The kings of Macedonia had also done their bit by taking wives from the upland nobility, luckily being allowed several at a time, and had appointed highland nobility to join their Companions. This had helped to spread Greek culture and a higher standard of living through most of the tribes, although few if any gave up hunting and heavy drinking for philosophy.

Traditionally, the Macedonian army consisted of all the able-bodied free lowland males of suitable age. All land was held in fief from the king and carried with it the obligation of military service and the privilege of voting in the assembly. It did not necessarily pass from father to son, so recruits from the highlands or from outside Macedonia could join the army and be given land if the king wished. The units were organised on a territorial basis, all the men whose land was in the same area serving together. If a vote had to be taken while on active service, those soldiers present with the king were taken to represent the whole army and their decision bound it.

Before Philip's day, the mass of the army fought as infantry. It was lighter in equipment than that of the southern Greeks, approximating more to the peltast than the hoplite type, and was not very efficient, although it could cope with raiding hillmen. Approximately 800 of the richer men fought as cavalry and enjoyed a high military reputation as well as increased status. They provided the army's main striking power. The 100 richest or otherwise most prominent of these provided an advisory council for the king. At the top of the tree came upwards of a dozen Guards of the Person. These were selected for ability, although if not already rich they rapidly became so, and might even be foreigners. They outranked all but the king, so could be employed as his deputies. Whether there was a lower semi-free class of serfs which looked after the land when the military tenants were on duty is disputed by historians. An alternative explanation would involve the land being granted to a family, only one member of which had to serve.

Macedonian politics tended to be eventful and her kings rarely died in their beds. Alexander's father Philip had followed two elder brothers to the throne. The eldest had overreached himself against the Thebans, was forced into becoming their ally, and had to provide his 13- or 14-year-old brother Philip as a hostage. This did not improve his internal prestige, and a year later he was assassinated by his brother-in-law, who then ruled as regent for the middle brother. He tried to assert Macedonian independence, was smartly put in his place by the Thebans, and had to provide fresh hostages in place of the old ones who had been chosen to influence the previous ruler. Philip came home after two years absorbing the new Theban military methods. Brother-in-law had now lost prestige, and was promptly slain by Philip's next brother. He now ruled for five years before dying in battle against invading Dardanians. The surviving soldiers rejected his infant son and elected Philip king at the age of 22 in 359 BC.

Not only had the invading Dardanians destroyed a third of the Macedonian army, occupied Lynkos and Pelagonia, and now had the obvious intention of taking more, but also two pretenders to the throne had appeared, one in the south-east backed by Athens and one in the north-east backed by a Thracian king and Chalkidike, while the wild Paionian tribes of the north were taking advantage of the confusion by raiding south. Philip had to act quickly. He started off by accepting Dardanian suzerainty, marrying one of their princesses and promising a heavy annual tribute. What Athens wanted was a free hand in conquering the independent city of Amphipolis, presently supported by Macedonia. He started negotiations and, while the Athenians were making up their minds whether Philip or the pretender were offering the most, he force-marched to attack the pretender and disposed of him. Chalkidike tried to organise joint action with Athens but, as the two were traditional enemies, failed to convince them. Bribes and presents sent the Paionian raiders home, and a bigger bribe to the Thracian king got the other pretender's throat cut.

Philip's position was now relatively good. He had won his first battle, raising his army's morale; all the foreign and internal threats were dealt with for the moment; Athens with her naval power was an ally of a sort; and he had earned an enviable reputation as a diplomat. He now had time for the army reforms he had been planning. These took several years to complete, each increase in fighting power in turn bringing more resources under his control to be used in increasing it still further. The final version of the army is described in detail later. For the moment, it is enough to say that his main innovations were to convert most of the infantry from peltast type to close fighting troops armed with a much longer spear than that usual at the time; to subject both infantry and cavalry to rigorous drill and discipline; and to organise a siege train capable of capturing a walled city without waiting for starvation.

His success in persuading the Macedonians to accept these changes illus-trates another facet of his character. Not only was he an energetic and fast-moving general, a devious and cunning plotter and an innovator capable of rethinking the entire military system of his day, but a man equally at home in any company, whether fencing verbally with Athenian politicians, talking to philosophers, carousing with Macedonian aristocracy or cracking jokes with the rank and file. His contemporaries considered his main faults to be excessive indulgence in women and wine, although not on campaign. Demosthenes, the Athenian politician, accused him of a lot more, but he is a far from unpre-judiced witness. His most impressive virtue to me was his ability to forgive enemies, a quality the Athenians should have been especially grateful for, but were not.

The first test of the new army came against the Paionian tribes to the north, probably because they were the easiest target. Paionia was a buffer state between Macedonia and Illyria, only dangerous when an unusually competent chief fought his way to the top and managed to establish control over a majority of the tribes. One such had just died, and Philip took advantage of the opportunity this provided for a short and decisive expedition north against the disunited tribes. These were forced to swear allegiance, to agree formal bound-aries, and to promise to send a small number of warriors to serve Macedonia as javelin-armed light cavalry if required.

Next came the Dardanians. The Dardanoi were one of the three most powerful tribes of Illyria, the others being the Autariatai and Adiaioi. Illyria bordered directly on Macedonia to the west and lay on the far side of the Paioians to the north. Its climate was much like that of Macedonia, and its main

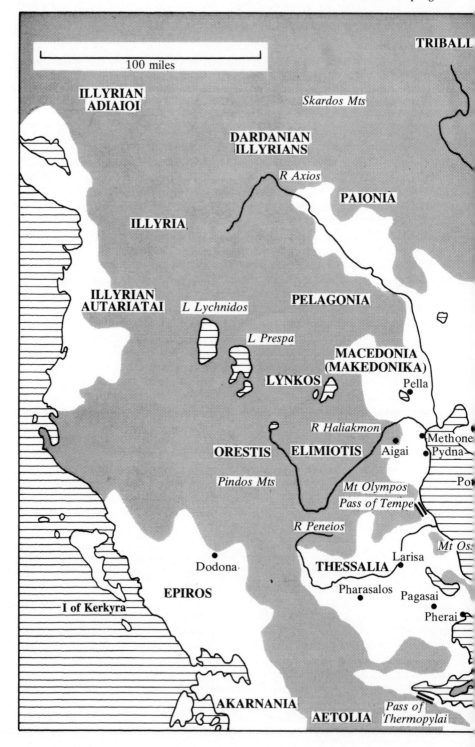

Macedonia and its neighbours

wealth derived from the large plains on the Adriatic coast. These were rather swampy, but provided good grazing for cattle, though poor corn land. Dardanian influence and territory had greatly increased in the last 40 years under their current king, now an old man of 90, and even the great Dionysios of Syracuse had been sufficiently impressed to offer them an alliance.

On hearing that Philip was mustering troops, had put away his Dardanian wife and was not sending the tribute, the Dardanian king, rather than fight a war, offered a compromise by which he should keep the captured territory but would forget about the tribute. This was not acceptable to Philip, a pitched battle was fought in which 10,000 Macedonian infantry and 600 cavalry largely destroyed a similar-strength army of Dardanians, and the conquered upland provinces of Macedonia were recovered. Philip immediately set about reorganising them to bring them into line with the lowlands and thus contribute to his new-style army. The hill chieftains were in no position to argue, having just been rescued from foreign occupation by a predominantly lowland army, and they gave up much of their independence in return for position and influence at court and high rank in the army. The most useful acquisition was Parmenion of Pelagonia, who was to become Philip's best general.

By 358 BC, the Macedonian army had grown sufficiently to allow it to be simultaneously used on two fronts. The Illyrians and Paionians were in no state to cause trouble to the west and north, and the death of the Thracian king meant that the north-eastern frontier was temporarily safe while the Thracian tribes fought for supremacy. Chalkidike to the east was still hostile but weakened by loss of the silver mines of Damastion, which were first cut off when Philip established control over the highlands, then quietly taken over by him. It was now time for Philip to look south.

Directly south of Macedonia lay Thessalia. This was a land of extensive plains surrounded by a ring of mountains, replaced on the east by a rocky and inhospitable coast. The climate was more extreme than that of Macedonia, being both hotter and dryer in summer and colder in winter. Thessalia was more than self-sufficient in corn, and this could act to the inhabitants' disadvantage by tempting invaders to winter their armies there, but her main wealth lay in cattle, sheep and horses. Most power resided in the hands of a feudal baronage ruling a population of peasants much more prosperous than those of most of Greece. The most important of the baronial families were those of Larissa, Pherai, Krannon, Pharsalos and Pelinna. Although most of these had a city as their headquarters, there was some friction with the city dwellers. Thessalia's main military strength lay in its superb cavalry, of which it could raise 2,000 for a foreign war, 4,000 together with 10,000 hoplites for home defence.

The southern Greeks thought of Thessalia as a bulwark against northern barbarians, rather than a genuine Greek state, and a study of its communications helps to explain why. There were four routes north to Macedonia, three of which were through very difficult mountainous terrain and blocked by snow during the winter. The other was easier and open all year round, but came through the easily defended Tempe gorge, so was avoided by invaders. There were two routes west through the mountains to Epiros, again difficult in summer and impassable in winter. A single route led south. This was not especially difficult, but led through sparsely populated mountainous country in which foraging was difficult.

Until this time, Pherai had controlled Thessalia. Now Larissa was disputing this, and Philip, while still involved with the Dardanians, weakened his main army by sending a contingent to assist the ruling family and took a wife from it. As his Thessalian in-laws controlled the Tempe pass, this gave him an easy all-year-round route into Thessalia to use whenever he wished.

The following year, in 357 BC, he acquired yet another wife, Olympias, daughter of the king of Epiros. They had met at a religious festival and it was at first a love match, but not without advantage for the two countries.

Epiros lay south of the Dardanians, south-west of Macedonia and west of Thessalia. It was a land of mountains and densely populated narrow valleys. It had more snow than Macedonia but was not as cold. The snow cut it off from both Macedonia and Thessalia each winter, and its rivers were dangerous obstacles in the spring when it melted. Corn did not grow well, but the land provided the best cattle in Europe, big horses, and upland sheep. Much of the land was covered with oak forest, but access from timber-starved Greece was too difficult for much of an export trade. Epiros exported cheese, olive oil and the great white Molossian dogs. Greece did not want these, routes to Thessalia were difficult, so the main customers were Macedonia and Illyria.

The people of Epiros were largely Illyrian in race, but had acquired a thin veneer of hellenic civilisation from Greek coastal colonies. They were good builders in stone and had walled towns. They could put 15,000 fighting men into the field, possibly 20,000 for home defence, but had suffered from Dardanian expansion. The reason is a little hard to make out, as the Dardanians only produced 10,000 men to fight Philip. The most likely explanation is that Philip caught the Dardanian king before he had all his troops assembled. The Epirotes do not seem to have used the hoplite system, and were probably armed much like their opponents, mainly with javelin and shield, but with a sprinkling of archers.

Meanwhile, Athens was in trouble. Her big problem had always been that she had a large population which could not be fed on home-grown corn, and depended on trading manufactured goods, wine and olive oil for it. The only sources that could supply on the huge scale required were Sicily, Egypt, Thrace and the north Black Sea coast. This obviously left the Athenians in a vulnerable position, and they were always tempted to bring the sources under their political control in order to safeguard them. They had already failed disastrously in attempts to conquer Sicily and Egypt, and there was no prospect of success for second attempts. Sicily was now divided between two far more powerful states than Athens, to wit Syracuse and Carthage, while Egypt was usually in the hands of the richest and most powerful nation of the world, the Persian Empire. Athens therefore decided to try and acquire as much as possible of the coasts lining her sea route to the remaining sources.

Unfortunately, Athens had lost much of her former power. The shift in farming to larger land holdings worked by slaves had made the rich richer and the poor poorer. Fewer men could now afford hoplite equipment, and she was hard put to get 10,000 hoplites into the field. Those men with a taste for military life who could not afford the equipment went abroad as mercenaries in very large numbers. At sea, where Athens had formerly maintained a fleet of 300 ships, she now had to strain to produce 120, while 60 was a much more normal-sized expedition.

If not strong enough for outright conquest, Athens had to acquire friends.

She had therefore organised a league of maritime states including most of the Aegean Sea's islands and many of the coastal city states of Greece, Thrace and Asia Minor. As by far the largest state of the league, she would naturally be its leader, and could steer it tactfully the way she wished it to go. Unfortunately, Athenians were not tactful, and started treating their allies as if they were subjects. With her finances overstretched by her military and naval efforts and bribes to the three kings currently dividing Thrace among them, she was faced by the revolt of three of her most important allies. It was imperative that she reduce them to obedience and also reconstruct the league in such a way that the allies should pay a larger share of the costs. She had no attention or resources to spare for elsewhere.

The price Philip had earlier paid for Athenian friendship had been the withdrawal of Macedonian guarantees of independence for Amphipolis. In spite of this, Athens had failed to take that city, and Philip saw now no reason why he should not try. After all, he was not now sworn to defend it! Realising his intentions, the Amphipolitans sent a delegation to ask Athens for help. Athens could provide none, and Amphipolis fell to the new Macedonian siege engines. Athens declared war, but could do even less, having just lost a battle to her revolting allies.

Philip now set to work to woo Chalkidike. His moderate treatment of captured Amphipolis, dislike and fear of Athens, and promise of commercial advantages within the new enlarged Macedonia, together with the return of some of the profits from the former Chalkidikan silver mines at Damastion, decided the issue. Chalkidike was now his ally, he had good ports at his disposal for the first time, and more important, he had deprived Athens of the Chalkidikan ports that would have enabled her sea power to be brought to bear on him.

An even better opportunity now came to Philip. One of the three Thracian kings allied to Athens, taking advantage of Athenian interest being concentrated elsewhere, moved into one of the other kings' territory and threatened mines established there by Greek colonists. Philip moved quickly to protect them, and combined the grateful colonists with Macedonian settlers to populate a new strongly fortified city which he named Philippoi. His share of the gold and silver extracted came to more than 1,000 talents a year, more than the entire revenue of the Athenian empire at its greatest extent. From now on, he had another weapon.

The deprived Thracian did not take this lying down, however. He formed an alliance with the chief of one of the Illyrian tribes which had benefited from Philip's curbing of the Dardanians. They were attacked before they could concentrate and forced to submit. The news of Parmenion's victory over the Illyrians, that Philip's horse had won at the Olympics, and that Alexander had been born to Olympias arrived on the same day. Although Philip had had plenty of wives, his only previous son had been born mentally subnormal, so the new boy would be Philip's heir. The omens were considered excellent.

Chapter 2

Macedonian expansion during Alexander's boyhood

After Alexander's birth, his mother Olympias was in a very strong position as both mother of the heir apparent and closely connected with foreign royalty. However, her relations with Philip quickly became strained. She objected to his continuing acquisition of fresh wives and more casual woman-chasing, and expected a bigger say in policy than traditional Macedonians or educated Greeks were willing to concede to a female. He objected to her temper, her enthusiasm for one of the wilder religious cults, and possibly to such uncouth habits as practising magic and taking sacred snakes to bed with her.

Philip may have worried about her possessiveness and growing dislike of her husband turning his heir into a cissy and prejudicing him against his father. At any event, Alexander was removed from her care at the age of seven and given a number of teachers supervised by a Spartan-influenced tutor. He was allowed no luxuries, given rough clothes thinner than the climate required, insufficient blankets and less food than he really needed. This regime may have contributed to his smallness as an adult, but it also made him at least the equal of his soldiers at bearing hardship.

Discipline was harsh, but he seems to have had teachers who could interest him in at least some subjects. We know that he acquired a lasting passion for literature, especially Homer's epic of the Trojan war, played a musical instrument well enough to disgust his father, and became a dedicated athlete.

When he was 13, his father persuaded the philosopher Aristotle to come and take over as tutor. Rather than teach the prince alone, Aristotle set up a school in which many of the sons of the nobility were enrolled. These first became Alexander's friends, then fellow-soldiers, then his generals, and finally some of them rivals or successors. Philosophy in those days did not confine itself to ethics, and Aristotle is likely to have taught the theory of government, geography, natural history and, above all, how to analyse a problem and argue logically.

Events were not standing still while Alexander grew up. By 355 BC, Athens had lost the war with her allies, the last straw being a threat of Persian intervention. She retained only the large island of Euboia, some smaller islands in the north Aegean and a few towns on the coast of Thrace. Her prestige had suffered disastrously and her financial state was even worse.

Attention now moved to Thebes. Simplifying the geography slightly, the main route south from Thessaly turned east to follow the coast through the famous pass of Thermopylai into the small state of Lokris. This pass was better for delay than for permanent defence, as there were several hill paths around it, and it was difficult to defend them all adequately without more troops than were usually available. Lokris was a long, thin, poorly populated coastal plain and the route passed down its length to its eastern end, then entering Boeotia, the territory ruled by Thebes, from the north.

West of Boeotia and south of Lokris, and separated from both by mountains, was the small state of Phokis, chiefly important for the great religious centre of Delphi. The plains of Lokris could be entered by two routes splitting off the main route from Thessalia north of Thermopylai, and by one route from Boeotia.

West of Phokis and south of Thessalia was Aitolia, and further west still and south of Epiros lay Akarnania. Both of these nations were largely mountainous, and their inhabitants mainly fought as javelin- or sling-armed skirmishers instead of in the close order hoplite style of most of southern Greece.

South and south-west of Boeotia lay the territory of Athens. South-east lay that of Corinth, controlling the narrow peninsula leading to the other half of Greece, of which the most famous state was that of the warrior Spartans. Across a narrow strait to the north-east of Boeotia was the large island of Euboia, stretching from Thessalia to Athenian territory, and presently controlled by Athens.

Thebes had until recently been the dominant military power of Greece, thanks to two inspired generals and their innovations. Thebans tended to be full-blooded, boisterous, domineering and aristocratic. They despised trade, had little interest in culture or art, and emphasised military training. They were not interested in hellenic unity or in the glory of leading the nations of Greece, but only in the advantages their pre-eminence brought them in robbing and bullying their neighbours. The other cities of Boeotia were forced to follow them in war, but were likely to change sides at the drop of a hat if it ever seemed safe to do so.

None of these characteristics was calculated to endear Thebes to the Athenians. While in favour of bullying the weak, they preferred to do it themselves, and the Thebans' pretensions, lack of culture and oligarchic government did not help. The contrast between the fertile Boeotian plain providing corn, meat, wine and horses in abundance with the skimpy and infertile Athenian farmland must have been another motive for jealousy. Small wonder that they disliked each other even more than was usual for neighbouring states in Greece.

Oligarchy, incidentally, means rule by a few. Thebes had a moderate oligarchy in which anyone paying taxes and able to afford hoplite armour could vote. Wars were therefore declared by the people that had to fight them and pay for them. Athens, by way of contrast, had a democratic government in which everyone voted, usually as the most persuasive, rather than capable, politician told them. The lower classes, safe in the knowledge that they would not have to pay or fight, but might benefit from exploiting other nations, showed a distressing tendency to take a hard imperialist line. The only counteracting force was that any attempt to increase military preparations by eliminating the free corn issue to the poorest class was immediately thrown out by the assembly, and its introducer stood a good chance of being impeached.

The present trouble arose from a Theban attempt to bully the Phokians. In 356 BC they had influenced an international religious council, meeting at the shrine of Apollo at Delphi and called the Amphiktomy of Delphi, to threaten

Phokis with a holy war unless certain members of the ruling group, hostile to Thebes, paid fines the council had previously levied against them. At the same time, the council censured certain other states that owed money to the shrine, notably Sparta. These were both mistakes. Instead of exiling its culprits as Thebes had intended, Phokis, provoked, elected one of them commander-in-chief. Backed by Sparta with promises of mercenaries, he seized the shrine and used its vast accumulated treasures to hire all the mercenaries he needed at half as much again as the going rate.

Thebes and Philip's Thessalian friends declared a holy war against Phokis. Phokis was joined first by Sparta, then by Athens after the citizens had decided that they hated Thebes even more than they did Sparta. Lokris came in on behalf of the Amphiktomy. The Persian king decided that anyone opposed to Athens could not be entirely wrong, so backed Thebes with a little of his huge pile of gold. Phokis now invested some of the temple loot in stirring up the Thessalian opposition. With Thessalia occupied with a brisk civil war, the Phokians took the offensive in 354 BC against Thebes, winning a couple of good battles before retreating once more back over their borders.

All this time, Philip had been working steadily at improving his position in Thrace. In his nibbling away at the Athenian-controlled Greek cities on the Thracian coast, he had to go a little carefully, in case he inspired the Thracian kings who regarded themselves as the cities' protectors to combine against him. So long as they saw him as a less dangerous opponent than each other, this was unlikely. A Greek once said that Thrace would have conquered the world – if the Thracians had the time to spare from fighting each other. The remains of the Athenian navy interfered as much as it could, which was not much, and Athenian diplomats tried to intrigue with Macedonia's other neighbours.

Philip could not ignore what was happening in Thessalia, so in 353 BC he marched south, quelled the opposition party, and got himself elected leader, or Archon, of the Thessalian league. He then moved against Phokis, but was beaten in a rather remarkable ambush which saw one of the very few massed uses of artillery in open battle of the ancient world. He withdrew, came back in 352 BC, chased the Phokians out of Thessalia, but was blocked from going further when their Athenian and Spartan allies came up in time to help them hold Thermopylai. Having at least sorted out Thessalia, he went back to Thrace.

He was interrupted again by a short war with Epiros which Athens managed to provoke in 350 BC. This ended relatively quickly with several Epirot provinces and their king's heir in Philip's hands, and a marked disinclination on the part of Epiros to tangle with Macedon again.

Shortly afterwards, he was again in a position to move south. By now, everyone was thoroughly sick of the Phokian war. Athens made a separate peace, leaving her ally in the lurch, while Sparta's help had mostly been of the 'Hit him and I'll hold your coat' type. It is fair to say, however, that Athens' help would have been much the same if her interests had not been threatened by Thebes' ally Philip. In 346 BC, her stolen gold gone, mostly spent on Athenian and Spartan mercenaries, Phokis collapsed.

Thebes and Lokris wished to destroy Phokis utterly, killing or enslaving all the inhabitants. Philip would not have this, and the Phokians were instead condemned to repay 10,000 talents to the shrine at 60 talents a year, starting in 343. Until this was paid off, they were to be deprived of all horses, weapons and fortifications. Sixty talents was roughly the amount needed to pay 1,000 soldiers for a complete year, so the exhaustion of Phokis can be seen from the fact that the sum had to be first halved in 341 BC, then reduced to 10 talents a few years later. While the hapless Phokians were saddled with this huge debt for centuries to come, their Athenian and Spartan allies, who had acquired much of the stolen temple gold in payment for their services, were not penalised. Small wonder if the Phokians began to think better of Philip, who had mitigated their punishment and might do so again, than of such friends.

With the south relatively peaceful, Philip could look again to the north and east, this time even further than Thrace, to Asia Minor. This was part of the Persian empire, specifically the provinces of Paphlagonia, Bithynia, Mysia, Lydia, Karia, Lykia, Kilikia, Phrygia and Kappadokia, ruled by governors called satraps. Their rural population was mainly Asiatic, but they were dotted with Greek city colonies, especially on the western coasts. To free these Greek cities from Persian rule had long been a dream of Greek politicians, and to do so would be a great source of prestige. There was also wealth to be gained, especially from the Persian king's local treasury at Sardis in Lydia.

There had been several abortive attempts to do something, the last being in 353 BC, when Thebes sent 5,000 men to assist Artabazos, the revolting satrap of Phrygia. This had failed when Artabazos came to suspect that the Persian king had got at the Thebans and they went home, either in disgust or clutching bags of Persian gold. Artabazos had been forced to flee and take refuge at Philip's court, where he tried to convince him of the opportunities offered. By the end of the Phokian war, he had succeeded.

Rather than trust to sea communications which would be at the mercy of the much larger Persian and Athenian navies, Philip set out to provide himself with a land route through Thrace and up to the narrow straits at the entrance to the Black Sea. His allies, the cities of Perinthos and Byzantion, already controlled the near side of the straits, and the small Macedonian navy could be based on them to provide adequate protection for a short crossing in such narrow waters. The far side was equally friendly, although without such excellent bases. He now had to complete the pacification of Thrace and to make some arrangement with the Skythians to the north who might otherwise disturb his communications by raiding into the settled parts.

Feeling in Athens, ably fanned by a smooth-talking and mendacious politician named Demosthenes, was now swinging against the treaty with Macedonia. One of the negotiators fled the city. Another was tried but found innocent by a narrow vote, the evidence against him being obviously false. Apart from unease at the thought that control of the Black Sea straits gave not only the power to cross into Asia but also the capability to starve Athens, the Athenians did not like the increasing friendship shown to Philip in the Peloponnesos, where the other states looked to him as a counterpoise to Sparta, nor that shown by the Euboian cities that Athens had managed to disenchant by overbearing behaviour in 349 BC. Philip's offers to submit to arbitration on matters in dispute, of co-operation in putting down the piracy that had greatly increased during the wars, and of commercial and legal treaties, although honestly meant, were all interpreted as disguised threats.

When in 343 BC Philip led a bloodless campaign into Epiros, dislodged the regent, and put the heir on the throne (a popular move with the Epirotes), Athens feared an attempt to expand south, sent troops to assist Akarnania should this occur, and started a diplomatic offensive. This succeeded in detaching Philip's friends in the Peloponnesos, who preferred him as a distant friend, but failed in attempts to start trouble in Thessalia and Illyria.

This did not distract Philip from Thrace. He set off again in 342 BC, leaving Antipatros as regent in Macedonia. Parmenion was left with another army in Thessalia, with orders to give minor help to the friendly Euboian cities, but not to threaten those still loyal to Athens which protected her corn route as it passed through the more sheltered waters between the island and the mainland. Steady progress was made in Thrace, both by arms and by diplomacy. Philip married yet another local princess, and planted colonies among the conquered Thracians to hold them down and help civilise them.

Another complication now appeared. In 341 BC, Athenian colonies in the Chersonesos, by the strait on the way to the Black Sea, started to lean on their barbarian neighbours. These appealed to Philip for help. Being short of troops and not wanting to offend Athens, he instead offered arbitration. Seeing this as weakness, the colonists leaned more heavily than ever, raided into Thrace, interfered with Macedonian shipping, and kidnapped and imprisoned Macedonian diplomats on neutral territory. Demosthenes visited Byzantion and other Athenian politicians went to Rhodes and other islands, seeking to win them over. The remaining Athenian allies in Euboia were reinforced, won some territory, and sent squadrons to raid Macedonian shipping and coastal towns.

Refusing to be distracted, Philip sent back to Macedonia for heavy reinforcements, and pressed on with the Thracian war. By the end of the year, the Thracian kings were finally defeated and only a little mopping up remained for the following year. Thracians were to pay tax to the Macedonian king, open their territories to trade and mining, and to furnish troops when required.

Worried in case they were to be next on the schedule of conquest, Philip's allies, Perinthos and Byzantion, turned against him. He laid siege to Perinthos, the worst defended, but it was supported by Byzantine and Athenian naval squadrons and Persian gold, mercenaries and food. Unsuccessful here, he marched to Byzantion and summoned it, without success.

Deciding he would rather have Athens as an open enemy, Philip arranged for his small navy to seize the Athenian grain fleet while its protecting squadron was aiding the besieged, capturing 180 Athenian ships worth 700 talents with their cargo. Infuriated, the Athenian assembly declared war. Seeing that the Athenians were now fully committed against Macedonia, the Persian king withdrew his support. The sieges dragged on through the winter, to be ended by a compromise peace, the two cities apparently resuming their position as Philip's allies. This may have been because the Athenians could not spare food for them, while the Persians were no longer interested.

His relative failure during the two sieges cost Philip much prestige and encouraged incursions into his territory. Alexander fought and won his first battle against one such. Philip attacked the Skythians before they could do as much to him, heavily defeating them, but was ambushed, wounded and lost much of his loot on the way back.

Trouble now sprang up again in the south. After a series of charges and countercharges of impiety, Amphiktomy had ruled against the Lokrian city of Amphissa, and tried to collect the fine. Athens and Thebes had abstained and refused to help. Philip was accordingly called upon. Neither Athens nor Thebes wanted a Macedonian army back in the south, the former because they were at war with Macedonia, the latter on the principle that 'nobody kicks my dog but me'. Thebes seized Thermopylai, but Philip moved by an alternative route and arrived in Phokis.

He was now faced by a particularly unholy alliance of the Athenians, his avowed enemies, and the Thebans, his official allies! He offered to let Thebes stand neutral. Demosthenes, telling the Athenians that Philip was there with the intent of wiping them out for good, prevailed on them to give exceptional terms of alliance to their Theban traditional enemies, the most startling of which was an offer to help them conquer Athens' own Boeotian allies. Thebes accepted, and the two armies marched to fight Philip. He manoeuvred them out of their initial position, and the two sides finally met at Chaironeia in 338 BC.

On one flank, Philip with the hypaspists and light troops allowed himself to be pushed back by the Athenians, exposing the flank of the Thebans grimly battling against the phalanx to a charge by Alexander and the cavalry. The ill-assorted allies went down to crushing defeat, and Macedonia controlled Greece.

Athens received generous terms, merely being deprived of the remnants of her island empire. Thebes, as a treacherous ally, suffered worst, being garrisoned by Macedonian troops and forced to receive back political exiles to form a pro-Macedonian government. The battle had political repercussions all over southern Greece. Akarnania and Euboia removed their anti-Macedonian governments without waiting to be told, and Corinth allowed free passage for Philip into the Peloponnesos, where he organised the lesser states into a proper counterpoise to Sparta.

He now called representatives of all the states of Greece to a meeting at Corinth. All but Sparta came, and they set up an organisation called the League of Common Peace. The member states were to have votes in the league council proportionate to their military strength. The council was empowered to adjudicate disputes between members, and an oath was sworn not to use either direct military action or support subversion against fellow-members. Finally, it declared war on Persia, and elected Philip its Hegemon, or commander-in-chief.

It was just after this that Philip married his seventh and last wife, the daughter of a prominent nobleman and minor general called Attalos. Any child of this marriage would be lowland Macedonian on both sides, unlike Alexander who was half Epirot, and Attalos provoked an unruly scene at the wedding by proposing a toast to a 'legitimate heir'. Alexander naturally objected to being called illegitimate, and rightly so; on that basis his father would also have been illegitimate, having a non-Macedonian mother. The implication was that Philip was not Alexander's father. Philip tried to calm the row, but only succeeded in getting insulted himself. Alexander stormed out, took his mother to Epiros, and went into voluntary exile.

It is hard to imagine that Philip really had any idea of not having Alexander as his heir. He had made him regent in his own absence on campaign, trusted him to command a wing at Chaironeia, and had sent him as his representative to make peace with Athens. A new son would not be of an age to rule for 20 years or so, and Philip was unlikely to last that long. A regency would be the best result that could be expected and, while Attalos would no doubt be delighted to wield power in his grandson's name, this would not be very satisfactory for Macedonia. Most likely the whole thing arose from the amount of wine being put away. In any case, Alexander was soon reconciled with his father and came home, although it is not certain that his mother did, and he remained at daggers drawn with Attalos and his faction.

Other important weddings about this time were those of Attalos to Parmenion's daughter, further increasing his influence by an alliance with Macedonia's most competent general after Alexander and Philip; and of one of Philip's daughters to Amyntas, the son of Philip's second eldest brother and rejected by the army as king in favour of Philip as an infant. The latter marriage could be looked upon as providing a counterpoise to Attalos, securing the loyalty of a possible pretender by linking him more closely with the ruling family, and providing a longstop in the event of Alexander's premature death. If Attalos had been thinking of arranging an accident for Alexander, it would certainly have given him pause for thought.

Philip's army was now nearly ready for the advance into Asia, but he gave it something of a work-out first with a short campaign against the Autariatai, the last of the three great Illyrian tribes to keep its independence. While thus engaged, he received an interesting proposal from the Persian satrap in Karia, one Pixodaros. Pixodaros wanted a powerful ally who could protect him in the unsettled conditions prevailing after the death of the Persian king two years earlier. He suggested that Philip's feeble-minded son Aridaios should marry his daughter.

Alexander got wind of this, and to his suspicious mind it seemed like another attempt to relegate him to the background. Without consulting Philip, he sent an embassy of his own, offering himself instead of Aridaios, Pixodaros immediately took fright and dropped the whole idea, possibly because a royal family with such dissensions did not look like a very safe ally, possibly because he did not believe the offer could be sincere, or possibly because the Persian succession seemed to be sorting itself out.

Philip was hopping mad with Alexander, partly for spoiling the opportunity and partly for his distrust. He explained that Alexander's marriage was too strong a bargaining counter to be thrown away on a minor satrap, who obviously had not considered his aid worth that much himself. In punishment, he banished those of Alexander's friends whom he considered had aided and encouraged him in his behaviour. He probably felt safer with such a clique out of reach.

In the spring of 336 BC, an advance party of 10,000 men left for Asia under the command of Parmenion and Attalos. They crossed over from Byzantion, and immediately the Greek cities started to rise against their Persian rulers. By midsummer, the coastal cities had all been liberated as far south as Ephesos, together with the islands of Tenedos, Lesbos and Chios.

All was now ready for Philip, Alexander and the main army to cross in their turn. First, however, another wedding had to be celebrated, that of the young king of Epiros to Alexander's sister. This would not only bind him more tightly to the family, but replace the link between Macedonia and Epiros formerly represented by Philip's somewhat shopworn marriage to Olympias. It was also a great propaganda occasion. Guests came from all over Greece to the Hegemon's court for the celebrations. Even Alexander was probably happy, as Philip's new wife had just given birth to a girl. Omens for the new campaign were excellent. The one from Delphi read, 'The bull has been garlanded, the end is coming, the sacrificer is at hand.'

As it happened, Apollo had it right, but not quite as people thought. Philip was stabbed to death by one of his own bodyguards in the most public manner at the height of the celebrations. The killer fled to waiting horses, but tripped and was killed by his pursuers. Suspects were many. Olympias had motive and opportunity and later arranged several other murders. Demosthenes hated Philip and forecast the exact moment of his death in a public speech. The Persians actually claimed responsibility. Possibly all were guilty of the plot, the Persians providing the gold, Demosthenes acting as middle man, and Olympias finding an assassin with a grudge against the king who was both a clansman of hers and a mutual enemy of Attalos. She was said to have honoured his remains to a totally excessive degree, almost, said one ancient historian, 'as if she feared people might believe her innocent'. The public nature of the murder also pointed at Olympias and Demosthenes. Certainly the bodyguard could have found easier opportunities offering a better chance of escape. How unfortunate that the killer should have been killed before he could be questioned! Or was this an accident?

No evidence points to Alexander. His only motive would have been to obtain the throne earlier than he otherwise would; his adherents were temporarily in exile so could not have made the arrangements, and he would certainly not have chosen such a public event. Far better for him if it had looked like an accident. He also seems to have liked his father, in spite of his mother's hysterical attempts to inculcate her own hatred in him, and had saved his life at risk of his own not long before.

What if Philip had not been killed at that time? Well, he was not an old man, only 45, so good for a few years yet. The chances are that he would certainly have conquered the whole of Asia Minor, but might not then have gone on beyond the Tauros mountains into Syria. That would have been left to an older, more mature Alexander after his father's death or retirement to Macedonia. Philip's quiet, step-by-step approach would probably have taken several years, during which Alexander would have been on campaign with him, removed from the influence of his crazy mother. A close partnership founded on mutual respect for each other's abilities might well have altered Alexander's personality for the better.

Would his conquests have been so great if he had had more commonsense and less of the divine fire? Probably not. Alexander did not accept the possibility of living through a defeat. He therefore took huge personal risks if they would increase the probability of victory and, although often seriously wounded, always got away with it. If he had been as cautious as Philip, he would probably have lived longer, but would not have gone as far or as fast. Of course, there was never any guarantee that he would be successful. He might have easily died in his first battle, and his name would then only be known now to dusty scholars.

Chapter 3

The armies of Greece

To appreciate Philip's innovations, it is first necessary to consider existing methods. Throughout most of Greece, the hoplite system still reigned supreme, though now often supplemented with supporting troops such as cavalry and skirmishing light foot. Basically, it consisted of a formal array of spearmen standing in line and thrusting with spears over the tops of their large shields.

The shield which gave the system its name, the hoplon, was stoutly constructed of wood, usually circular, and about three feet in diameter. It was often faced with a thin sheet of bronze to encourage enemy weapon points to glide off if the shield was held at a slight angle. The shield's not inconsiderable weight was supported by a double grip, the left arm being pushed through the main one behind the centre of the shield so as to take most of the weight on the elbow, the other at or near the rim and grasped by the left hand. Earlier shields had either been supported by a neck strap or by a single hand grip behind the centre. The first method carried the weight well, but the shield could not be easily moved around to intercept a blow. The second one made the shield very manoeuvrable, but very tiring unless small or of light construction. The double grip to a great extent combined the advantages of both systems.

The hoplite shield also provided opportunities for decoration, either painted on or cut from thin bronze sheet. Some of the Greek cities had a standard pattern which everyone had to use. The Spartans had a letter Lambda, looking like an inverted V. Sikyon and Messenia also used the initial letters of their names, a W tipped 90 degrees to the right and an upright capital M respectively. Thebes used a Hercules club as its symbol, and Mantinia a trident head. Other states such as Athens, and mercenaries, left it up to the individual, and devices could include birds, snakes, animals, gorgon heads, obsolete shields, incense tripods or drinking goblets.

In addition to his shield, the hoplite was protected by a helmet, some kind of armour for his torso in case he failed to block fast enough with his shield, and usually greaves for his legs.

There were a number of types of bronze helmet in use. The Corinthian provided the most protection, but interfered excessively with vision and hearing, so was losing ground to other types such as the Boeotian, the Attic, the Thracian and the Pilos. National preferences existed, Athenians liking the Attic, Thebans the Boeotian and Spartans the Pilos, but it is doubtful if there was any real uniformity. More likely, an army would have a mixture, possibly with the favourite sort showing a clear majority.

Like shields, helmets lent themselves to decoration, this time in the shape of tall crests of horse hair or feathers. There were many different patterns. Not much is known of colour choices. We do know of one mercenary force which had all-white crests, and that citizens' wives dyed their crests for them. The commonest colour for horses' manes and tails is black, which must have been exceedingly difficult to dye in bright colours.

When the hoplite first came in, his standard body armour was the bronze bell corslet. This was heavy, cumbersome, and did not provide especially good protection, unbacked thin bronze being easily penetrated by a strong thrust, as many corslets recovered by archaeologists prove. By Philip's time it had long disappeared, being initially replaced by a composite armour of bronze scales on a leather or textile backing. This was stronger, lighter and considerably more comfortable to wear, and we now read of hoplites charging long distances at the run, previously a most unlikely feat. Further protection was provided by leather reinforcements at the shoulder, especially useful against downward sword cuts, which might otherwise break a collar bone even if they did not penetrate the armour. A kilt of heavy leather straps called pteruges might also be worn to protect the abdomen and thighs where the corslet did not reach.

Further changes were now taking place. It had become obvious that the shield was the most effective defence for a well-trained man, and there was an increasing tendency to lighten body armour still further. A new type of corslet, moulded to fit the wearer as closely as possible and showing heroic muscles on the outside, was coming into fashion. This is usually thought to have been bronze plate, but that is unlikely. It almost certainly was of rawhide leather, soaked in water and left on a wooden former to dry, or of many layers of canvas soaked in glue and similarly dried. Either of these would provide a light, cheap and relatively tough defence, inferior to the other armours against a powerful spear thrust, but reasonably effective against a sword cut or a missile from long range.

Even more popular was a body defence called the spolas. This could be a short leather jerkin or a slightly longer garment of quilted cloth. Its defensive value approached that of the muscled cuirasse. It was especially popular with mercenaries, these being mainly recruited from the less-prosperous elements of the community. It was worn, for instance, by all the rank and file of Xenophon's 10,000.

The remaining defence consisted of thin bronze greaves, sprung on to protect the leg from the knee down, and sometimes supplemented by an ankle and foot protector. Similar defences for the upper arm and thighs had never been very popular and were now long obsolete. Even the greave was starting to be discarded in some quarters, mercenaries especially tending to prefer the Iphikratean marching boot.

Passing from defensive to offensive equipment, the hoplite's main weapon was a long spear. This is difficult to scale from contemporary illustrations, most of which are on vases, but was probably about eight or nine feet long. We do know that it was considerably longer than the spear carried by Persian infantry, which appears from contemporary Persian monuments to have been between six and a half and seven feet long, depending on how tall we assume the men carrying it to have been.

The hoplite grasped his spear near the point of balance with his right hand and thrust it overarm over the top of his shield. Counting the length of his arm, this gave him a maximum reach of about seven feet. If fencing with a single opponent instead of fighting in ranks, he might also use an underarm thrust, or even throw the spear, but these tactics were not employed in regular battle. When hoplites were first introduced, they had carried a single javelin as well as their spear, but this had long ceased to be the case.

The hoplite secondary weapon was a short sword, worn fairly high up on the left. This was usually a cheap, crude affair with a straight blade less than two feet long, but was sometimes a very efficient reverse-curved cutting sword of about the same length called the kopis, very similar to the Gurkha kukri in shape. However, except among the inhabitants of Euboia, the sword took a very back seat, the hoplite whose spear had broken preferring to reverse the part he had left and use the bronze buttspike as a point.

The hoplite's formation was dictated by his weapons. He needed a three-foot frontage to provide room for his shield, and five feet clear behind him for the backswing of his spear. The drill books made provision for closing up to half the frontage with shields overlapping, the back ranks also closing up to brace their comrades with shields against their backs, for instance to receive a determined cavalry charge. However, few cavalry would dare charge home frontally against hoplites in any formation, and such close-packed troops could neither move nor fight effectively, so it is not surprising we read nothing of this being employed in battle.

The most usual formation was in eight ranks, but this might be reduced to four against poor-quality opponents or to overlap a flank, or greatly increased to weight one flank. The only contribution made by the rear rank men, apart from stepping forward to replace losses, was moral support, ie, by making it more difficult for those in front to run away. Formations therefore usually disintegrated from the rear, and it was accepted practice to put the best men in the front rank, the next best in the rear rank, and the worst troops in between.

Of the citizen armies, only the Spartans and possibly the Thebans had properly organised units, with sub-units, junior officers and NCOs. The Athenians, for instance, had no grouping smaller than the tribal regiment of up to 1,000 strong, and sneered at the Spartan army, saying that every second man was an officer. The convenience of such sub-divisions in speeding manoeuvres was obvious to professionals though, and mercenaries had adopted a variant of the Spartan system. Such troops stood at least a good chance of turning to meet a threat from flanks or rear.

Other hoplites were formidable only to the front, but were an exceedingly tough proposition for those who had to face them so. While other troops skirmished from a distance, the hoplite line pressed forward, confident that only fellow hoplites would dare get in the way. Surviving poems of Tyrateus of Messenia emphasise that those who go forward the most firmly suffer the least casualties and that the most dangerous proceeding is standing still to be shot at, points many a wargaming Greek general would do well to take to heart.

Although hoplite armies had taken over from earlier forms in most parts of Greece, other types survived in a few areas. The mountainous states of Aitolia and Akarnania still relied heavily on light skirmishing infantry armed with javelins or slings. Although these could not stand against hoplites on level ground, they were more mobile, so could fall back before them, inflicting a constant trickle of casualties as occasional lucky missiles got past shield and armour. The hoplites might be lucky enough to push them against an obstacle, whereupon a brief massacre would follow until the survivors managed to extricate themselves and flee. The lights might stand to defend their villages rather than give them up to pillage and arson, with the same result. They might run short of missiles and lose heart, their tactical retreats turning insensibly into a real rout. All these could be hoped for in the plains. In the difficult and broken country of Aitolia, it usually went the other way, with the hoplites harassed from all sides, tired out with vain pursuit, and finally overwhelmed by emboldened mountaineers at close quarters.

In Thessalia, there was another military anachronism. Before the hoplite era, Greece had been ruled by a horse-riding aristocracy, supported by undisciplined light-armed clansmen on foot. The hoplite system, by enabling infantry to resist cavalry, had downgraded the nobles and sown the seeds of democracy. On the Thessalian plains, with their wide scope for manoeuvre so unlike the cramped flat lands huddled between mountains of the rest of Greece, the horseman retained his ascendancy, and the hoplite states learned to leave him alone.

The most famous test of the hoplite came with the great Persian invasions of the 5th century BC. Persia had no equivalent infantry to the hoplite, her own relying mainly on their bows. The Greek habit of closing fast gave the archers little opportunity to shoot, while the numbers of the Persians hindered them from evading the charges. At close quarters, the Persian short spears and flimsy wicker shields designed to catch arrows put them at a great disadvantage. Their cavalry, which in more open country could have protected the foot by threatening to envelop the hoplites' flanks, were reduced to frontal charges with little hope of success. They took the hint, and future Persian armies were to use Greek mercenary hoplites to complement the excellent native cavalry which they now concentrated on developing.

The early Greek aristocratic cavalry outside Thessalia had transformed themselves into hoplites who rode to battle, then dismounted and fought with the poorer hoplites who could not afford horses. There are many contemporary illustrations of such hoplites accompanied by an unarmed mounted groom to take charge of both horses. When experience against the Persians and Thessalians decided the southern Greeks to start raising their own cavalry again, it seems to have evolved from these grooms.

The new cavalry started off without armour, helmets or shields, and armed only with a pair of javelins. As time went on, helmets and defensive armour were increasingly worn, although shields were not used by European cavalry until after the period covered by this book. By the time of Philip, there were two main types of cavalry in use by the Greeks and their immediate neighbours.

The cavalry used in small numbers by the southern Greeks and in larger numbers by Macedonia wore a metal-reinforced corslet similar to that of the hoplite and a crested helmet of one of the open-faced types, mainly the Boeotian and Attic among southerners, with the Thracian and its Macedonian development in the majority among Macedonians. Xenophon, the only contemporary writer on cavalry equipment and tactics, recommends a tubular leather protection for the bridle arm, a combined protection for the rider's thighs and the horse's flanks, and armour pieces for the horse's face and chest. However, this is something of a red herring. He had seen such equipment in use while serving as a mercenary in Persia and obviously liked it, but all the evidence we have points to it failing to win adoption elsewhere.

The masses of Thessalian cavalry and the small mounted contingents of Illyrian and Thracian nobles remained much lighter in type. The many vase illustrations of Thessalian cavalry sometimes show helmets and short leather or quilted jerkins but, more often than not, just a simple tunic and hat. Some modern popular historians have stated that the Thessalian cavalry which fought under Alexander was just as heavily armoured as the Macedonian Companions. If so, it is surprising to say the least that no evidence at all can be discovered for this, while there is an abundance pointing the other way. Most likely, the authors assumed this to explain the Thessalians' undoubted efficiency. Such an explanation is unnecessary. Good light cavalry are just as effective an arm as heavy if used properly, as Roman experience against Hannibal's Numidians showed.

The normal armament for a cavalryman at this time was a pair of fairly heavy javelins, suitable either for thrusting or throwing, and averaging somewhere between five and six feet long. These were backed up with a cutting sword such as the kopis. When fighting other cavalry, it was usual to throw one of the javelins just before contact, then thrust with the other until it broke, finally taking to the sword. If fighting hoplites who were facing them in good order, they would throw both javelins from a distance, keeping out of reach of their spears. If the javelins opened a gap, if the enemy became disordered, or if the infantry were not hoplites, they might charge home, using the horses' weight and momentum to shoulder men off their feet and hacking down with their swords.

It is often stated that cavalry could not charge home until the introduction of the stirrup in the 6th century AD, despite the fact that history is full of such occurrences and illustrations show precisely that happening! Modern tests have, in fact, shown that the stirrup is largely irrelevant when charging with a lance, a hindrance when throwing javelins, but an appreciable help when striking downward cutting blows with a sword. A more crucial invention than the stirrup, and equally lacking until a century after the period of this book, was the saddle, the main function of which is to take the rider's weight off the horse's spine and transfer it to the pads of muscle lying at the side, reducing fatigue for man and beast.

Although the pair of heavy javelins was the normal cavalry armament from the Pillars of Hercules to India and beyond, some nations did substitute other weapons. The probable Macedonian use of a single much longer lance is discussed in the next chapter. Some nations substituted a bow for the two throwing weapons, skirmished at a greater range, and were even more reluctant to come to close quarters. The nearest of these to Greece were the Skythians just north of the Danube, who were occasionally used in small numbers as mercenaries. Other such nations could be found inside the Persian empire and sent contingents to fight in its armies. The bow used in each case was a composite type of horn, sinew and wood, short and handy for mounted use, and shooting arrows very much smaller and lighter than those of Greek archers, 50 or more being carried in a quiver instead of half that amount.

There were also variations in the formations used. Thessalians fought in a rhomboid, Skythians, Thracians and Macedonians in a wedge, Persians and Sicilians in a rectangle with the same number of ranks as files, Greeks in a rectangle with three times as many files as ranks, so square in dimensions. The parade frontage for heavy cavalry was three feet per horse but it is very doubtful if this could be maintained moving over broken ground or at speed. Half as much again would just allow enough room in the ranks for the horses to turn 90 degrees, and seems to have been standard for later heavy cavalry. Light cavalry would have a six-foot frontage. A horse's depth was reckoned at nine feet, which today would be considered tight and risking a kicking match. The rhomboid formation gave the best control, the wedge almost as much but was better for shooting and charging, and the rectangle best for shooting, worst for control and charging, the Persian version being a little less extreme than the Greek.

The other main adjunct to the hoplite was the foot skirmisher, or psilos. Spurred by unfortunate experiences fighting Aitolians and other such peoples, the Greeks had long had a small proportion of men armed with missiles to fight at a distance and lightly enough equipped to move easily across rough ground and keep out of enemy hoplites' reach. Their main duty was to protect their own side's hoplites from interference by enemy skirmishers and to assist the cavalry if it was outnumbered by enemy horsemen. Naturally, if they managed to establish an ascendancy over their opponents, they would then go on to worry the enemy hoplites.

Our natural tendency today is to think of the bow as the most important missile weapon, brought up as we are on tales of French knights being brought down in heaps by fast-shooting English longbows. What these stories do not stress is just how many arrows had to be shot to achieve such results or that the victims were the unprotected horses and not the armoured riders. The small numbers of archers available to the Greeks could never have produced the volume of arrows possible to an English army of which two-thirds were archers. In addition, their weaker bows and lighter arrows lacked even the longbow's armour-piercing performance, while the targets were not horses but shielded and armoured infantry.

Instead of shooting off long-range massed volleys to soak an area of ground with missiles in the English style, the Greek archer was a sniper, shooting at an individual target with careful aim which, however, was easily upset by charging him. Ancient archery manuals, admittedly from considerably later than this era, suggest that 80 paces was about the limit for this sort of accurate shooting, with 240 and 180 paces possible against group targets for foot and mounted archers respectively. The main source of archers for the Greeks was mercenary recruitment from the island of Crete. Cretans seem to have used the same sort of composite bows as Asiatics, but their arrows were heavier. However, this did not help penetration, as they were broadheads designed for maximum wounding effect against unprotected flesh. This reduced their armour penetration to much the same as the lighter Asiatic arrow with its more suitable point.

The other common long-range weapon was the sling, whirled around the head to throw either a round stone or an egg-shaped lead shot. Of these, the shot was much the more efficient, while it lasted. Stones were rather more plentiful! The effect on the target was considerably more severe than that of an arrow. Shot often penetrated deep into unprotected flesh which then closed around it, necessitating a special surgical instrument for extraction. Even long-range shot and stones could incapacitate a limb with extensive bruising, and the best-armoured hoplite or cavalryman could be knocked out and concussed by a strike on the helmet. While the extreme range of the hand sling was considerably less than that of the bow, probably about 120 paces, its greater target effect made it superior beyond the bow's 80-pace effective range.

Slingers were even rarer in Greece than archers. The barbarous Agrianians could provide some, but these were usually to be found in Macedonian service, hurling lead shot with the cast-in inscription 'A Present from Philip'. Others came from the Greek islanders of Rhodes or from Achaia. The famous Balearic slingers did not penetrate so far east, and the Persian king would not have taken kindly to attempts to recruit in his territory.

The most important missile weapon among the Greeks was undoubtedly the javelin. The practitioners were available in quantity from such states as Aitolia, while its capabilities were not as inferior to the bow and sling as is usually supposed. Its maximum range against a massed target was probably in the region of 50 paces, although considerations of ammunition expenditure probably encouraged a much closer advance where this was safe. This willingness to get close often upset archer or slinger opponents and served a useful end in keeping them away from the hoplites. Javelinmen often carried a light shield called the pelta, usually small and round, but sometimes crescent-shaped. As its use spread, this and the employment of the javelin as a hand-to-hand thrusting weapon led to the introduction of a new troop type.

This was the peltast, a compromise between the javelin-armed skirmisher and the hoplite, equally willing to fight at close quarters if a suitable opportunity occurred, or to skirmish with javelins if it did not. The first peltasts were Thracians. These were armed with a cutting sword and either a long spear or javelins, and carried the pelta. By Philip's time, peltasts had become extremely fashionable among the Greeks, and a large proportion of Greek mercenaries were armed in their fashion. They now carried a larger oval shield, called the thureos, of the same light construction as the pelta. They wore a helmet, possibly a spolas, and carried both long spear and javelins in addition to their sword. They could be an exceedingly dangerous menace to hoplites caught disordered or in unsuitable terrain, and because of their cross-country mobility, were ideal for supporting or driving off skirmishers.

The formations envisaged by the manuals for these types of lighter troops were naturally both less dense and less deep than those of hoplites. Psiloi were allowed an average of six-foot frontage and depth, although they presumably did not stand in rigid ranks, rather operating as a swarm of individuals. Peltasts might have the same frontages as hoplites if fighting at close quarters, but would maintain formation more loosely, splitting to pass an obstacle, or opening out to move fast across difficult ground or to skirmish. Formations were usually four-deep to allow all weapons to be used effectively and prevent troops evading a charge getting in each other's way. The manuals stress the inadvisability of placing missilemen behind other troops where they will be unable to shoot effectively.

Although Greeks serving abroad as mercenaries were increasingly likely to do so as peltasts, at home the hoplite was still the most common type, for both social and economic reasons. Possession of hoplite equipment was usually the qualification to vote and Greeks were passionately devoted to politics. It also distinguished the upper and middle classes from their inferiors. From the ruler's point of view, it was also cheaper. The citizen hoplite provided his own equipment and had to be paid only when called out for service. Mercenary peltasts had to be paid for the whole campaigning season, although they were usually paid off in autumn and re-enlisted next spring, living on their savings during the winter. It was also unfortunate that Philip's new gold mines enabled him to pay mercenaries all the year round, giving him an unfair advantage in recruitment.

Most cities owned some artillery, large cumbersome giant bows shooting javelin-like missiles to about 480 paces. These were almost invariably kept at home for siege defence. They were highly accurate, capable of penetrating any shield or armour, but strictly for anti-personnel work. Philip was experimenting with stone throwers to batter city walls, but they had not taken Perinthos and Byzantion for him. No need for civilised cities to copy semi-barbarians yet. It was rumoured that his machines were powered by twisted sinew, but why depart from the tried-and-tested giant bow? Lot of new-fangled nonsense, most of them thought and anyway they were bound to be expensive. The citizens might yet learn that being sacked was an even greater expense.

Chapter 4

The Macedonian army after Philip's reforms

The most striking difference between Philip's army and that of his predecessors lay in his substitution of a new soldier type for the standard Greek hoplite. This type is usually known as the phalangite from the formation employed. This is slightly illogical as hoplites also fought in phalanx, the term basically meaning a formal arrangement with front rank men evenly spaced in line and rear ranks covering off at regular intervals. Philip and Alexander called them foot companions.

Instead of being armed with a spear grasped only in the right hand and thrust overarm, the phalangite was armed with a weapon called the sarissa. This was much longer and needed to be held with both hands, making it technically a pike rather than a spear. In passing, I might mention that modern non-military historians and translators are often unfamiliar with the technical names of weapon classes and misuse them horribly, so that it is often better to stick to the ancient names to avoid confusion.

There are three Ancient authors who specify the length of the sarissa. Theophrastos, the nearest to Philip's time, said that the longest sarissae were 12 cubits or 18 feet. Polybios, writing considerably later, said that a 16-cubit sarissa had been replaced by a 14-cubit type which was now standard. Asklepiodotos, writing a little later still, said that the minimum length should be ten cubits, giving a projection of eight cubits in front of the rank, and the maximum 12, giving a projection of ten, the same claimed for Polybios' 14-cubit type. It seems likely that the length varied over the period the weapon was in use.

There are a number of modern quibbles over the length, some authors maintaining that cubits must be a mistake for feet, and one going so far as to invent a short Macedonian cubit. Their reason for distrusting the length quoted by the Ancients is mainly the existence of a body of cavalry called sarissophoroi, the argument being that a cavalryman could not manage a weapon of such dimensions. These objections are dealt with later, but suffice it to say here that they have no substance. The use of pikes of such sizes by a large proportion of infantry throughout the 16th and 17th centuries AD demonstrates conclusively their practicality for men on foot.

Some of the Ancient texts also mention a grading of sarissa length according to the rank in which the soldier fights, so as to meet the enemy with a single dense row of points. As each rank needs about three feet depth, there must have been practical limits to this technique if the front rank were not to be outreached by their opponents. The one period in which this would not have been so was that of Philip and Alexander, as their phalangites were not opposed by other pikemen but by hoplites.

This may give a clue as to the derivation of the phalangite. The longest spear which can be used in one hand is about 12 feet long, and the Athenian mercenary leader Iphikrates is said to have introduced the use of spears, variously stated as twice or one and a half times the length of the normal hoplite spear, a few years before Philip's accession, which would make them about that length. If Philip had set out to make his front rank decisively outreach such troops, a ten-cubit or 15-foot weapon would have been ample. Having once gone to using both hands, it would be obvious that the length could be further increased, and that giving the second rank 12-cubit weapons would enable them to thrust simultaneously at the same targets. It would then become apparent that a method originally meant to enable Macedonian peltast-type troops to outreach Iphikratean peltasts had also made them into troops who could not only outreach hoplites in the same way, but bring twice as many men into action on the same frontage, thus creating a new and superior type of close combat infantry.

The sarissa had, of course, some compensating disadvantages. Because both hands were needed for his weapon, the phalangite could not control a hoplon, so was forced to change to a smaller two-foot diameter bronze shield which could be pushed up the arm to leave the left hand free. This reduced his protection, the shield being not only smaller but impossible to move around to intercept a hit while his pike was levelled. This was not so important when engaging hoplites who first had to fight their way past two lots of pike points before they could reach him, but could be nasty when fighting other pikemen or being shot at with missiles. This led to a reintroduction of the metal corslet later on, but in Philip's and Alexander's time the phalangite had to make do with a spolas supplemented by bronze helmet and greaves.

Another disadvantage was that the long pike was not only heavy to carry but awkward. The rear ranks had to keep them vertical, and any failure to do so had a horrible effect on changes of formation and direction. Drill had to be of a high order, leading to a need for proper regular soldiers paid all the year round. Conversely, phalangites were extremely vulnerable to other troops if they became disordered and thus no longer presented an unbroken double row of points to the enemy. If opponents penetrated a gap, they might have no other alternative but to drop their pikes and take to their swords. Hoplites, with their larger shields and handier spears, could then have a decisive advantage.

Alexander took six units of foot companions with him to Asia, totalling some 12,000 strong. Another 12,000 infantry were left behind in Macedonia, so the presumption is that the whole army had 12 taxeis of foot companions, each taxis being probably organised as a double chiliarchia of 2,048 rank and file, plus officers, who on the basis of later manuals should add about 50 more. Each taxis seems to have had its own recruiting area, and they are sometimes referred to by this, although more often by their commander's name.

The other Macedonian infantry type is the hypaspist, which translates roughly as 'shield bearer'. There were three chiliarchia of these, of which one was called the agema of the hypaspists and acted as foot guards.

The equipment of the hypaspists is a matter of dispute. Tactically, they were used as a link between the cavalry and the pike phalanx, so must have been more mobile than the latter. However, on occasion, phalangites appear to have

Left to right *Macedonian phalangite and Hypaspist, Greek hoplite, and Agrianian javelinman* (all figure drawings by Ian Heath).

been used in preference to hypaspists on forced marches against lightly armed hillmen. This implies that if the phalangites temporarily discarded their pikes, they became more lightly equipped than hypaspists. It may seem unlikely that pikemen would discard their pikes in this way and leave themselves only with swords, but this must have in any case been normal procedure when assaulting fortifications, as it is difficult to visualise men climbing ladders carrying 18-foot weapons, let alone using them at the top.

The shield referred to in their title, the aspis, could be any round bronze-faced shield. However, as it is stressed as a point of difference in title, it seems unlikely to have been the same as the two-foot diameter shield of the phalangite. A near-contemporary monument, the so-called Alexander sarcophagus at Sidon, showed unarmoured men on foot using a shield similar to the hoplon, which suggests that this may have been the hypaspist shield. This has probably been confirmed as I write by the very recent discovery of a grave thought to be that of Philip. This contained all the occupant's weapons and armour, including a shield which, scaled from photographs, appears to be of hoplon size. As shields were not used on horseback and a Macedonian king is likely to have fought on foot with his foot guards, it seems equally likely that his shield would be similar.

The other equipment in the grave included an iron helmet of standard Macedonian type decorated with gold, an iron corslet like that of Alexander in the mosaic mentioned below, a composite garment of textile and leather, probably a spolas with attached leather pteruges worn under the corslet as an equivalent of the mediaeval aketon, gilt bronze greaves, and several long spears. It seems unlikely that the corslet had any place in hypaspist equipment, but the helmet, greaves, spolas and spears would fit in well.

The spear shafts had all rotted away, but the head of one spear was rusted to the tomb wall at a height suggesting that the shaft may have been 12 feet long. The Macedonian cavalry spear was called a xyston and is usually said to have been six feet long, although there appears to be no evidence to support this and a great deal to the contrary which we will have to go into shortly. For the moment then, it is enough to say that if it were really 12 feet long, it would be equally suitable as a hypaspist weapon.

Hypaspists often seem to be grouped or confused by ancient authors with peltasts. This is understandable if they were a direct development from the earlier traditional Macedonian peltast-type infantry, updated with the fashionable new peltast spear adopted by Iphikrates, an intimate of the Macedonian royal family, but otherwise kept both as a sop to traditionalists displeased with the new phalangite innovations, and to be used in difficult ground unsuitable for pikemen. They differ from the peltast in that there is no evidence for their carrying javelins, and from the hoplite in that they probably fought in a looser order more suitable for rapid movement over difficult terrain.

It is fair to say that the picture of a fighting man in helmet, spolas and greaves, carrying a large round shield and long spear would not satisfy all historians, but would content the vast majority. The minority view of Berve and Tarn that the hypaspist was armed and operated identically to the foot companions and based on the negative grounds that no ancient author says they were not, always unlikely on tactical grounds, must now be regarded as untenable in the light of the grave find.

With the Macedonian companion cavalry, we are on much stronger ground. Apart from anything that can be learned from Philip's grave goods, we have four useful pictorial sources. One is a mosaic pavement at Pompei copied from a contemporary painting and showing Alexander charging against Daraios. The equipment and dress depicted confirm its authenticity, agreeing exactly with information from other sources, while bearing no resemblence to anything contemporary with the construction of the mosaic. The second is a medallion showing Alexander attacking Porus. The other two are painted funeral stele from a little after Alexander's time found at Alexandria in Egypt.

These show cavalrymen wearing metal corslet, pteruges, tunic and cloak, armed with an approximately 12-foot long lance and a sword, but lacking greaves and shield. The only problem here is the spear, and we must ask ourselves if this is the xyston mentioned in various texts and usually considered to be shorter? All of our four representations come from after the start of Alexander's campaigns, so it is possible that the longer spear had replaced a shorter version previously in use. There are several reasons for rejecting the idea of a replacement. The first is the long spear in Philip's grave. The second is that the ancient historians tell us that the Macedonian cavalry spear was decisively longer than the Persian weapon, itself between five and six feet long, and that Daraios finally made a despairing effort to get his cavalry to adopt it. Finally, the late Macedonian tactical manual which survives in three versions equates troops carrying the xyston with those carrying the kontos, known to have been 12 feet long.

The other type of native Macedonian cavalry was known alternatively as prodromoi, which translates as 'scouts', or as sarissophoroi, which translates as 'pikemen'. These continue to be a real puzzle, simplified though by the thorough discrediting of Tarn's contention that they were Thracians.

Their scouting role suggests that they were light cavalry, but it is hard to see how this fits in with their other name. It is not, of course, necessary to suppose that this implied them carrying a weapon as long as that of the infantry

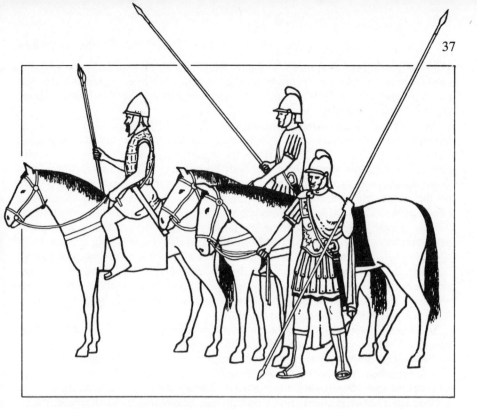

Left to right *Thessalian cavalryman, Macedonian Prodromoi light cavalryman, and Macedonian companion heavy cavalryman.*

pikemen, but if it was in fact the same length as that of the rest of the cavalry, why should they have a special title? A number of possibilities exist. One is that their true title was prodromoi sarissophoroi, and that half the name was used on different occasions. They might then have been armed as the companions but without metal body armour. Another is that they were an experimental force with a longer weapon which turned out to be a failure. Another is that they adopted the 12-foot spear before the rest of the cavalry did, but had been caught up with since. Finally, and I think my favourite, prodromoi might be their official name and sarissophoroi a rude nickname invented for them by the rival Paionian light cavalry armed with orthodox javelins. In any case, they were certainly light skirmishing cavalry armed with a spear at least as long as that of the companions.

Nineteenth century Argentinian gaucho's used a long lance of up to 15 feet in length, grasped with both hands to thrust rather than rigidly couched. This was extremely effective in skirmishing and could be whirled helicopter fashion as a defensive ploy. Although gauchos normally rode with stirrups, they took them off for greater freedom of movement when carrying this weapon.

Alexander took eight ilai of companions, one of which was the royal squadron, and four ilai of scouts to Asia. The royal squadron was probably about 300 strong, the other ilai of companions probably about 200 each, and the scouts possibly rather less. He also took 1,800 Thessalian cavalry, 600 allied Greek cavalry and a single ila of Paionian light javelin cavalry. Another 1,500 cavalry were left behind in Macedonia. If these included the 200 Thessalians and 500

Thracians later sent to Asia as reinforcements, that leaves 800, just enough for four more ilai of companions to bring the total number of companion ilai to the same as that of the foot companions and confirming the theory that these shared recruiting areas.

As well as taking foreign cavalry to Asia, Alexander also took non-Macedonian infantry. The contingents of the allied Greek states provided 7,000 men, probably hoplites. Greek mercenaries, probably peltasts, initially came to 5,000, but were reinforced later by batches totalling a further 7,700. Some of these may previously have been in Macedonia, but most probably became available as the news of success and easy pickings spread. Thrace and Illyria provided 7,000 barbarian equivalents of the peltast, and the Agrianians 500 good light javelinmen, later to be reinforced by a further 500. Archery was provided by 500 Cretans, later to be reinforced by a further 500 archers from the army left in Macedonia. Some of the Agrianians may have been slingers.

Philip had also introduced limited numbers of two new types of troops, skirmishers utilising the staff sling and a primitive crossbow respectively, but whether Alexander took any of these with him is uncertain. If he did, they may have formed part of the siege train.

The staff sling consisted of a sling on a four-foot pole. It shot much heavier missiles than the ordinary hand sling including stones up to one pound in weight and a Roman author gives its practical range as 240 paces, the same as a bow.

The crossbow was called the gastrophetes, which translates as 'belly bow'. This comes from the loading method, which started with putting the end of the slide against the ground and pressing with hands and abdomen on the butt until slide and string were cocked and held by the trigger catch. Like its mediaeval equivalent, it outranged the bow and could penetrate most armour, although not usually a heavy shield.

The javelin-throwing giant bow type of artillery, of which the gastrophetes was a miniature variant, had also been improved by Philip's engineers. By substituting twisted sinew for bent wood as the energy storing medium, they had managed to make the catapult much lighter for the same range and power. The name incidentally comes from katapeltes or 'shield piercer'. The javelin-like missiles could penetrate shield and armour and even kill a second man standing behind. The rate of shooting was quite good with a well-drilled crew, and the accuracy sufficient to pick off a single man at 160 paces or so or hit a group at 480 paces.

Philip's engineers had also applied the same principle for the first time to throwing stones. These engines were two-armed like the javelin-shooter, not with a single arm like the late Roman onager and mediaeval mangonel. They came in various sizes, but even the smallest was much heavier than the javelin-shooter. However, unlike earlier engines, they could damage constructions as well as kill troops. They were graded according to the weight of the stone flung, expressed in minae (roughly one pound) or talents of 60 minae. The smallest was sometimes later used as field artillery and could smash palisades. It was rated at 10 minae. A 30-minae engine could damage strong wooden constructions such as siege towers, and was useful for counter-battery fire. The smallest useful against stone city walls was the one talent, and the largest ever built were rated at three talents. Alexander may have used some of these in his sieges. To break down a wall, however, they had to be brought up to within about 160 paces in order to get a trajectory promising a near right-angled impact.

The stone missiles were something of a problem, as they had to be chipped by skilled workmen to near-perfect roundness. One cheat to get past this problem was to use a rough stone as the centre of a baked clay ball. This had less effect at the receiving end, but had the incidental advantage of breaking up on impact so that it could not be shot back. Other special ammunition types included sacks of stones or lead shot as an equivalent of shrapnel, fire missiles, and even biological warfare in the shape of baskets of hornets' nests or poisonous snakes, especially interesting to men who did not wear trousers! I hate to spoil a good story, but dead horses were not used. The smallest horse weighs a lot more than three talents.

Although Philip's men were mostly regular in the sense of being paid all year round and dri'led, it is a matter for conjecture whether they wore uniform and carried standards. It seems likely that many of them did. Spartans, Xenophon's mercenaries, and successor armies all wore red tunics, and these were probably also worn by Macedonian regular infantry. However, the Alexandria stele of a companion cavalryman mentioned above depicts a white tunic, bronze corslet, red-brown cloak and purple saddle cloth, so this may have been their uniform. The Macedonian shield device was an eight-pointed star. Philip's shield has this inlaid in ivory, but it was probably usually painted on, possibly in varying regimental colours, as we hear of bronze, silver and white shielded units in successor armies. The stars were later sometimes supplemented by crescent moons, between four and seven of these being distributed around the outer edge. However, this may not have applied in our period.

A near-contemporary painting shows a soldier in a Macedonian-type helmet wearing a dark red tunic and a white corslet apparently made up of four-inch wide horizontal sections with similarly coloured shoulder pieces and short pteruges, probably a form of spolas. His crest is white, his helmet and greaves bronze, and the interior of his large shield pale blue. The Alexander mosaic shows him in a white tunic, whitish coloured corslet, apparently a light purple cloak, and bare headed. His chestnut horse has yellow leather harness, except for a rather broad breast strap of black or purple criss-crossed with yellow.

I know of no evidence of standards being used before Alexander's time by either Greeks or Macedonians. The standard usually associated with Alexander, the figure of an eagle mounted on a pole with a snake in its talons, was probably taken over from the Persians after they had acknowledged him ruler.

The drill movements taught to the foot companions included left, right and about turns, wheeling to left or right on a flank pivot, opening and closing files and ranks, doubling and halving ranks, various kinds of countermarch, and inclining. The cavalry had their own specialities. The Macedonian wedge formation lent itself to quick changes of direction by simply maintaining position on the commander riding at the point of the wedge. The Thessalian rhomboid took this further, it being possible to swap leaders and follow one of the other three points. The circling movement later known as the cantabrian circle had not yet penetrated to Greece and Persia, although probably in use in Italy and Sicily. Although I have used the terms left and right, the ancients did not. Right was 'to the spear', left 'to the shield' for infantry and 'to the rein' for cavalry. The movements must have been fascinating for an uncouth barbarian to watch, because later on I shall be telling you how Alexander hypnotised some with a drill display until they forgot to watch what the rest of his army was doing!

Chapter 5

Securing the home base: Alexander's Greek and Balkan campaigns, 336 BC to 335 BC

Although Alexander was obviously the front-runner, he was not the only possible candidate for the throne of Macedonia. The mentally subnormal Aridaios could safely be ignored, but there was still Amyntas, son of Philip's predecessor. Attalos' schemes had suffered a setback when his daughter had borne Philip a daughter instead of a son but, having earned Alexander's enmity by attempting to supplant him as heir and publicly insulting him, his only chance lay in backing some other candidate. Incidentally, it is sometimes stated that Attalos' grandchild was a boy. This is not possible. There was only time for one child, and we know it had a girl's name. Another complication was that Parmenion's daughter was married to Attalos and his son Philotas was a friend of Amyntas. As the most respected Macedonian general, Parmenion's influence could be very important.

We do not know exactly what happened, but one of four brothers from a noble Lynkestian family immediately announced his support for Alexander, two were seized and executed along with Amyntas, and the fourth fled to the protection of the Persian king. It seems likely that the first brother in return for advancement had betrayed a plot between the other brothers and Amyntas, and that his evidence was convincing enough to justify the killings in the public eye. Legally, of course, no Macedonian could be executed without the consent of the army, and any cutting of corners by Alexander might have been dangerous. The army at home was commanded by Antipatros, who now backed Alexander.

All the possible opposition leaders were now concentrated with the advance party in Asia, namely Attalos, Parmenion, and the son of one of the executed Lynkestids. With Antipatros and the much larger main army backing Alexander, and his own three sons possible hostages at court, Parmenion chose not to intervene when a friend of Antipatros arrived secretly with a party of soldiers to arrest Attalos. Attalos chose to resist arrest and was slain. Now both parts of the army were Alexander's.

Alexander then acted to conciliate the great families of upland nobles. His action against two of the Lynkestids had been cancelled out by the rewards achieved by the other. The Orestids could hope to gain from their connection with Olympias, who could now return from Epiros, and were pleased to have three nobles enrolled among Alexander's intimate companions. The Elimiots not only had a representative among Alexander's friends, but had been enemies of Attalos. Eordaia claimed two more of Alexander's friends, and the

Tymphiots were friends of Parmenion and followed his lead. With army, people and nobility all firmly behind him, it was time for Alexander to look abroad.

When Alexander was later asked how he managed to keep the Greeks under control, he answered 'By never putting off what needs to be done today.' Some of his advisers thought he should sit still and write diplomatic letters. Instead, he marched south for Thessalia. The long and narrow pass of Tempe into Thessalia had been occupied by Thessalian troops, not so much because they were hostile as to gain time to bargain and make up their minds. Alexander turned the pass by cutting a stairway over Mount Ossa, and the Thessalians came off their fence with a rush and recognised him as ruler like his father before.

Alexander was officially Hegemon of the League of Common Peace, his father having specified when the league was formed that the Hegemony would pass to his heir, but the Greeks were now busy trying to wriggle out of this commitment. They did not have time. Force-marching, Alexander was through the pass of Thermopylai before anyone could muster to block him, summoned the Delphic council, and overawed them into confirming him.

Continuing south at high speed, he frightened Thebes into abject surrender, and arrived at Athens as the assembly was voting a shrine in honour of his father's killer. This motion was quickly dropped, and replaced by others showering honours on Alexander, including Athenian citizenship.

At Corinth, he summoned the League of Common Peace, and set up arrangements for keeping the Greeks quiet while he was in Asia. His main actions were to order the break-up of the pocket empires by which the larger cities enforced their will on the smaller ones surrounding them, and to set up provisions for arbitrating quarrels between cities. He made it plain that Macedonia was going to stay in control, but would not exploit Greece in any way. He would be content with a grudging passive acquiescence to his operations in Asia, where the propaganda value of having all the Greeks theoretically united behind him might be considerable. After all, those thousands of Greek mercenaries in Persian service would want to go home some day, and might think twice about annoying the ruler controlling those homes.

On the way back, Alexander stopped at Delphi to consult the oracle. He was told that this could not be done because he came on an unfavourable day, a concept previously unknown and possibly inspired by Persian gold. He dragged the priestess towards the shrine, and she finally gave in, saying 'Alexander, you are invincible.' On hearing that, he pressed her no further, saying that this prophecy was quite good enough for him!

The south now as secure as Greece could ever be, Alexander wintered briefly at home, and then marched north against a Thracian people called the Triballoi. These had ambushed Philip on his return from his Skythian expedition and had stolen most of the loot. The expedition had the twin aims of teaching them not to 'meddle with the Mafia', and of safeguarding the Persian expedition's lines of communication. The only serious attempt to withstand him came in a narrow defile blocked at its highest point by a line of carts. He guessed that these were not meant to be a static defence but to be rolled down on him, and so ordered precautions. The carts were safely dodged by men mostly in dispersed formation, and the Triballoi decided not to wait.

Alexander kept pushing on, using his light troops as ferrets to chase the

Greece and the islands

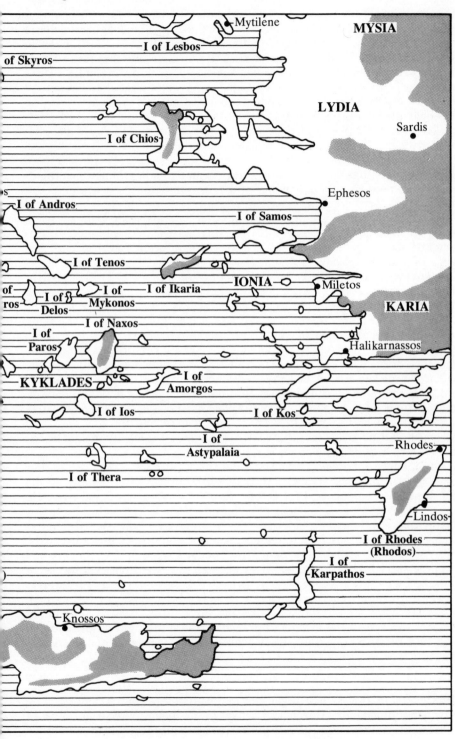

Thracians out of their woods to where his heavier infantry and cavalry could get at them. The plentiful loot was not kept with the army to risk another debacle like Philip's, but sent back home in advance. The fugitives finally took refuge on an island in the Danube. Alexander sent for his ships, but they proved to be too few for an adequate assualt landing against opposition. Alexander instead improvised rafts from tent skins stuffed with hay, and floated and swam the whole army across the river at night, not to the island, but to the far bank. The Skythian inhabitants formed up to fight, broke, made a stand to defend a fort, broke again and fled on horseback into the plain. After this display of amphibious ability, the Triballoi surrendered, and other river tribes sent goodwill gifts. These included a band of Kelts, forerunners of the later Galatian migration. Alexander was slightly put out when they claimed that the thing which frightened them most was the possibility of the sky falling on their heads, as this implied they were not especially scared of him.

Having dismissed the Keltic ambassadors and recrossed the Danube, Alexander received news of trouble in Illyria. King Bardylis, who at Philip's accession had been close to conquering Macedonia, had recently died aged 90. His son was now out to make a similar reputation.

A few weeks later, Alexander had junior pinned in a fort inside a narrow mountain valley, only to have another Illyrian king turn up and occupy the hills overlooking the only way out to his rear. This was a wooded ledge just wide enough for four men. On one side of it was a river. On the other, the ground rose, first gradually, then steeply towards mountain crests. Alexander could not stay where he was without supplies and could not get foragers through the defile. He formed his phalangites into a four-wide column and headed for the exit, covering the rear with light troops and cavalry. The phalangites now proceeded to put on something of a drill display, wheeling in both directions and pointing their pikes to left and right. As the foe watched fascinated, suddenly what had appeared to be a column marching towards the defile became a four-deep line assaulting the hills, joined by some of the light troops and cavalry who had moved during the distraction.

The enemy on the hills immediately fled, and it was some time before they could be brought back. By then, Alexander had his heavy troops down off the hill, through the defile and formed up on level ground across the river. He himself was covering the movement with most of the light troops. The enemy charged as he withdrew the screen, but were stopped by a threatened counterattack by the phalanx, by the retreating archers shooting from the centre of the river, and by the artillery attacking from the far bank.

Three days later Alexander, hearing that the two Illyrian kings were camped carelessly without proper palisades or sentries, decided the time was ripe. He launched a night attack covered by his archers and javelinmen. However, when he found just how lax the Illyrians were, he decided not to wait for the rest of the army and pressed on with the light infantry alone. The two Illyrian kings fled, their armies killed, captured or utterly dispersed.

Alexander now heard news of more trouble at Thebes. The politicians exiled on Philip's orders had sneaked back and, encouraged by a rumour of Alexander's death in Illyria, had organised attacks on the Macedonian garrison occupying the citadel. Alexander's arrival by the back route from Illyria 14 days later took them utterly by surprise. However, they rejected his ultimatum to hand the exiles over, called for help from other cities and sent skirmishers to attack the Macedonian camp.

The Thebans had built a double palisade around the citadel to keep the garrison in and Macedonian relief out. Three days after Alexander's demands had been rejected, an officer called Perdikas commanding that day's pickets saw evidence of slackness among the Thebans manning the palisade and attacked on his own initiative. He got inside the first palisade and was joined there by the unit in immediate support. Alexander now ordered up the rest of the army, but sent only the javelinmen and archers inside the palisade, keeping the hypaspists and companions just outside in close support.

At first all went well, then Perdikas was wounded, the Thebans counter-attacked, and the assault force fell back outside and rallied on the hypaspists. The Thebans followed up in disorder, were charged by the phalanx and broke. They fled to the city gate near by. Mingled with the fugitives the Macedonians entered before the gate could be shut, while others stormed the now largely undefended walls. The Macedonians garrisoning the citadel also joined in. A general massacre and sack followed, not so much on the part of the Macedonians as by the Phokians, Plataians and other exploited neighbours of Thebes.

It was thought by the rest of Greece that Thebes was finally being punished by the gods for a very impressive number of impieties which were listed at length, and that the said gods had employed their usual method of first sending the Thebans mad. One of the impieties, interestingly enough, was helping Xerxes in his invasion of Greece. Alexander left the question of punishment to Thebes' neighbours. These decided that the citadel should be garrisoned, the city destroyed, and all inhabitants without a Macedonian friend to vouch for them should be enslaved. This was a punishment of almost unprecedented severity, but all agreed it couldn't have happened to a better set of victims.

A number of states had, in fact, supported Thebes. The Aitolians now sent messages to say they were sorry. The Arkadians who were marching to Thebes' aid halted, organised a court, and condemned their own leaders to death for persuading them to go! The Persian king had sent Demosthenes 300 talents to organise support at Athens. He does not seem to have spent any of it for the cause, but instead treated it as a personal fee. Alexander demanded that he be handed over with several other like-minded politicians, but dropped the demand when the Athenian assembly pleaded mercy for them.

Alexander now returned to Macedonia, to find that his mother had taken advantage of his absence to have Attalos' daughter and her baby killed. He was annoyed, but this did not stop him leaving her as queen regent in Macedonia during his absence in Asia. However, she was counterbalanced by leaving Antipatros at home in charge of nearly half the army. They did not get on. The size of the force that Alexander left behind is somewhat surprising at first unless one has paid the close attention to Greek politics which we have had to in previous chapters, in which case it seems almost optimistic!

It was now too late in the year to start for Asia. The advanced force had been having difficulties owing to the Persian counter-moves made possible by the two-year delay in the main expedition, but it would have to maintain itself a little longer yet, until the winter gales were over and the spring grass began to grow.

Chapter 6

The Persian Empire and its army

Kyros, the founder of the Persian empire, was son of the king of Anshan. Anshan lay north of the western end of the Persian Gulf. Its coast was rocky and treacherous, lacking harbours, and the narrow coastal plain stiflingly hot and infertile. It was cut off from the north and east by deserts, its only good access being by mountain roads north-west. The interior was a country of fertile valleys, high plains and mountains, breeding good horses and strong men.

The kings of Anshan were vassal to the kings of Media, and Kyros started his career by becoming an indispensable assistant to the Median monarch. When the latter woke up to the fact that his subordinate had greater support among the Median nobles and army than their rightful ruler, it was already too late. By 549 BC, Kyros had defeated him, was accepted as king of Media, and was busy extending his rule over the other provinces which, with his own Anshan, made up Persia. By 548 BC he had added the title of king of Persia.

The other major states in the area were Lydia and Babylon. King Kroisos of Lydia, feeling nervous, wondered if he should do before being done to, and asked the oracle at Delphi. The oracle told him that if he made war on Kyros a mighty empire should fall. He made the mistake of assuming that it would be Kyros', secured alliances with Babylon, Egypt and Sparta, then commenced hostilities. Spartan promises proved to be worth about as much as usual and, before Babylon or Egypt could move, Lydia had been conquered and added to Kyros' growing collection of states. After Lydia fell in 546 BC, Babylon was given a few years' respite before falling to a short sharp campaign in 539 BC. Kyros now set himself to conciliate the conquered and appears to have done so successfully. He died in battle in 529 BC trying to extend his rule over the Skythians east of the Caspian Sea.

Kyros' son Kambyses succeeded to the throne in 529 BC, and had added Egypt before dying in 522 BC. He had been considering an attack on Carthage, but had been hampered by the traditional friendship between that power and the Phoenician cities which provided his fleet. As the land route was too long and desert-like to be practical, the project was dropped. However, Kyrene and Libya were frightened into submitting to Persian rule.

The direct line having been extinguished by murder and intrigue, the throne was now taken by one Daraios, and the empire immediately dissolved into a succession of rebellions. By about 516 BC these had been put down, and Daraios set himself to round off the empire. He pushed it into India on the east and through Thrace to the Danube on the west. Crossing the Danube, he had a rather nasty experience with another Skythian tribe, and decided not to chance his luck further.

Among the territories conquered by Kyros in Asia Minor were a number of Greek cities. These were left pretty much on their own apart from having to pay a modest tribute, but the Persian reverse north of the Danube started them thinking independently. Encouraged by some of the mainland Greeks, rebellion started to break out in 500 BC. By 492 BC, a combination of Persian arms and Greek treachery and indifference had quelled the rebellions, and Daraios had amazed the conquered rebel cities by restoring democratic government and letting them carry on as before.

He now planned a punitive expedition against the mainland Greeks. Thrace and Macedonia were reoccupied by Persian troops and the larger of the Aegean islands brought under Persian control. All was now ready for a seaborne attack against Athens. Something like 15,000 men were landed at Marathon and were opposed by the Athenian army. The Athenians' Spartan allies had what an unkind commentator might term their usual good religious reasons for not being able to come but, as it happened, the Athenian army managed to defeat the Persian force on its own, and the survivors re-embarked and sailed home.

Daraios would certainly have mounted a larger expedition, but was first delayed by a revolt in Egypt, then died in 486 BC. His son Xerxes had to finish off the Egyptian business, but finally marched on Greece with a huge army and fleet in 481 BC. An attempt to block him at Thermopylai by a small force of Spartans and allies failed when an outflanking force marching by mountain paths came in behind them. All the Greek states north of Athens submitted, most of the Athenians evacuated, and Athens fell. However, the combined southern Greek fleets won a decisive victory over the larger Persian navy at Salamis, and Xerxes, faced with the prospect of the Greek admirals cutting his lines of communication and a consequent flood of rebellions in other provinces, returned home. The army he left as a covering force was badly defeated by the Spartans while the Athenians held their Theban allies, and the remnants also made for home.

The 170-year expansion of the Persian empire was now over, but it continued to hold its own on the defensive up to Alexander's expedition 144 years later. From time to time provinces would rebel or the mainland Greeks would stir up trouble among their compatriots under Persian rule, but the provinces would be recovered, and equal trouble stirred up among the quarrelsome and lamentably sticky-fingered Greeks by massive injections of Persian gold.

If the Persian strength had declined somewhat from its peak, so had that of the Greeks. A long and destructive war between Athens and Sparta had crippled the former and given even the latter a distaste for foreign adventure. Thebes had expanded to fill the power vacuum, only to be surpassed by the formerly insignificant state of Macedonia. For a time, Philip of Macedonia had seemed a dangerous threat. A statesman as well as a military genius, he had unified Greece and harnessed much of its strength for an offensive against the Persians. He had been aided in this by Greek preconceptions of Persia, to wit that Persia was hostile, could not stand up to Greek arms, and was emphatically worth looting. However, the leader had been removed by a combination of the usual internal opposition and external bribes, leaving as heir an untried lad who seemed to lack his father's judgement and could not count on the same support.

Since gold seemed to be the most important resource of the Persian empire, both for bribery and to pay mercenary Greek soldiers hopefully as good as those of the enemy, it is worth taking a look at where it came from. Daraios had organised the empire into large units called satrapies. Originally there were 20 of these in addition to Persia itself which paid no taxes. According to Herodotos, the Greek historian and geographer, the peoples included, and their taxes converted from Babylonian talents into Greek talents, were as follows:

1) Ionia, the Magnesians of Asia, Aeolians, Karians, Lykians, Milyans and Pamphylians paid 520 talents; 2) The Mysians, Lydians, Lasonians, Kabalians and Hytennians paid 650 talents; 3) The Hellespontians, Thracians of Asia, Paphlagonians, Marianynians and Syria Kappadokia paid 467 talents and 1,500 horses, plus other livestock; 4) Kilikia paid 650 talents, of which 140 went to the cavalry guarding the province and the rest to the king, plus 360 white horses; 5) Phoenicia, Palestine and Cyprus paid 455 talents; 6) Egypt, nearer Libya, Kyrene and Barka paid 910 talents, plus 120,000 bushels of grain for the army of occupation at Memphis; 7) The Sattagydae, Gandarii, Dadikae and Aparytae paid 220 talents; 8) Susa and the rest of the Kissian country paid 390 talents; 9) Babylon and Assyria paid 1,300 talents; 10) The Medes, Paikanians and Orthokorybantians paid 585 talents and 3,000 horses; 11) The Kaspii, Pausikae, Pantimathi and Varitae paid 260 talents; 12) Baktria as far as the land of the Aegli paid 467 talents; 13) The Paktyic country, Armenia, and up to the Euxine Sea paid 520 talents; 14) The Sagartii, Sarangeis, Thamanaei, Utii, Myki and colonists in the southern sea islands paid 780 talents; 15) The Sakae and Kaspi paid 250 talents; 16) The Parthians, Chorasmians, Sogdi and Arii paid 390 talents; 17) The Parikanii and the Ethiopians of Asia paid 520 talents; 18) The Matieni, Saspiri, Alarodii paid 260 talents; 19) The Moschi, Tibareni, Makrones, Mossynoeci and Maris paid 390 talents; and 20) India paid 467 talents. I assume that Herodotos here mistook 'talents in gold' for 'talents of gold'. As gold was worth about 13 times as much as the equivalent weight of silver, it seems to me that the alternative would make the parts of modern Pakistan which were all the Persians held in India unrealistically valuable. I do this with trepidation, and await correction.

The grand total of taxes thus comes to 9,452 talents a year. It was not an excessive burden on the taxpayers but, as the precious metal was mostly hoarded rather than put back into circulation, it hindered trade by restricting money supply. The opposite occurred when Alexander got his hands on the hoards and spent them, the huge increase in money supply without a corresponding increase in productivity then causing rapid inflation.

Apart from money taxes, there were also taxes in kind. Each satrapy had to support its satrap and his household, feed armies passing through it or stationed within it, and contribute food for the royal household and troops in attendance. Some outlying nations not under direct rule also paid tribute. This included 200 slaves a year from the Kolchians of the Caucasus, 1,000 talents' weight of frankincense from the Arabs, and four quarts of gold, ebony and 20 elephant tusks from the Nubians.

As an indication of how gold and silver had accumulated in the Persian treasuries, there were still 180,000 talents left for Alexander in the central reserve after Daraios had paid for his war and fled with a further 8,000 talents, apart from the sums at provincial capitals.

Herodotos' list also gives an impression of the number of races the empire had to govern. On the whole, they were content with Persian rule, only those races which had formerly enjoyed dominion, such as the Egyptians and Babylonians, or those opposed to strong government, such as the Asian Greeks and mountain bandit tribes, being likely to rebel. However, this compliance was equally likely to work in favour of a new ruler, especially if he reintroduced a few traditional liberties.

Each satrapy was governed by a satrap, usually of noble Persian birth, but sometimes a Mede or descendant of the pre-conquest royal family. The satrap was expected to command the troops of his province as well as administer it, so had a considerable potential nuisance value under a weak Persian king. Under a strong king, he was kept in line by messengers travelling at high speed between post stations on the great road which had been constructed from Sardis to Susa and by occasional surprise visits from an official with the ominous-sounding title of the King's Eye.

The Persian culture was in many ways less advanced than that of the Greek world. The education of an upper-class Persian in theory concentrated heavily on riding, archery and speaking the truth. Although Persian could be written using an adaption of the Babylonian cuneiform, the administration was mainly carried on in the Aramaic language and script by clerks from the subject races, which often had cultures of respectable antiquity.

The Persians' own chief religion was the worship of Ahura-Mazda according to the teachings of the reforming sage Zoroaster whom they believed had lived about 300 years previously. This was much simpler and purer than that of the Greeks and encouraged what we would consider moral behaviour much more strongly. Indeed, so far from persecuting the religions of the conquered races, they even occasionally gave them government financial support. One notable example of this was the help given to the Jews of the captivity in rebuilding their temple at Jerusalem.

The same attitude of tolerance can be found throughout their dealings with other races. Where the Greeks divided other nations into Greeks, whom they hated, and non-Greeks, whom they despised, the Persians considered the Medes their equals, all others on the same level and only slightly below to be ruled justly rather than ruthlessly exploited in Greek fashion. Of course, this did not stop the king having someone impaled if he answered back, was found in the royal harem, or was caught diverting the revenues.

In such an absolute monarchy, much obviously depended upon the character of the man currently occupying the throne. The able King Ochos had died shortly before the Macedonian invasion was to be launched. According to court gossip, he had recently begun to suspect the activities of his Grand Vizier, but ate or drank something unlucky before he got around to doing anything about it. The heir also died of indigestion when he started taking an independent stance. The direct line being now extinguished, the vizier picked a distant royal relation called Daraios. His main qualifications apart from a modicum of royal blood were the echoes of Daraios the Great which his name aroused and the fact that he was a very big man who had once slain an enemy champion in single combat. He could not have been as stupid as is generally supposed, as he had the presence of mind to swop drinks with the vizier, who promptly expired.

The army the new king had at his disposal to fight off the invasion was very

Left to right *Greek or Macedonian general, Skythian horse archer, Persian extra heavy cavalryman, and Persian foot archer.*

different from that which Xerxes had led to Greece. The failure of the earlier Persian infantry to stand up to hoplites had led to large numbers of Greek mercenaries being imported in their place. There may have been as many as 48,000 Greeks in Daraios' service, nearly seven times as many as fought for Alexander as official war leader of the Greeks! How many of these would have been hoplites and how many peltasts is uncertain, but Xenophon's troops, also raised in the service of the Persians, had roughly one peltast to four hoplites. The proportion of peltasts may have increased somewhat since then, but the Persian experience of fighting against hoplites would have favoured them obtaining as many as possible. It must be remembered that in Greece the citizen militia would normally provide enough hoplites, and mercenary peltasts would be hired to support them. This was not the case in Persia, where on the contrary light troops were plentiful, hoplites non-existent.

The main strength of a Persian army lay in its cavalry. A typical heavy cavalryman wore an iron or bronze scale armour corslet over a long-sleeved tunic. Helmets were unusual, although some individuals had adopted them from the Greeks. Most wore a cloth tiara. This was something between a balaclava helmet and a pixie hood with its tip lying over in a fold, except in the case of the king, who had the tip of his tiara stuffed to stand up. Persian legs were clad in trousers, a practice the Greeks considered especially barbarian. The standard armament consisted of two javelins suitable for thrusting as well as throwing, backed by a sword. As with Greeks and Macedonians, shields were not carried.

Some Persian cavalry were heavier still in type. Their horses were armoured with metal-embossed leather face-pieces and with similar or metal scale armour for their breasts. Their riders would mostly wear helmets, might have a tubular leather protection for their rein arm called a cheir or 'hand', and would most likely wear parapleuridia, a sort of metal or leather scale armour cowboy chaps which protected the rider's whole leg and some of the horse's shoulders and ribs. The usual armament was carried.

This extra-heavy cavalry was not, however, as common as many authors suggest. The royal bodyguard might have had armour, as the usurping prince for whom Xenophon fought had 600 men so equipped. However, the Alexander mosaic does not show it on the Persian cavalry trying to cover the retreat of Daraios' chariot. Officers might well have had it, and the use during the next century of a further development of such armour by Kappadokians and Armenians suggests that at least a proportion of their troops might have had it. That it was not used by the majority of Persian cavalry is confirmed by the way that the ancient writers have the Macedonians deliberately striking at the Persian horses' heads with their spears, a practice which would be less productive if that part were armoured.

One part of the Persian army which almost certainly did have horse armour was the Massagetic Skythian contingent, some 2,000-strong. These would have differed from other Persian extra-heavy cavalry in having pointed Skythian hats instead of helmets and, according to Herodotos, in that they had no iron or silver, substituting bronze and gold. Their secondary weapon was a chisel-bladed axe called the sagaris, instead of a sword. Herodotos implies that some of their cavalry substituted a bow for the javelins. If so, the archers may have ridden in rear ranks where their need for horse armour would have been less pressing. Alternatively, the heavier cavalry might have been supported by separate bodies of skirmishing horse archers.

Not all Persian cavalry were armoured. The Dahae Skythians were light skirmishers with bow and axe, intent to stay out of harm's way and shoot from a safe distance. These could gradually wear down an infantry force with a steady trickle of casualties as the occasional shot slipped past guarding shields and armour, or could tempt heavy cavalry into repeated vain charges to be evaded easily, the horse archers then having a simple target as the scattered troopers rallied back. However, if their opponents could retain cohesion and morale until the archers had empty quivers, they would often just go home, possibly to collect more arrows, but the result was just the same. Horse archers were also very vulnerable to equally speedy light cavalry armed with javelins. These, being anxious to close, would charge at speed, and their pursuit could be swift enough to push the horse archers out of a tactical evasion into a panic flight. There were 1,000 Dahae fighting for Daraios at Gaugamela.

The favourite type of javelin light cavalry in a Persian army was the Paphlagonian, but a reconstruction of the battle line at Gaugamela suggests that the Arachosians and some other contingents also fell into this class. Except for the lack of corslets they were very similar to the heavy cavalry in dress and equipment.

One type of cavalry which did differ was the 1,000-strong Indian contingent, who alone among the two side's armies carried shields. They wore no armour, but cannot really be classed as light cavalry due to their poor manoeuvrability. Their lack of agility may have been due to their regard for fat horses, or it may have been because of their practice of trying to make their mounts drunk with wine before battle! India also provided Daraios with a small number of elephants, and possibly some infantry.

Left to right *Persian Kardakes, Paphlagonian light cavalryman, Greek mercenary Peltast, and Cretan archer.*

The Persian king traditionally rode to battle in a chariot rather than on a horse. Another variant of the chariot was also occasionally used, 200 of them being deployed for Gaugamela. These were each drawn by four partially armoured horses, manned only by a single heavily armoured driver, and liberally equipped with scythe blades and spear points. They were meant to be driven headlong into an enemy body in an equivalent of the 20th-century Japanese kamikaze attack. Sometimes this worked. More often, the drivers, instead of staying with the vehicle, bailed out too soon before contact and the horses swerved away into gaps between enemy units like show jumpers running out. Chariots also needed flat level terrain to charge over, so that signs of obstacle clearing work could be a tip-off that their use was envisaged. They could also be countered by light infantry who were agile enough to dodge their charge, then fling javelins from close range as they whizzed past. The most diabolical of all anti-chariot gimmicks was that later used by a Roman army against Mithridates the Great of Pontos. As the chariots charged, each legionary took one pace sideways and two backwards, revealing the thick stake set in the earth behind him!

The traditional royal infantry guard, the Immortals, were still represented by 1,000 men known as 'bearers of the golden pomegranate' from the counterweight on the butts of their spears.

The only good native Persian infantry available in numbers, to the tune of some 60,000, were a mysterious body known as Kardakes, one possible translation being 'picked young men'. From their positioning and fate at Issos, these seem to have been more equivalent to peltasts than hoplites. The Alexander sarcophagus shows Persians fighting on foot with hoplite-style shields, and the Kardakes seem to be the only candidates. If this is indeed them, we can take them to be roughly equivalent to the hypaspists in function, the main difference apart from the substitution of tiara, long sleeves and trousers for Greek dress, being the use of javelin instead of long spear.

The great majority of the Persian infantry were lighter troops, armed mainly with missile weapons such as bows, slings or javelins. Some of these were dressed much as the Kardakes except for having small shields or none. Others wore a variety of native costumes. Many were competent practitioners with their weapons, but the very number of men available could be a crippling disadvantage, few being able to see the enemy to shoot, and the press preventing them evading an enemy charge. Many came from timid or unwilling nations, and these could be a source of weakness for the rest; for if one man runs away, others are tempted to follow.

Except for the mercenary hoplites, none of a Persian army could be considered regular. Some troops were kept permanently embodied and regularly paid but were not drilled. Others came from small royal land holdings allotted to families in return for the obligation to provide a mounted warrior, chariot, or infantry archer when called upon to do so. Such land was known as horse land, chariot land or bow land respectively. Much of the cavalry consisted of semi-feudal levies which followed a prominent local nobleman to war. Some of the infantry might even be conscripts, routed out of their villages, handed a spear and told they were now part of the ever-victorious army of the Great King.

Permanently embodied bodyguards sometimes had uniforms in a common colour, white and red being known examples. However, the Alexander mosaic shows Daraios' horse guards in a variety of colours, patterned or plain except that they all wear yellow head-dress, as does the king, who in addition has a light-grey gown with a broad white stripe down the front and a purple cloak. His chariot horses, like most of the guardsmen's mounts, are black. Other horses colours are bay and chestnut. None of the horses is very big. Most other cavalry would dress as they pleased, usually in bright colours with complicated patterns. Colours and patterns grew darker and simpler the further you got down the social scale, and many of the poorer infantry probably wore natural linen and wool.

Standards were extensively used, mostly in the form of a small flag hanging from a crossbar on a pole like the Roman vexillum. The devices carried are unknown, but the symbols of Ahura-Mazda and other local gods are obvious possibilities. The group of standards accompanying the king included a gold sun disk on a pole, an antique shield with the Ahura-Mazda symbol on a pole, and the eagle with serpent mentioned earlier.

Most cities had some giant bow-type javelin-shooting engines available to be mounted on their walls if besieged. The Phoenician cities of the Syrian coast generally had pretty competent engineers, so might have already acquired a few of the new torsion-powered models that Philip had developed. As far as is known, none of this municipal artillery was ever dismounted for field use.

Before leaving the Persians, I should stress that the personal names in this book are the Greek forms. This is because Daraios is better known and more easily pronounced than Darayavaush, Kyros than Kurush, Xerxes than Khshayarsha, Ochos than Vauhaukash, and Zoroaster than Zarathoushtras. I might also add that there are alternate versions even of the Greek forms!

Chapter 7

Sea fighting, siege warfare and logistics

Vessels in the ancient world were divided into long ships intended for war and round ships designed to carry cargo. The round ship was not really round, but about four times as long as wide. It depended on the wind for propulsion, the usual rig being two square-cut sails on transverse yards, the larger on a vertical mast stepped just aft of midships, the smaller on a mast well raked forward in the bows. This was an efficient and practical rig, and Roman illustrations often show the main yard braced right round with the tack made fast near the stem. This implies that it was capable of working to windward to some degree, although not as well as modern fore-and-aft rigged vessels. It would, however, be faster than these with the wind behind the beam as would normally be the case given the methods of the age. Its biggest disadvantage compared with a modern schooner was the larger crew required for sail handling. Ancient literary sources indicate an average run of some 60 miles per day.

The largest commercial cargo ship of the period would probably have had a cargo capacity of about 250 tons. A more average large ship had a capacity of 150 tons, a length of 100 feet and a crew of ten to 15 men. The smallest decked ship, as opposed to open boats, would have had a capacity of 40 tons, a length of 40 feet and a crew of six or seven. Ships were to grow rapidly in size after Alexander opened up the sea routes to India, and Roman cargo vessels 180 feet long carrying 1,200 tons were not uncommon. Shipment by sea had huge advantages over land transport where it was possible. A large ox-cart with two men might carry a one-ton load ten miles in a day, working out at five ton/miles per man/day. A large ship could achieve 600 ton/miles per man/day, a massive saving in labour costs.

Where there was valuable cargo, there were also pirates to prey on it. The most dangerous areas were wild indented coasts and sea narrows, where small rowing vessels loaded with armed men might suddenly appear to seize ship and cargo and hold passengers and crew for ransom or sell them into slavery. At the lowest level, these would be open boats with 15 oars on each side manned by 40 or overmanned by 50 men and called triakonter or lembi. These were in essence little different from fishing boats and, indeed, the same people might well indulge in both activities. Similar boats were used by navies as despatch vessels and Alexander was to rely on them as his main fighting vessels for river warfare, although he also seems to have used craft up to triremes at times. A square sail could be hoisted to rest the rowers on long trips. More ambitious pirates used a special breed of ships called a hemiola, of which more later.

The first specialised warship had been the pentekonter. This was an open boat 100 feet long by 14 feet beam, with a gangway running down its centre line to a fighting platform at the bow protected by wicker screens, 25 oars on each side and an innovation in the shape of a wicked bronze-shod ram at the waterline to provide an alternative to boarding tactics. The crew consisted of 50 rowers who, like all oarsmen of the ancient world and contrary to popular opinion, were free fighting men, plus ten others, some of whom were fully armoured marines. The pentekoner was long obsolete as a general warship in Alexander's time, but a few were still used as scouts, patrol ships and despatch boats.

As ramming tactics came more into favour efforts were made to increase the speed and handiness of warships. Speed could be enhanced by increasing the ratio of length to beam, squeezing in the maximum number of rowers, and lightening the structure. Unfortunately, such increases in length actually detracted from handiness and, combined with the need for light construction, sadly weakened the structure. Experimental craft lengthened to give twice the number of oars and rowers were a failure. Then some unknown Phoenician hit on the idea of having two vertical rows of oarsmen, one over the other. This was a limited success, doubling the power without any great increase in length, but the extra height caused stability problems. These had to be compensated by greater beam, which in turn needed extra length to maintain a good ratio. Obviously, further development was yet required.

This culminated in the trireme or trieres, still the standard warship in Alexander's era. This had three levels of oarsmen and oars but not vertically over each other. The rowers were instead staggered at slightly different heights, the lowest row being the furthest inboard. The two outboard rows were given adequate leverages for their oars by a rectangular outrigger projecting beyond the ship's sides. There were 31 upper row oarsmen on each side and 27 in each of the two lower rows, making 170 in all. The crew also included 20 sailors and officers. Athenian triremes relied mainly on ramming as did the Phoenician navies, but carried ten hoplites and four archers to discourage boarding. The hoplite complement could be doubled if land operations were envisaged. States which relied on boarding rather than ramming and therefore did not mind the loss of speed caused by extra weight used up to 40 hoplite marines. The trireme's length was 120 feet, its true beam 13 feet and its beam over the outriggers 18 feet.

Progress had not stood exactly still though, and efforts to produce larger ships had recently been successful following the adoption of a new principle, that of having more than one man pulling the same oar. The first model had been the quadrireme, probably with two rows of oars on each side, each pulled by two rowers. This had been followed quickly by the quinquereme or penteres with three men on each of the top oars and two on the lower. This had a total of 300 rowers, 20 sailors and officers, and between 75 and 120 marines depending on the kind of fight envisaged. There was now a complete deck over the rowers to protect them and provide a platform for the marines. The dimensions were not much greater than those of the trireme at 120 feet length, 14 feet true beam and 20 feet over outriggers, but construction was much stronger, making the ship less vulnerable to ramming. As yet, such ships were mainly in use as flagships, but Syracuse, Carthage and Sidon were already moving towards standardising on them. Athens was not impressed by the idea of big ships, and when she did change she chose the quadrireme as her standard type.

Unlike the Athenians, Alexander thought big. By the end of his reign, he had ordered a large fleet of septiremes or hepteres. These were never to be built, but a few years later seven such ships played a big part in Demetrios Poliorketes' great naval victory off Cyprus. These had four men on each top oar, three on each lower, and had a crew of 350 rowers, 20 sailors and officers, and 200 marines. They were 140 feet long, 23 feet true beam and 30 feet over outriggers, and were almost impervious to ramming. Even this was not the ultimate limit. Demetrios later had a 16er as his flagship which seems to have been quite practical, 10ers were almost commonplace, and a single twin-hull 40er proved impractical only on economic grounds.

The use of quinqueremes and larger ships brought one other change to naval warfare. It was possible to mount artillery on such ships. These were nearly all anti-personnel bolt throwers, only the very largest ships having a small stone thrower which, however, had very little ship-sinking power except against the lightest of opposition. Much larger stone throwers were occasionally used from the sea in sieges, but this will be covered later.

The speed of ships under oars did not vary greatly with their size. The trireme and quadrireme were probably a little faster than larger or smaller ships, but this variation was dwarfed by that caused by rower fatigue. Full speed of around eight to nine knots could be achieved for only about 20 minutes. Fast cruise of four to five knots could be maintained for about three hours. Slow cruise involved taking some half or more of the oarsmen and oars out of action to rest in relays, and the ship could keep up two to three knots all day. Turning circle and speed varied with the ship's length. The oars could be used differentially to back up the steersman, so both radius and time taken were quite moderate. Even at high speeds a 360° turn of 250 feet diameter could be completed in one minute.

Warships could also move under sail. They had, in fact, two sets. The first was used only under passage and would ideally be landed with its mast to save weight before battle. A fleet arriving by sea to fight one already on the spot could therefore be at a disadvantage if engaged immediately. If in an otherwise straight fight one admiral retained his sails, it would depress his side's morale and raise that of the enemy, as he obviously lacked confidence in his propects and was prepared to flee. The second, which was retained on board, was a much lighter affair called the boatsail. This could be hoisted when all appeared to be lost and the rowers were too tired to escape and would then take the ship downwind, hopefully too fast for the equally tired enemy to follow. Warships were slightly faster than cargo vessels under sail, probably doing a maximum of six or seven knots compared with the merchantmen's maximum of five knots and average of three knots, wind permitting of course. However, they could not sail into the wind, and because of their shallow draft made excessive leeway. Clever use of the oars could partly compensate for this. It was possible to row at an angle into the wind, then sail back with it, thus progressing in a zig-zag almost as if tacking. Leeway under sail could be minimised by rowing with some of the lee oars.

The pirate hemiola was designed to use oars and sails together either to overtake a merchant ship or escape an avenging warship, reaching as much as ten knots. It was 70 feet in length and ten feet in beam. Its name means 1½er, and it has been postulated that it had two banks of single-manned oars of which half a bank could be rapidly drawn in to provide men to lower the mast for action. It had a total crew of 62. The answer to it was a craft specially designed by the Rhodians, who took it on themselves to clear the trade routes of such vermin. This was the triemiola or 2½er, designed on similar principles but with a much larger crew of 200 or so.

Merchantmen often made direct trips across open sea and war fleets occasionally did so, but a more usual method was to follow the coastline or hop from island to island. It is, in fact, quite hard to get out of sight of one or more islands off the Aegean coasts of Greece and Asia Minor. A warship could carry stores and water for three days in emergency but normal practice was to land each night for foraging, cooking and sleeping. A land force could often severely hamper a fleet by depriving it of these facilities. Because rowing vessels went to leeward so badly, a rocky lee shore was a dangerous neighbour indeed. However, being designed to be hauled up stern first on the beach each night, a sandy shore instead was considered a welcome refuge from storms. That this was so was largely due to the almost complete lack of tides in the Mediterranean. The discovery that such tides existed was to be a terrible shock to Alexander's fleet when it first encountered them, just as it was a surprise to find that all winds did not blow steadily from northerly points throughout the sailing season.

Battle formations were mainly line abreast, with much backing and turning to prevent the enemy from getting his rams into your vulnerable sides. Navies specialising in ramming would either attempt a manoeuvre called the periplos to get around the enemy flank or one called the diekplos to break through his line then turn to attack in rear. Both these really required the enemy to be less skilled. Navies preferring boarding tactics would try to make contact bow on and turn the fight into a land battle. The advent of the big warships greatly favoured the latter tactic.

Some nations were undoubtedly more skilled at sea than others. They included the Athenians, Rhodians, Cypriots, Phoenicians and the former Phoenician colony of Carthage. The advent of the big ships provided some relief, as only one man on each oar needed to be highly skilled. Not all the skills required were those we might think of today like rowing and seamanship. The ability to throw a javelin sitting down was apparently one thing that distinguished a proper marine from a drafted land soldier. Altogether, a couple of months' hard practice might be the minimum required to make a raw fleet of men lacking previous experience fit to meet bad weather or an enemy.

Ships could be built much more quickly than crews could be trained, on some occasions in as little as one and a half months from starting to fell timber to launching. Of course, ships hurriedly built in this fashion from green timber might last no more than five years instead of the 25 years possible with a properly constructed and maintained vessel.

The cost of constructing and fitting out a trireme in Alexander's time can be taken as two talents. Proper maintenance could cost a talent a year, or skimped at half a talent. The crew provided their own food and were only paid for the eight months of the sailing season. At the standard rate of half a drachma a day, this comes to another four talents. Costs for other ships would be in proportion to their sizes and crews. A skilled shipwright's pay can be taken as twice that of a labourer or oarsman, which will give a pretty close idea of the number of man/days involved in construction and fitting out. Just as there were mercenaries on land, there were on sea. On one occasion the Rhodians hired out a number of triremes at 10,000 drachmae a month which, even allowing for inflation, represents a handsome profit!

Before going on to consider siege methods, we had best look at the sort of defences to be attacked. The lowest class is represented by field defences constructed by digging a ditch, casting up the earth removed into a bank on the inside and then planting stakes on this to form a palisade. This might protect a temporary camp against attack or even surround an isolated farmstead. It can be quickly smashed by stone-throwing artillery of even the lightest kind, the palisade chopped by axes or set on fire or pulled over with ropes, or at a pinch climbed by assaulting troops without special equipment, although at considerable personal risk.

The next class has deeper and possibly multiple ditches, perhaps dry stone ramparts, complicated entrances, sometimes wooden towers, and access is made difficult by cliffs, ravines, water or steep slopes on some or all of its sides. The barbarian hill fort of which we have so many in Britain is a good example. Once access has been gained and artillery or missile troops brought into position to shoot in the assault, this presents few problems to a regular army.

The third class has regular tall walls with rampart walk and battlements, studded at intervals by taller towers to give extra command and provide flank protection. These can be weakly constructed of stone or thick constructions of sunbaked mud brick. They must either be escaladed with ladders or breached.

The last category is much the same but is well constructed with thick stone walls offering much greater resistance to seige equipment, so is correspondingly harder to breach, although no more difficult to escalade.

It is with the last two, more formal, classes that we shall be primarily concerned. Alexander treated the others with considerable disdain, and they rarely held him up other than while he constructed an approach across the obstacles separating him from them. The most common siege method before Philip was to sit down and starve the defenders out. This was all very well if you had time to spare, help was not on the way to the garrison, you had enough money to pay your own troops, and disease did not decimate the besiegers before the garrison hungered or despaired. Philip's favourite method was to deliver a mule load of silver to the fortress commandant's quarters but, for occasions when this would not be possible, he got together an imposing collection of talented and original engineers.

Alexander preferred to take fortresses with a rapid escalade if he could. With a large number of ladders up against the enemy walls and massed archery and artillery keeping the defenders' heads down, the chances of getting a foothold on the ramparts which could then be rapidly expanded was often reasonably good, especially if the defenders' morale had been reduced by previous defeats. On the other hand, a failure could be very costly. Alexander did not have many of these, mainly because he only made such attacks when conditions were favourable, but partly because he was given to getting up the ladder himself and leading from the front. General Eisenhower once said that the troops liked to see him up near the front line in World War 2 because they figured out that their position could not be all that dangerous if there were senior generals hanging about!

Another favourite method could only be used against mud brick walls and also involved keeping the defender's heads down. Once this had been accomplished, the infantry closed up to the foot of the walls along a wide stretch and proceeded to undermine them, with whatever tools they had and with their weapons. Wooden stakes would be used to support the weight above, then set fire to once the excavation was deep enough. This could often bring down enough wall material to make a climable slope up the rest.

More formal mining with a tunnel driven from a distance up to and under a section of wall or an interval tower was a slower but potentially much more dangerous form of attack. It was slower because only a few men could be employed at a time and these had to be highly skilled. It was dangerous because the usual target was a tower. If the burning of the props did not bring down the tower and a good section of wall with it, it often left it teetering dangerously and unable to be manned. However, the miners did not necessarily have it all their own way. If the defenders suspected mining, they would set out basins of water along the defences, and start digging a countermine when they saw the water repeatedly quiver from faint underground vibrations. As the countermine tunnel neared the other, the miners would hear the sounds of tools. Finally, there might be a breakthrough and a deadly fight in the dark with weapons and tools. An especially rough trick was for the counterminers to introduce a maddened bear into their opponents' tunnel. One of the most dramatic finds ever made in archeology was at Dura, where the tower collapsed on Sassanid miners and Roman counterminers as they fought, leaving their corpses to be found together one and a half millenia later. Even if countermining was ineffective, the mine might still fail. It might have gone off course and be too far away to do serious damage. Almost as bad, the burning of the props was always unpredictable, and it could happen that the breach was made in the middle of the night and successfully obstructed by the defenders before a dawn assault could be launched up the tumbled slope of debris. Mining was made infinitely more difficult by rock foundations or a ditch, impossible by a wet moat.

Another old technique was the use of a battering ram. This could be as simple as a tree trunk carried against a door by a dozen men, but was usually far more elaborate. Much ingenuity was put into defending doorways and even with the first door burst down there would likely be a further one with a death trap in between commanded by arrow slits and murder holes in the roof for such kindnesses as boiling oil or water, melted lead or red hot sand. The walls offered a better prospect as support could be had from missiles against the defenders at the top. The usual method was to construct a wheeled shed or penthouse of heavy timbers draped with green hides as a defence against fire missiles. This would be pushed up against the wall, then the ram set continually swinging from its roof against the wall until the constant impacts made first a crack, then a breach. The biggest of these ever to be constructed was used by Demetrios Poliorketes at the great siege of Rhodes. The ram itself was 180 feet long and was worked in relays by 1,000 men.

A related device, more used in earlier times and most often against brick walls, substituted a sharp pick end for the blunt end of the ram, and could be used to dig out a cavity. This is often seen in Assyrian sculpture.

The effectiveness of stone-throwing artillery against walls depended on the size of the engine, the strength of the walls and the range. As described earlier, a strong stone wall needed a one-talent or three-talent engine at close range to breach it and even then it might be a long job. Against weak stone or brick walls, even a 30-mina machine might be effective and results could be obtained in a single day. However, an artillery battle would have to be fought and the defending engines silenced before breaching could be attempted. The attackers could use 30-mina and 10-mina stone-throwers to try to smash defending engines, and the former could smash up the lighter stone of the battlements as well. The defenders would use 30-mina engines and larger against targets such as siege towers and penthouses, 10-mina machines for counter-battery. Both sides would use bolt-shooters to pick off artillery crew and other exposed personnel.

The final and most advanced siege technique grew out of the combination of the penthouse and the scaling ladder. In its simplest form, it was a wheeled tower higher than the defences. The top storey accommodated archers who could shoot down on defenders who at such angles would not be protected by their battlements. The next contained a drawbridge which could be let down to enable stormers to rush across it on to the wall. Ladders from the remaining floors enabled other men to reinforce success. The problem lay in getting the tower close to the wall under artillery fire. Towers became steadily heavier and more strongly constructed, equipped with water tanks to fight fire, plated with iron and draped with hides. The final development was to give them their own artillery so that they could fight their way forward. As usual, Demetrios Poliorketes lived up to his nickname 'City Taker' by establishing a record at Rhodes. His machine was 100 to 150 feet tall, 50 to 75 feet square at its base, had nine storeys, weighed 180 tons or $3\frac{1}{2}$ times the weight of a trireme, but was pushed fairly easily by 3,400 men. On its lower floor it had two three-talent and one one-talent stone-thrower, on the next it had three one-talent stone-throwers, and on the other storeys a further 14 smaller stone-throwers and bolt-shooters. The engines were protected by heavily padded hatches which opened to shoot, then closed for reloading. It was finally defeated by diverting water to turn the ground between it and the defences into a swamp.

None of Alexander's towers were that big, although he used artillery-armed siege towers on at least one occasion. Mostly the opposition did not justify them, and the kind he used most often probably corresponded to the size later quoted as the minimum by the Roman engineer Vitruvius. This was 90 feet high, 25 feet square at the base and 20 feet square at the top. Judging by the speed with which Alexander's engineers got these into action, it is likely that they kept all the necessary metal fittings in stock so that they only had to cut the wood. They may even have transported whole towers in disassembled form as they are not likely to have weighed more than 30 tons.

If towers or penthouses were to be brought up to an enemy's walls by land, it was first necessary to fill in any ditches in their path. The method used was for the whole army to work at this every waking moment during which they were not committed to other duties. Somewhat surprisingly, this brought reasonably quick results with only minor losses. They could also be brought up on ships against seaward walls. To gain adequate stability, two ships would be fastened together as a base. This technique could also be used in mounting large stone-throwers on ships. Yet another technique was the installation of a single bolt-shooter in a sort of wooden gunhouse in the bow of a small cargo ship or trireme. This could then annoy the defenders in relative safety from light weapons, and could simply move out of angle if engaged by something big. Such converted ships were, of course, vulnerable to ramming attack and needed to be protected by unconverted vessels.

Soldiers were largely responsible for supplying themselves. Their pay was made up of two components which we can call ration allowance and salary. Ration allowance was paid monthly in advance, usually as cash but sometimes as food. Troops were expected to start a long march with food for 15 days and cash to buy it from the sutlers who accompanied the army for a further 15. This was usually left to private enterprise but commanders occasionally collected food from the countryside, then sold it to the sutlers to resell to the men. If a commander had no money, his only recourse was to allow the men to plunder the locals, whether these were friendly or enemy. If the troops managed to feed themselves in this way, it was generally accepted that they could not expect to be paid the ration allowance for that period at a later date, although it was not completely unknown for troops to try this on, especially if they were discontented for other reasons. However, if ration allowance had been paid and the troops then plundered, it was equally accepted that the commander could not seek to have it repaid out of future entitlement.

The salary component was in theory paid monthly in arrears, but in practice got behind more often than not. The troops usually accepted this state of affairs, provided that all arrears were paid off at the end of the campaigning season. If they were not, trouble would erupt on a massive scale with rioting, murder, looting of the locals and possibly an outright revolution to seize control of the state. The reason for both the temporary forbearance and the end of season deadline lay in the custom of hiring troops for only ten months in the year. Once this time was up, they were no longer entitled to ration allowance, so normally took their pay and went off for a holiday. Without it, there was not only no holiday, but nothing to live on.

The actual amounts paid are hard to sort out because the information surviving is fragmentary and partly comes from the time of rapid inflation following Alexander's conquests. However, the following figures are probably not too far out. They are quoted in Athenian obols per day. Remember, 6 obols = 1 drachma, 100 drachmae = 1 mina (one pound weight of silver), and 60 minae = 1 talent.

	Ration allowance	Salary
Rower or light infantryman	2	1
Peltast	2	2
Hoplite	2	3
Cavalry	4	4

These are only averages. An impecunious state could try to get away with paying an obol less and might well collect enough troops if there was little fighting going on that year. However, if there was plenty of alternative employment, it would go short or get only the dregs. A state might also get away with paying its own citizen troops the lower rate, or bully junior members of a confederation into supplying troops for less, but this would obviously tend to produce political repercussions. At the other extreme, states that could afford to do so might increase pay by one or two obols to get a better share or to deprive opponents of troops. The Persians paid up to 5 obols plus rations for mercenaries, Alexander's hypaspists got 6 obols, and the Athenians sent home a bunch of Thracians hired in an emergency because, on more sober reflection, pay and allowances totalling 6 obols seemed excessive. The Phokians gave double pay, but that was partly to soothe the mercenaries' fears of the divine consequences of serving impious temple robbers. One is reminded of the English free company which later held the Pope to ransom and which, when offered 5,000 crowns and his blessing or 10,000 and his solemn curse with bell, book and candle, opted for the latter!

A state which lacked money to pay its troops could, of course, try to get it from its allies, steal it, or all else failing, borrow it. I say all else failing, because the normal rate of interest was likely to be about 20 per cent, rising considerably if the risks seemed greater than usual.

The supply of mercenaries was not unlimited. It would tend to increase if there was peace at home, if harvests were poor, if especially good pay was being offered or if there were exceptional prospects for loot. Alexander's conquests were to tempt many more men into the profession. It would also increase if some state was trying hard to put down Aitolian or Cretan pirates and was thus driving potential recruits into the only other congenial occupation for those nations. Strangely enough, there seems to have been a sort of mercenaries' labour exchange. This was at Tainaros on the central southern peninsula of the Peloponnesos, approachable by land only through Spartan territory. Both prospective employers and employees would go there to seek each other.

Like any other impedimenta, a general's war chest had to be carried, so this seems a good time to mention the loads which could be transported other than by ships. The most basic method of all is, of course, on the back of a human porter, who might at a pinch carry 100 pounds. A pack mule's load can be taken as 250 pounds, a camel's as 500 pounds, and that of a pack elephant as 1,000 pounds. A light cart drawn by two oxen could also carry 1,000 pounds, and a larger one drawn by six or more oxen twice or three times that. Bad terrain or lack of food would either lessen these loads or lead to increased losses in animals. Animal losses would also be enhanced if loads were increased in good conditions.

Do not image that animals can always pick up enough grazing to keep themselves in condition. In general, they are likely to deteriorate from November onwards if kept working unless fed grain, and will be incapable of any hard work before the grass starts to grow again in April. As nomads did not grow grain, winter was always the best time to attack them, while they lacked mobility.

Chapter 8

The conquest of Asia Minor: the Granikos campaign, 334 BC to 333 BC

Alexander finally set out for Asia in early May of 334 BC. He marched along the Thracian coast to Sestos in the Chersonesos, where only a few miles of water separated Europe from Asia. Here he met the combined Macedonian and allied Greek fleet of 160 warships. The Persians had a fleet of 300 or more ships recruited from the Phoenician ports and Cyprus, but these were engaged elsewhere. A revolt had broken out in Egypt two years previously and mopping it up had delayed the Egyptian fleet past the end of the sailing season of 335 BC. It could not now intervene in time some 700 miles to the north-west, especially as the prevailing winds were northerly.

Parmenion had returned to meet Alexander, so was left with 100 warships and numerous transports to ferry the army over to the bridgehead secured by the advanced force at Abydos on the Asian coast. Alexander took the remaining 60 warships and sailed some 20 miles down the coast to opposite the traditional site of Troy at the entrance to the strait. Here his small force could watch out for a possible Persian naval response where the narrow waters would hinder the enemy from deploying their full superiority. At the very least he should be able to delay them long enough to bring up the remainder of his warships and get the transports out of the way. While he was there, he took advantage of the opportunity to make a propaganda visit to Troy, site of an earlier Greek victory over an Asian power. This was an outstanding success in morale-boosting and helping to establish his theoretical role as the champion of Greek civilisation against the foreign barbarian, so much so that his equally sound tactical motive has been ignored by historians.

How much of the coast was still held by Macedonian sympathisers is unknown. As we have already seen in Chapter 2, the first wave of enthusiasm resulting from the advanced force's landing had led to the gaining of coastal cities as far south as Ephesos, plus the important islands of Tenedos, Lesbos and Chios. Much of this territory appears to have been lost again during the two-year delay caused by Philip's murder, partly no doubt due to political troubles among the force's multiple command, some of whom were probably too busy looking over their shoulders at Macedonia to take any very energetic action, but mainly because of the counter-attack by the local satraps. We can guess that Ilion near Troy and Abydos were still friendly, and we know that the island city of Kyzikos had held out against Persian attacks. This was especially awkward for the Persians as their only mint for the area was at Kyzikos and they had many mercenaries to pay.

The advanced force had originally included 1,000 cavalry, of whom 600 were probably Macedonian prodromoi, and 10,000 infantry, probably mostly mercenaries and allied Greeks. When the main expeditionary force had joined them, the troops at Alexander's immediate disposal totalled some 5,100 cavalry and 35,000 infantry. These figures were made up roughly as follows:

Macedonian companion cavalry	1,800	Macedonian foot companions	12,000
Macedonian prodromoi	600	Greek mercenary peltasts	5,000
Thessalian cavalry	1,800	Greek allied hoplites	7,000
Greek allied cavalry	600	Thracian peltasts	6,000
Paionian light cavalry	300	Illyrian light javelinmen	1,000
Macedonian hypaspists	3,000	Agrianian light javelinmen	500
		Cretan archers	500

Alexander now advanced with these north-east along the coast to Lampsakos, a distance of about 16 miles which took him two days. Lampsakos would not admit him. The Persian commanders had borrowed money there to pay their troops, which the city would hardly get back unless it proved loyal. Also, the rival city of Kyzikos had declared for Alexander and the Greeks of Lampsakos did not care to be on the same side. He continued on along the coast to the city of Priapos which did submit to him. A short distance ahead lay the River Granikos, Kyzikos was about 30 miles further, and the city of Daskylion yet another 50 miles along the coast. He sent the four ilai of prodromoi and Sokrates' ila of companion cavalry ahead to scout.

We must presume from Alexander's line of march that he knew the Persian army had been encamped at Daskylion waiting for his landing. It had, in fact, advanced a little since then and was currently at Zeleia debating its next actions. The army consisted of the Persian nobles of Asia Minor, their mounted followers, military colonist and stray courtiers come to see the fun. It totalled 20,000 cavalry, together with 18,000 Greek mercenary hoplites. The hoplite commander was Memnon, originally from Rhodes but a veteran in Persian service and married to a Persian wife. He advised declining battle against the stronger Macedonian army, instead retreating and laying waste the countryside, thus gaining time for Daraios to arrive with reinforcements and presenting Alexander with supply difficulties. This was hotly disputed by the nobles who did not fancy destroying their own estates and their subjects' crops. Finally, Spithridates, satrap of Lydia and Ionia, who commanded the army, ruled in favour of fighting a defensive battle on the Granikos.

When his scouts sighted the Persian army, Alexander also met with quibbles from his generals. The first was that it was the month of Daisios, during which Macedonians traditionally avoided fighting. Alexander was prepared to compromise. He issued a decree cancelling Daisios, and instituting a second month of Artemisios instead! The other was worthy of more consideration and originated from the skilful veteran Parmenion.

Parmenion pointed out that the army could not reach the river until early afternoon and would then need time to deploy, so that the battle would inevitably start late in the day. The river, although not especially deep, was some 60 feet wide and had steep and slippery clay banks. An immediate attack would have the Macedonians emerging from the crossing tired and disordered, so at a disadvantage to the defenders. He thought the army should encamp and attack at dawn. The Persian cavalry would not dare bivouac near by, as it would be in grave danger if caught with its horses unharnessed or if it kept them harnessed all night without proper rest. The Macedonians could therefore force a crossing against the infantry alone, assuming they were not withdrawn with the cavalry, then form up in good order on the far side to fight on equal terms.

All but one of the ancient sources say that this advice was rejected. The remaining source says it was followed, and one modern writer not only believes this, but also suggests that the other accounts are deliberate official lies intended to show Parmenion in a bad light. This is inherently unlikely, if only because it does not reflect badly on Parmenion, but proves him to be a competent tactician. It is rather Alexander who is shown up as acting rashly and getting away with it by sheer luck and the heroism of one of his friends, a friend moreover who, from his later actions, could not expect kindly treatment from an official historian. This, of course, supposes that all the facts are known.

One of the curious things about the majority account is that it shows both sides apparently using bad tactics. The Macedonians attack rashly in disorder, but the Persians, instead of defending the bank with infantry and counter-attacking any foothold the enemy gain with cavalry, thus using the two arms in the optimum way, line the bank with stationary cavalry and keep the infantry some distance to the rear. The version I now propose is consistent with the known facts and at the same time makes both sides act sensibly.

I postulate that the Persian cavalry reached the river before the Macedonian scouts could cross, but that the slower-moving mercenary hoplites were still some distance away. The Persian cavalry command therefore decided to man the river bank to delay the enemy until the hoplites could come up and take over. The cavalry could then withdraw and be reformed into a counter-attack force. The mere fact of showing the cavalry on the bank might make the enemy hold off long enough. If it did not, they had at least the advantage of height and would have ideal javelin targets as the enemy were slowed by the river and its banks, and might well turn them. If they did not succeed in this, then hopefully the disorder of the Macedonians would compensate for the impetus they got from moving forward against stationary defenders.

We already know Parmenion's advice. It was sensible as far as it went, but included one very real risk. If the hoplites were not withdrawn but kept position on the river bank all night, they would have been a very dangerous nut to crack for either disordered phalangites or peltasts next morning. The chances of disposing of them before the Persian cavalry return were not good. Hoplites were to demonstrate their worth both against disordered phalangites and charging companion cavalry in good order before the war was over.

Alexander's choice was instead to launch an immediate attack, and we can see from his dispositions that he wasted no time in shuffling units about, but deployed them as they came up and launched the attack as soon as all were ready.

The prodromoi and Sokrates' ila of companion cavalry had been the first to arrive and were to lead the attack, reinforced by the Macedonian light cavalry's Paionian rivals. Next were the remainder of the companion cavalry who came up with Alexander. These fell in on the right of the prodromoi, supported by the Cretans and Agrianians. Next came the hypaspists, who fell in on the left of the scouting force. Half the phalangites continued the line to the left, then an

The Battle of Granikos

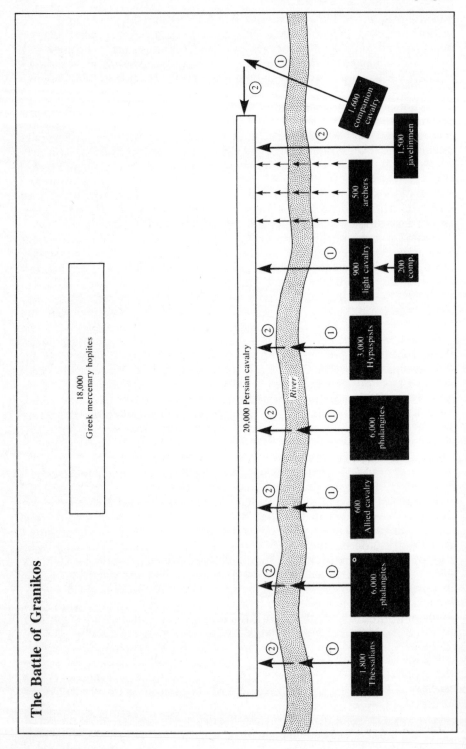

18,000 Greek mercenary hoplites

20,000 Persian cavalry

River

1,600 companion cavalry

1,500 javelinmen

500 archers

900 light cavalry

200 comp.

3,000 Hypaspists

6,000 phalangites

600 Allied cavalry

6,000 phalangites

1,800 Thessalians

unspecified body who may have been allied Greek cavalry or peltasts, then the rest of the phalangites, the Thracians and the Thessalian rearguard.

The light prodromoi and Paionians led the attack supported by Sokrates' companions. Being more agile than the other cavalry, they managed to get a footing on the bank in spite of the showers of javelins, and a scrimmage commenced. The light troops suffered badly and were pushed back.

Alexander had meanwhile headed across, aiming a little upstream and to the right. By now the light cavalry had probably received many of the javelins which would otherwise have fallen on the companions, and the defenders were probably distracted by the bother around the initial point of contact, as well as by the change in direction and archery from the far bank. The Macedonian artillery would also have been useful here but did not seem to have got into action. Presumably they did not wait for it. The combination of these factors seems to have got the companions across without being opposed on the bank. Possibly the defenders fell back in the face of the archery. Whatever the reason, the companions quickly sorted themselves out and charged in obliquely towards the enemy centre where their leaders were concentrated.

Meanwhile, the infantry were also crossing, as were the Thessalians further down. At first they were checked by the javelins but, when these ran short, the horsemen could not stand against the long infantry pikes and began to give way. If the fight had been on level ground, the Persian cavalry could have charged in to take advantage of the infantry disorganisation and might have broken them. As it was, if they had charged down the slippery bank into the river, they would have been, if anything, even worse off themselves.

Alexander, charging at the tip of a Macedonian wedge, was at one time in considerable danger himself. The shorter javelins of the first Persian unit he struck could not cope with the long Macedonian lances and it had to give way. Alexander's own lance broke and had to be replaced. Charging again with a new lance into a fresh body of Persians led by Daraios' son in law, he killed him with a thrust to the face, but then was struck at with a sword by another prominent noble, the blow shearing off part of his helmet as he rode past. Turning on this man, Alexander thrust him through the corslet and chest, but exposed himself in the process to the sword of the Persian commander Mithridates. He was saved by a blow from Kleitos which cut off the Persian's arm and mortally wounded him.

Other senior Persians including more of Daraios' relations, had also perished, disheartening their men, and they were having trouble with the Agrianians who were now mingling with the companions and interfering with a private fight. The centre was the first to give, and then the wings followed in flight. There was little pursuit, as the Persian hoplites were now close enough to need attention. About a thousand of the Persians died. As usual in an Ancient battle, the defeated suffered disproportionately high casualties, even a minor wound to horse or man being sufficient to prevent escape.

Now it was the turn of the hoplites. Alexander charged them with the companions. He made no impression on them and his horse, not the famous Bukephalos, was killed under him. However, his attack delayed them long enough for his infantry to surround them. According to our sources, he refused at first to accept their surrender on the grounds that they were traitors to Greece, and all but 2,000 were dead before he relented.

Macedonian losses were said to have been 25 killed among the companions,

60 from the other cavalry, and 30 infantry. These figures may not be very reliable, and in any case at least four times as many could be expected to have been temporarily disabled by wounds. Ancient armour protected the fatal areas relatively well, but tended to leave the extremities exposed.

The difference between the casualties to the mercenaries and those of their opponents is particularly disquieting, and one is tempted to wonder if the majority of them might have got away. If they kept their heads and moved off in a body, they might have been considered too dangerous to meddle with, especially as the Macedonian cavalry horses were probably not in a good state for pursuit after a difficult river crossing and battle. It is also likely that darkness was not far off. One reason for supposing that this might have been the case is the variant source mentioned above. This is commonly supposed to have derived from one of the mercenaries opposed to Alexander, hence his thinking that the Macedonians had crossed the river at dawn, as all he would know was that they had crossed before he had arrived. If the official story was true, he must have been one of the 2,000 prisoners, yet he seems to have fought in later battles as well.

One very important Greek escapee was Memnon, who was to become the life and soul of continuing Persian resistance in Asia Minor. However, he did not fight with the mercenaries but on horseback with the other senior generals. His deputy Omares was not so lucky, and died with his men.

Next day, Alexander appointed Kalas, the commander of the Thessalian cavalry, as satrap in place of Arsites, and sent Parmenion to Daskylion with part of the army to install him. This was easily accomplished, Arsites having evacuated and fled into the interior, where he shortly after committed suicide in remorse for his bad advice before the battle. This was the satrapy which comes third in Herodotos' list. In addition to the Greek coastal cities opposite Europe, it controlled much of the interior hill country which was mainly inhabited by Phrygian mountaineers. Delegations from these now began to come in to submit, to be told that taxes would be identical to those paid to Daraios and sent back to their homes.

Alexander himself marched south towards Sardes. This had formerly been the seat of Spithridates, who had perished in the battle. He had controlled both the first and second satrapies of Herodotos' list as well as acting as overall commander in Asia Minor, and Sardes housed a rich central treasury. Mithrines, the commander of the citadel garrison, came out with the senior citizens to submit when the army was still nearly ten miles away. He henceforth accompanied the army as Alexander's honoured friend and good example to other garrison commanders. Sardes was not a Greek city, but the former capital of Kroisos' Lydia. Alexander restored a traditional form of self-government abolished by the Persians, but installed a garrison of Argive Greeks under a Macedonian commander, and kept it a regional administrative centre. A Greek named Nikias was left there in charge of Asia Minor's finances, and Parmenion's brother Asandros became satrap in Spithridates' place with a force of cavalry and light troops to enforce his will in the countryside.

Alexander now sent the remainder of his allied troops on a subsidiary mission to 'Memnon's country'. We now know that Memnon was busy reorganising fugitives about 100 miles south at Halikarnassos, so this expedition may have been a flank guard pushed out in that direction.

The main army marched south-west to Ephesos, a distance of about 50 miles which it covered in four days. The Persian garrison and a small squadron of light warships had already evacuated when he arrived. Ephesos had declared for Philip two years previously, but had been recovered for the Persians by Memnon. Alexander now expelled the oligarchic government which had been co-operating with the Persians and set up a democratic one in its place. There were scenes of wild lower-class enthusiasm, and Alexander had to intervene to put an end to bloody reprisals against the oligarchs, who had probably not had much option in the matter of co-operation in the first place.

This democratic enthusiasm seems to have given Alexander ideas. He now recalled the allied infantry, and sent out two forces, each of 2,500 Greek allies, a taxis of phalangites and an ila of companion cavalry. One of these was to head west under Pharmenion, the other north-west under Alkimachos, an experienced diplomat as well as a general. Their missions were to free all the Greek coastal cities still held by the Persians, to expel all oligarchs, and to institute democratic government. The public enthusiasm for this might well be a temporary thing, but it made good propaganda for mainland Greece and, more important, placed governments in power in every city which must be firmly committed to his support. If the Persians regained control, the best the democrat leaders could hope for would be exile, the worst, impaling.

Meanwhile, Alexander took the rest of the army towards Miletos, about 40 miles to the south. This was still garrisoned. The Greek mercenary holding it for Persia, a man named Hegesistratos, had written to Alexander surrendering the place, but had then changed his mind on hearing that the main Persian fleet was shortly to arrive at last. However, Alexander's admiral Nikanor arrived three days earlier with 160 warships with troops on board. The harbour of Miletos was controlled by the offshore island of Lade. With the island now held by 4,000 Greek and 6,000 Thracian peltasts, Nikanor could deny both battle and access to the 400 Persian warships. Seeing themselves cut off from help, the garrison withdrew from their outer walls to an inner circuit they could hold more easily.

Parmenion now suggested a naval attack on the Persian fleet. If the Macedonians won, he argued, they would have command of the sea and would find it very useful, while if they lost they would be no worse off than at present, as a fleet forced to huddle in harbour could not be said to be doing much good. As a clincher, an eagle had been observed perched on the shore behind the flagship, a perfect omen promising victory!

Alexander saw it differently. He thought it lunacy to attack an experienced Cyprian and Phoenician fleet of more than twice the strength of his own partly trained force. If the battle were lost, it would seriously damage the troops' morale, at present so high, and encourage dissident Greeks at home to revolt. He also took a different view of the omen. An eagle ashore meant that they should seek victory on land.

The eagle must have known what it was doing. A messenger now came jointly from the mercenaries holding Miletos and the town council declaring that the city was prepared to be neutral and let both Macedonians and Persians inside its walls if Alexander would raise the siege. This exceedingly impractical proposal can hardly have been meant seriously. Alexander replied to the effect that if the citizens wished to prevent him entering they had better be on the walls armed by dawn. The walls must have been fairly antiquated, as they were easily breached in a number of places by Alexander's stone-throwing artillery

SARMATIANS

CASPIAN SEA

(Euxine)

Artaxata

ARMENIA

Sinope

lis

ΟΝΙΑ

PONTOS

L Thospis

L Matianos

Mazaka

Gaugamela

MEDIA

KAPPADOKIA

Arbela

Gates pass KILIKIA

ASSYRIA

Issos

Tarsos

Syrian
Gates pass

Thapsakos

R Tigris

R Euphrates

PHOENICIA

Palmyra

Babylon

Arados

Salamis

Tripolis

Kition

Byblos

Damascus

BABYLONIA

Sidon

Tyre

ARABIA

Jerusalem

Gaza

500 miles

Pelusion

mphis

in a single day. The breaches were assaulted later that day and carried. Most of the citizens then surrendered, but the oligarchs and garrison tried to get away by water. None appear to have escaped the Macedonian fleet, but 300 mercenaries reached a small island and, as they seemed prepared to die fighting, were granted terms.

The Persian fleet had attempted to intervene but had seen it was hopeless to try and get through, and so desisted. Basing themselves near by at Mykale, they tried again to tempt the Macedonian ships to give battle. Instead, Alexander sent a land force to deprive them of their base and watering facilities. This forced them to withdraw to the island of Samos, too far off to be a convenient base for action in the Miletos area. However, they tried once more. This time they varied their tactics by sneaking five ships past Lade in an attempt to catch the Macedonian ships beached with their crews ashore foraging and cooking. Unfortunately, ten Macedonian guard ships remained manned, and these chased the five Persians off, capturing the slowest.

Alexander now decided to disband his fleet. It obviously could not withstand the Persian fleet in open waters, and was extremely expensive to maintain. This does not mean that he scrapped it. He merely told the various contingents they could go home. With the Persians based too far away for a close blockade, they could slip away in small groups quite easily. If the Persian fleet turned its attention to mainland Greece, Antipatros would be glad to have the constituents available for a fleet of his own. As for the army in Asia, the recent experience had shown that it could take most walled cities with little trouble, and that a hostile fleet could not operate without a base. When all the coastal cities were in Alexander's hands, the Persian navy would be hard-pressed to continue at all. He kept 20 Athenian ships as coastwise transport – and hostages.

In pursuance of this policy, the army now marched south-east towards the next great seaport, that of Halikarnassos in Karia. This was a much harder nut to crack. Its position and its walls were equally strong, and the latter were being strengthened daily under the supervision of the loyal and talented Memnon. Memnon had recently been appointed by Daraios to overall command of both all the troops remaining in Asia Minor and of the fleet. Daraios had also taken the precaution of retaining Memnon's family as hostages. The city was now garrisoned by a large number of Greek mercenaries who might have included many of those allegedly slain at the Granikos. Those of the Persian cavalry which had not scattered to their homes had also mainly congregated there, and the fleet had fallen back to the city to help out.

The garrison carried out an active defence. Even when the Macedonian army first approached, a sally was made to annoy it with long-range shooting, although this party was quickly driven back inside the walls. A few days later, Alexander took the companion cavalry, the hypaspists, three taxeis of phalangites, the Agrianians and the Cretan archers round to the far side of the city, partly to examine the defences, but also to make an attempt on the small neighbouring town of Myndos. He had been in contact with a pro-Macedonian faction there, who had agreed to let him in if he came by night. in fact, the promised aid did not materialise. An attempt was still made, and a tower brought down by the infantry undermining it with improvised tools, but the wall failed to collapse with it. The garrison resisted stoutly, and was heavily reinforced from Halikarnassos by sea. Alexander gave up and returned to the main siege.

His first step was to fill in the ditch to enable him to bring his siege towers up to the walls. It was about 45 feet wide by 22½ feet deep, but this was still relatively quickly accomplished. As the machines were brought up, the defenders made a night sally to try and burn them. The guards were on the alert, and the attempt was a failure, many of the sallying troops being caught in a jam as they tried to get back in. This episode cost the defenders 170 killed, the Macedonians only 16, although many more were wounded.

Yet another sally was provoked by two drunken Macedonians who attacked the wall unsupported. A party dashed out, killed them, then held off fresh Macedonians as they came up by throwing javelins from a superior height, the ground sloping down from the walls. This fracas was further reinforced by both sides, and a fierce fight continued for some time before the defenders had to retreat inside. So many of the defenders had become involved that it was later thought that a simultaneous assault on the denuded walls by the rest of the Macedonian army might have carried them.

The defences had by this time been much weakened by battery. In one place, two towers had collapsed, bringing down the curtain wall between them, and a third was badly shaken. However, as the attackers pushed up to the wall, they saw a further half moon-shaped brick wall had been improvised behind the gap. Alexander brought up his engines against the brick wall next day, and yet another sally was made in an attempt to burn them. One siege tower was set alight and destroyed and a row of mantlets for covering archers damaged, and the remaining engines had to be withdrawn to save them. The sortie was greatly aided by flanking shots from the towers on each side of the breach, which were now almost in the attackers' rear.

The engines were brought up to the brick wall again a few days later, and this time there were two sallies in response. One was at the breach itself, and was defeated by much increased engine guards supported by slings and artillery from the siege towers. The salliers lost heavily, especially during their retreat. The other sortie was from the city's main gate. This took the Macedonians by surprise at first, but was then driven back by reinforcements. Many were trapped when a bridge broke under the load of fugitives, and more when the gates were closed prematurely to prevent the Macedonians mixing and entering with the rout. This episode cost the defence 1,000 dead, the Macedonians 40.

It was now becoming obvious to Memnon and Orontobates, the Persian commanders, that the condition of the fortifications and the cumulative losses in men were such that the siege could not last much longer. They decided to cut their losses and get out, which they did with great skill. They set fire to the city and retreated, a minority to two fortifications at the harbour mouth which they hoped to hold with naval aid, the larger number to the heights behind the city.

When this was reported to Alexander, he organised fire-fighting and civilian relief operations. When dawn broke, showing the Persians on the heights, he decided against interfering with their escape. He left a garrison of 3,000 mercenary infantry and 200 cavalry under Ptolemaios, but appointed a Karian as satrap. This was Ada, a lady who had already occupied that position after the death of her husband, the satrap Hidrieos. She had then been pushed aside by Pixodaros, whom we have met before intriguing with Philip. He in his turn had been replaced by Orontobates, who had now fled. All Ada had left was the city of Alinda, an even stronger fortress than Halikarnassos, so difficult to take from her. She had already offered it to Alexander, been given it back, and had adopted him as her son. She must have been a nice old soul, and he did not argue about it, although at times was embarrassed by her Aunt Ada-like conviction that he was half-starved and needed fattening up!

It was now late autumn, and some of Alexander's further troop dispositions were influenced by this. He sent the seige train back to Tralles near Ephesos to refit for next year. He also granted home leave for all the recently married among the Macedonians, and they marched off in a body under Ptolemaios son of Seleucos. They were instructed to return in the spring bringing reinforcements. Pharmenion was sent to Sardes with one ila of companions and all the Thessalians. His orders were to patrol the whole coast as far as Lykia and Pamphylia, and as far as possible to make the Persian naval command's life a misery.

Alexander did not plan a winter rest for himself and the rest of the army. He continued along the coast eastward for some 200 miles to Phaselis, all the cities and peoples on the way submitting. At his point he was distracted by a plot. You may remember the loyal one of the four Lynkestid brothers. He had been promoted to command the Thessalians when their former commander had been made a satrap. A messenger from Daraios intercepted by Parmenion was bringing him an offer of 1,000 talents and backing for the throne of Macedonia if he would kill Alexander, and there were indications that he had been in previous correspondence with his brother at the Persian court. This was not conclusive, but the risk of leaving him in such a powerful position was too great, so he was arrested and imprisoned to await more evidence one way or the other. He was finally executed four years later, after Alexander had inherited the Persian royal archives.

The march continued to Aspendos, where the inhabitants submitted, but begged not to be garrisoned. Alexander agreed on condition that they gave him 50 talents for the army's pay and all the horses which had been bred as tribute for Daraios. They agreed, and he marched a little further along the coast. News then reached him that they had in fact now refused to pay up, and were busily repairing the city walls. He doubled back, got the horses and double the money out of them, set an annual tribute, took hostages, and set up a judicial enquiry into lands they were accused of stealing from their neighbours. Such comprehensive misfortune may well have discouraged other clever fellows.

Alexander had now done as much as he could to hinder Persian naval passage along the southern coast of Asia Minor to attack his home base and line of communications. The winter trip through the coastal hills must have been arduous. He was blocked from going further along the coast by the mountains of Kilikia, so turned north across the central plateau. Near the Pisidian city of Telmissos, his path was blocked by mountain tribesmen holding a defile. He encamped and, seeing this, most of the tribesmen went back to their city comforts. Alexander immediately launched an attack on the remainder with his lighter troops, brushing them aside and seizing the defile. Passing the army through, he decided not to spend time on besieging the Telmissians, but instead to attack the most powerful and warlike of the Pisidian tribes, the Sagalassians, hoping that defeating them would encourage the rest to submit. He quickly acquired loyal allies in the shape of the Selgians, another tribe at odds with the first two.

The Sagalassians formed up for battle on the steep hillside in front of their city, reinforced by volunteers from Telmissos. Alexander deployed with the hypaspists on his right, the phalangites continuing the line to the left. In front of the main line, he had a skirmishing screen of archers and Agranians on the right, Thracian light javelin men on the left. His cavalry were kept out of action, the terrain being unsuitable. The Greek and Thracian peltasts would have been ideal if present. Since they were not used, we must conclude that they were still garrisoning previous conquests.

The battle was fairly short and sharp. The Pisidians waited until the advancing light troops had reached the steepest part of the slope, then charged downhill, enveloping their flanks somewhat as well as hitting them frontally. The archers were driven back, but Alexander's javelinmen held firm. When the heavier Macedonian infantry joined in, the Pisidians broke and fled, scattering over the hillside with a loss of some 500 dead. Alexander did not waste energy on chasing light infantry with heavier, but went straight for the city and carried it by assault for the loss of 20 men, including Kleandros, the commander of the archers.

Alexander now spent a few days mopping up the Pisidians, capturing some forts and receiving the submission of others. He then continued north, and five days later reached Kelenai. This was a strong hill-top fortress acting as headquarters for the satrap of Phrygia, implying that Herodotos' third satrapy had split into eastern and western parts. It had a garrison of 100 Greeks and 1,000 Karians. Thinking support unlikely at that time of year, the garrison offered to surrender if no relief had been heard of by a specified date. Alexander did not fancy besieging such a site, so agreed, detaching 1,500 troops to watch it until the date came. He spent the next ten days reorganising. He appointed Antigonos, son of Philip and surnamed 'One Eye', the new satrap, then put Balakros, son of Amyntas, in command of the allies in his place. He then set off for Gordion.

The importance of Gordion was that it was on the great royal road from Sardes to Susa. From Sardes to Gordion was 220 miles covered in 12 daily stages. From Gordion to the fortress protecting the crossing of the River Halys on the border of Kappadokia was 135 miles and eight stages. From there to the two fortress-protected defiles on the Kilikian border was 390 miles and 28 stages. From the defiles to the Armenian boundary on the River Euphrates was 58 miles and three stages. Across Armenia, passing at least one major fortress en route, was 212 miles and 15 stages, and across the Matienian land including four ferries was 515 miles and 34 stages. To Susa from there was 160 miles and 11 stages. All these stages represent day's marches for small parties of ordinary travellers. Persian royal messengers managed two stages per day, while a large army might cover only half as far.

Spring was now coming, and Alexander's reinforcements and returning leave party would soon hopefully be appearing along the road from the direction of Sardes. The army rested, waited, and wondered what the Persians were doing. The men from home grew steadily more overdue, and rumours spread about hold-ups caused by the Persian fleet at the straits.

In May, the leave men finally turned up, bringing with them 3,000 Macedonian infantry, 300 Macedonian cavalry, 200 Thessalian and 150 allied Greek cavalry and 500 Agrianians. There were also less welcome visitors, a delegation from Athens to plead for the freedom of the Athenians among the 2,000 mercenaries captured at the Granikos and now in forced labour in Macedonia. Having found official records at Sardes of the exact amounts the Persians had paid Demosthenes to work against him, Alexander showed commendable restraint in merely telling them that, with thousands of Greeks still fighting for Persia, it was not yet time to consider this, and that they should ask again later when the situation had been cleared up.

By late May, Alexander was ready to start. Before leaving, however, he went to see the local tourist attraction. This was a chariot owned by the legendary King Midas. Its yoke was fastened by a most complicated knot, and the story went that the man who unfastened it would rule Asia. Alexander unfastened it in typical fashion, with a sword cut, and the army left Gordion to make the legend come true.

Chapter 9

Persian counter-attack: the Issos campaign, 333 BC

While Alexander had been waiting for his reinforcements at Gordion, Daraios had been planning possible counter-moves. Up to now, the Macedonians had been fighting against the satraps of Asia Minor, reinforced by mercenaries and the fleet. In general, the Persians had been more successful at sea. They had lost many of their possible bases, but still had Cyprus and the harbour fortifications of Halikarnassos as possible staging points, and could expect to be able to use isolated beaches from time to time in spite of harassment by Parmenion's cavalry. The Macedonian fleet had been disbanded rather than face the Persian superiority in ship numbers and technique, and the Persian sea strength had been increased still further by incorporating the mercenaries from abandoned garrisons. On land, a full local levy had proved insufficient to face the Macedonians in battle, fortresses had imposed only minor delay, and important recruiting and tax collection areas had been lost. The only course now promising any chance of success would be for Daraios to bring up the main army, and even this would be weakened by the lost resources.

A sea attack might well succeed in capturing an island base near the straits which would be immune to counteraction from land forces, particularly as Memnon had shown himself to be a most able commander and now had a high proportion of the empire's prized Greek mercenaries on board his ships. From such a base, he could interfere with Alexander's communications with home, block his reinforcements and, by intercepting the Athenian corn fleet, make that city desperate enough to revolt openly against Alexander.

A land campaign would be terribly risky. The Persians would have a sizeable advantage in numbers, especially if the less efficient troop types were called up with the good ones, and time was allowed to bring up contingents from the furthest parts of the empire. Against that, the king knew that the mercenary hoplites were the most useful part of his army. He also realised that the Macedonians had been continually beating hoplite armies. In addition, there was the strong possibility of revolts springing up where troops were removed, while the political effects of a defeat could be disastrous, even if Daraios himself managed to get away. It was true that most of the subject races passively supported their foreign rulers and would fight for them, but the same would probably apply once they came under Macedonian rule. It may also have been that Daraios recognised that he himself was not an especially good general. It was all very well for him to delegate command to Memnon, a Greek ineligible for the throne, but it would be risky indeed to give it to a talented noble Persian, who might then decide he wanted the privileges of rule as well as its responsibilities.

The decision was accordingly made to act by sea. Memnon first sailed to the island of Chios, which was delivered up to him by treachery, and then landed on Lesbos. Most of the cities of that island surrendered to him, but Mitylene, the largest, resisted with the aid of mercenaries in Macedonian pay. Memnon started to blockade it, but while doing so fell ill and died. This was a stunning piece of bad luck for Daraios, as it was, of course, for Memnon. However, he handed over his command on his death-bed to his Persian nephew Pharnabazos and another Persian named Autophradates. They continued the blockade, and Mitylene submitted on generous terms. However, these terms were broken as soon as the Persians got possession, a local tyrant and Persian garrison being installed and a heavy fine exacted. One hopes the Persian pair were better archers and riders!

When Daraios heard in June of Memnon's death, he was shattered. Lacking the same confidence in the fleet's new commanders, he decided to switch to the alternative land strategy, and by doing so fell between two stools. On the one hand, he had to recall the Greek mercenaries with the fleet to his main army, thus depriving the naval effort of much of its fighting power. On the other, he now had insufficient time to get the more distant contingents of the empire to the decisive point.

On receiving his instructions, Pharnabazos sailed with most of the fleet to Tripolis in Syria, where he handed over the mercenaries. Autophradates kept another 100 ships to look for more opportunities in the islands. He was rejoined by Pharnabazos, although apparently the latter only brought ten of his ships back. Possibly their crews had also been impressed into the army, or perhaps their fighting value without mercenaries did not justify their expense when a giant army had to be put together. It must be remembered that most of the Persian gold and silver was in ingots, and that it took time to convert it into coin for paying troops.

The two admirals now sent ten ships to the Kyklades, the group of islands forming a chain from the south-western tip of Asia Minor to the Attic peninsular of Greece, and then sailed with the rest of the island of Tenedos. This they quickly overawed in spite of its Macedonian sympathies, giving them an ideal base from which to control the straits.

The detached squadron was not so lucky. Its depredations were reported, and a Greek local defence squadron caught it by surprise at dawn off the island of Siphnos. The 15 Greek warships took eight of the Persian vessels with their crews, but the squadron commander got away with a pair to take the news to the admirals.

However, we have got ahead of ourselves, and it is time to go back and find out what Alexander was doing. In spite of the rumours, the Persian fleet had not occupied a suitable base in time to stop the reinforcements; the taxes from the conquered provinces had been collected by Alexander's staff, leaving him prosperous enough to send 600 talents home to raise a new fleet and 500 for Antipatros' use as well as provide for his own army; and he was on the march eastward to Ankyra.

At Ankyra, he was met by a Paphlagonian delegation offering submission. This made it unnecessary for him to detour north into their country and deprived the Persian empire of some of its best light cavalry. He put the

Paphlagonians under Kalas' satrapy, and turned south-east into Kappadokia, a country of desolate plains which he put under a locally born satrap called Sabiktas.

The Persian satrap of Kilikia was holding the defiles called the Kilikian Gates, but was brushed aside by a night attack with the hypaspists, Agrianians and Cretans. He fell back towards his capital of Tarsos, burning the crops behind him. However, the Kilikian plains beyond the mountains were so fertile and well watered that enough food was left to keep the invaders going. Hearing that Arsames, the satrap, was planning to sack Tarsos, then evacuate by sea, Alexander pushed him so hard with cavalry and light troops that he fled to Daraios withoug having time to harm the city.

It was now time for Alexander to have ill luck. Having taken Tarsos in early July, he fell seriously ill with fever, and was out of action until mid-September, his life being despaired of at one stage. Parmenion thought he had evidence that Alexander's doctor had been bribed by Daraios to poison him, but Alexander chose to ignore this, and recovered largely through the doctor's efforts. Of course, with rumours like that flying about, the poor man would have been unlikely to survive his patient, so he had to try hard!

As Alexander lay recovering, he sent Parmenion with the Thessalian cavalry, Sitalkes' Thracians and the Greek allied and mercenary infantry to seize the other Kilikian defile, the one called the Syrian Gates and lying on the army's route into the heart of Persia. Once he himself was back on his feet, he spent a little time subduing mountain tribes which confused liberty with licence. He now received two lots of news. One was from Ptolemaios and Asandros at Halikarnassos. Orontobates, the Persian satrap of Karia, who had been holding on to the harbour defences of Halikarnassos and had even spread over a few local islands with the aid of the fleet, had been defeated in a pitched battle with a loss of 50 cavalry, 700 infantry and 1,000 prisoners. With luck, the whole coastline might soon be under control. The other news was to have an even more galvanising effect. Daraios was coming.

Daraios had moved west to Babylon in June, and summoned his troops to meet him there. After two months, he dared not wait longer for late-coming contingents from far afield, and advanced to Sochi, two days' march on the Syrian side of the Syrian Gates defile. He arrived there in late September, joined up with the mercenaries which had been landed near by at Tripolis, and established his supply base at Damascus. His intention was to wait there, in open plains in which his superior numbers and cavalry could be used to full effect, until Alexander should come to meet him. He was still there when Parmenion's scouts discovered him in October.

The Syrian Gates were not, in fact, a single pass, but a number. Heading from Tarsos to Sochi, an army would first come to the Karakapu pass, then to the town of Issos. The main route then followed the shoreline of the Gulf of Issos south along a narrow coastal strip with mountains to the east, then turned east to climb over these by the Beilan pass. However, there was a longer route. This went north-east from Issos, over a low pass called the Kalekoy, then east over either the Bahche or Hasanbeyli passes.

On hearing the news, Alexander set off force-marching by the southern or main route. The pace he set was too hot for some of his men, and a number of invalids and stragglers had to be left at Issos. He met up with Parmenion, who was holding the narrowest part of the coastal strip, and their combined force pushed on for the Beilan. After two days' fast marching, he chose to halt for the night before turning up to the summit. That night brought gales and torrential rain which delayed next morning's start. As they waited for the weather to clear a little, fresh news arrived.

Shortly after being spotted by Parmenion's scouts, Daraios had got tired of waiting and had advanced himself. However, he had not moved by the Beilan pass over which the scouts had come, but over the northerly passes. This made a great deal of sense, as there were many places on the southern route where he could have been delayed long enough by small bodies of enemy for the Macedonian army to reach him while he was still cramped by the mountains and unable to deploy his full strength. By taking the northern route, he would emerge in the plain by Issos between Alexander and Parmenion and would have the opportunity of defeating them in detail.

This plan had been spoilt by Alexander's forced march and by the weather. Instead of being between Alexander and Parmenion, he was behind them both. He hurriedly marched after them, hoping to catch them from the rear while their army was entangled in the pass, although he found time for a little mutilation of the sick he discovered at Issos. However, some of the stragglers had got away from Issos in a small boat and carried the tale to Alexander. At first he did not believe it, and sent some of the companions back in the boat to check. When the news was confirmed, he blessed the weather that had kept him out of the mountains, and started the army retracing its steps. Both armies were now marching to meet each other and both in each other's rear. Fugitives would have a hard time getting away whichever side won. However, when Daraios realised that Alexander had reversed and that he himself was committed to the battle in cramped terrain which he had wished to avoid, he chose to halt and occupy a defensive position behind the River Payas.

The size of Daraios' army is a matter of extreme doubt. The ancient writers put it at 600,000. This is universally pooh-poohed by modern writers on the general grounds that it is a lot of men. To this, one may reply that most of the levy of the great Persian empire would be a lot of men! I am personally very reluctant to demolish such a figure unless I can put something constructive in its place. However, let us assume that this was the maximum figure that contemporaries would consider credible, and that it has been inflated by including every slave, cook, camel driver, bottle-washer, etc, who could be inserted at the back as a spear carrier in the theatrical sense. Even in the 19th century a British army in India could have four hangers-on to each fighting man, and slightly earlier Asiatic armies had a considerably higher ratio. If we add together the numbers in the units actually mentioned as doing something constructive, it comes to 140,000 providing an interestingly similar ratio.

According to the Ancients, the battlefield stretched some 3,700 paces from the edge of the sea on the west to the foothills of the mountain chain on the east. Daraios started by sending his 30,000 cavalry and 20,000 good light infantry over the river to cover his deployment. He then formed up his 30,000 mercenary hoplites behind the river bank in the centre, and put 30,000 Kardakes on each side of them. The cavalry were now brought back. Most of them were put on the left of the infantry by the sea, the others on the opposite flank. The light infantry were also withdrawn, to the hills on the right flank. These curved in an arc, so that some of the troops on them would be behind the Macedonian flank.

Alexander's strength would have been the same as at Granikos, minus

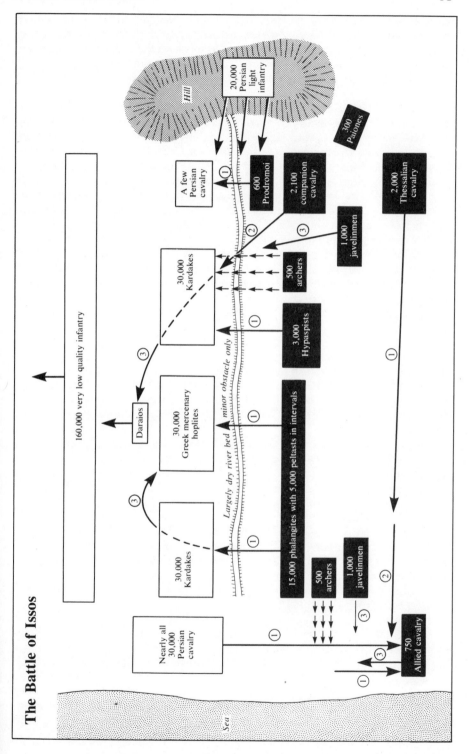

The Battle of Issos

casualties, sick and garrisons, but plus the reinforcements received at Gordion. As the coastal strip broadened out, he started to deploy his infantry from column into battle formation, with the hypaspists on the right, the phalangites continuing the formation to his left. As it opened out still further, he also deployed his cavalry, sending the Greek allies to his left by the sea, the rest on his right.

As the two armies came in sight, Daraios had second thoughts and transferred even more of his cavalry to his right, leaving very few by the hills. Alexander now thought he should strengthen his left to face the mass of Persian cavalry opposite it. However, he did not want to be seen doing it, so he first pushed forward the prodromoi and Paionian light cavalry on his right, and then withdrew the Thessalians and moved them to the left concealed from view behind his infantry. It may seem strange to you that footmen should have been able to conceal cavalry in this way, but the reason is simple. It was the dust clouds raised by marching men, hiding all but the front ranks. He now moved two of the ilai of companions outward to fill the gap left by the Thessalians' departure. The two wings were now slightly advanced, each with half the light infantry following the cavalry in support. On the right were the Agrianians, now 1,000-strong, and half the archers. On the left were the Thracian javelinmen and the other half of the archers. The mercenary peltasts were placed in bodies between the units of the phalanx. No mention is made of the allied infantry or the other Thracians.

By now, the Macedonian army was passing the hills occupied by the Persian light troops and Alexander deployed the right flank's supporting light infantry as a screen. These feinted an attack on the Persians, who evaded back up to the crest of the hill. Alexander therefore decided that they were unlikely to come down and attack. He told off the 300 Paionians to watch them, then withdrew the light infantry and sent it forward on his extreme right to threaten the enemy flank.

Alexander now charged with the right flank cavalry. The few Persian cavalry on that wing were swept aside, and the archers on the hill were too distracted by the speed of his charge and the threat from the Macedonian light troops to achieve anything notable against it. He struck the Kardakes, broke them, and kept on, angling to head for Daraios in his chariot behind the enemy centre. If he could kill or capture the Persian king, the war would be as good as over.

On the far flank, it was the Persian cavalry who charged in an attempted hammer and anvil manoeuvre intended to sweep round and drive the Macedonians against those light infantry-populated hills. If only the allied cavalry had been there to receive them, they might well have managed it, but the advent of the Thessalians taking them by surprise, and the support of the Thracian and Cretan light troops, enabled the Greeks to hold.

The Macedonian centre was not doing so well. The phalangites had been disordered by crossing the stream, and the mercenary hoplites of the Persians were taking full advantage of this and fighting furiously to avenge past humiliations. The support of the less-affected hypaspists and peltasts may have been crucial, but these too suffered.

If all the Persian infantry had been hoplites, they might well have won. As it was, the Kardakes on the left of the hoplites had been broken by the companions, and those on the right were not coping with the phalangites as well as their Greek comrades. Meanwhile, behind the centre, Daraios' bodyguard was fighting desperately to save him.

As the Kardakes gave way, the outer units of the phalangites swung in upon the gallant mercenaries, until they, too, started to crumble. Seeing this, and Daraios driving off at speed while his bodyguards threw themselves in Alexander's path, even the staunchly fighting cavalry of the Persian right gave up and made for home.

Alas, they not only had the mob of poor-quality infantry and servants to their rear, but a long circuitous route through mountains before they got to safety. Daraios had to abandon his royal chariot, shield and robe as a prize for Alexander, and take to a horse. The pursuit went on until nightfall. By the time Alexander had called it off, 10,000 cavalry and 100,000 foot were said to have been slain. One noble Persian among them who would be badly missed was Sabakes, the satrap of Egypt.

Even now, Alexander had not yet finished. Returning from the pursuit, he stormed the Persian camp, capturing Daraios' mother, wife, infant son, two daughters, and 3,000 talents in coin.

Daraios fled almost alone through the night, but started picking up fellow-fugitives, both Persian and mercenary, when daylight came. He soon had 4,000 with him, but kept going for the Euphrates, meaning to put the river between Alexander and himself as soon as possible. Another 8,000 of the fugitive hoplites stuck together and managed to fight their way to the ships which had brought them to Tripolis. They launched enough of these to carry them, burned the rest to discourage pursuit, then sailed for Egypt by way of Cyprus.

Chapter 10

Gathering the fruits of victory: Phoenician and Egyptian campaigns, 333 BC to 331 BC

Alexander now appointed Balakros, son of Nikanor, as satrap of Kilikia and Menon, son of Kerdimmas, as satrap of the Syrian plains, giving the latter the Greek allied cavalry to rout out any opposition not already cowed by Daraios' defeat. Parmenion was detached with a force towards Damascus, where the main part of the Persian army's funds, wealth, baggage and womenfolk had been abandoned. Despite a sword wound in the thigh, Alexander then found time to visit Daraios' captured family and promise them safety and honourable treatment.

He now marched south, meeting the son of the king of Arados on the way, Arados was a small Phoenician state consisting of a fortified island city with subsidiary possessions on the adjacent mainland. Its king was currently with the Persian fleet, but his son yielded the fortress on his behalf.

While near Arados, Alexander received an embassy from Daraios. This offered recognition of Alexander's rule over Asia Minor west of the River Halys and an indemnity of 10,000 talents in return for peace and the return of the royal family. Daraios must have still been hoping that the activities of his fleet could give him some bargaining power. Alexander in return offered Daraios safety in return for unconditional surrender, saying that he was now the overlord of Asia, not Daraios. If Daraios wished to dispute this, he should come back and fight. If he did not come, Alexander would fetch him. However, the details of the Persian offer were hushed up in case they caused dissension in the army.

Alexander now learned that Parmenion had made a rich haul indeed at Damascus. It included 2,600 talents in coin, sufficient to pay off all the army's arrears of wages and the next six months' as well, eight talents of uncoined silver, 7,000 pack animals, 329 female musicians, 306 cooks, 13 pastry cooks, 70 wine waiters, 40 perfumiers, and a number of prominent noblewomen with their children. These included the wife and three daughters of the previous Persian king, a wife, son and grown-up daughter of the elderly satrap Artabazos, and Memnon's son and two nieces. Alexander had known and liked Artabazos and his daughter Barsine during their exile 20 years previously at Philip's court. Barsine was now Memnon's widow, and Alexander made her his mistress. Being intelligent, bilingual, and used to the ways of both nations, she may have been more important politically than she is usually given credit for by male chauvinist Greek authors. He also captured envoys from Athens, Thebes, and most important, Sparta.

Alexander could now afford to spread himself a little, and founded the first of what were to be many Macedonian/Greek colony cities. This was Alexandria-by-Issos, on the site of the battle. Among other functions, it was to house a mint for turning conquered bullion into coins. In the ancient world, coinage had a propaganda as well as a trading function. Alexander's new coins, based on the popular Athenian standard, could be expected to spread out in slowly widening circles across the world as they changed hands, and everyone who handled them would have solid evidence of his successes in Asia.

His men were not forgotten. As after Granikos, he visited the bedsides of the wounded, encouraged them to talk of their exploits and experiences, and honoured and rewarded those he had seen or heard of distinguishing themselves. Fancying himself as an amateur physician, he even took a hand in their treatment. This may or may not have helped their recovery, but certainly increased their affection for him.

Proceeding south down the coast, he received the submission of Byblos from the son of another king absent with his ships in the Persian fleet. A little further on, he came to the great port of Sidon. Sidon had rebelled against Persia 12 years previously and had been savagely repressed and a puppet king installed. The king was absent in the fleet with a contingent of 50 ships, and the Sidonians took advantage of this to go over to Alexander. The roots of Persian sea power were now being grubbed up with a vengeance.

In the meantime, the main Persian fleet had moved south and occupied the island of Chios. They now left a shore party in control there, and moved further south to the area where their detached squadron had been destroyed, at the same time sending minor detachments to Kos and Halikarnassos. The fleet was now joined by Agis, king of Sparta, in a single ship, which had come to collect promised aid for a war against Macedonia and her allies. This happy gathering was shaken by the arrival of the news of Daraios' defeat at Issos. Pharnabazos loaded 1,500 of the fleet's remaining 3,000 Greek mercenaries on to 12 triremes and headed for Chios, nervous lest his base change sides behind him. Agis got 30 talents out of Autophradates, borrowed ten triremes off him to take it home, but stayed with the fleet himself. Shortly after, the fleet started for Halikarnassos but, instead of wintering there, broke up into national contingents and headed for its home ports.

Anyone who was popular with Sidon was very likely to be less so with the equally influential and rival city of Tyre. Tyre now offered to accept Alexander's rule, but on condition that he did not enter or garrison the city. This could not be accepted, as he could not afford to leave any such important base in his rear for the Persian fleet to exploit. The Tyrians consequently defied him, confident in their walls, their position on an island, and their fleet. They may not have counted on the wholesale desertions of naval contingents to the Macedonians which were shortly to take place.

It was a difficult place to beseige, standing on a walled island nearly three miles round. There was half a mile of sea between it and the mainland, and the defences rose in some places as much as 150 feet above the sea. It had only once been captured, and that by sea, and had once been unsuccessfully besieged for 13 years. The Tyrians' justifiable confidence led them to an excess remarkable even by contemporary standards. They seized Alexander's emissaries, and hurled them from the walls. This breach of the inviolability of heralds meant that they could expect little or no mercy if the city fell. They would have to fight all the harder.

As Alexander had only his 20 Athenian transports, he would have to walk to the island. In mid-January, he started to build a connecting mole out from the land. Most of the sea gap was quite shallow, although it started shelving rapidly during the last 100 paces, reaching a maximum of 18 feet. The mole therefore went well at first, stone from the nearby old city and timber from the local forests being easy to obtain. However, as the mole got within 400 paces of the walls, the workers began to come under catapult shot. As they got nearer still, other missile troops joined in from the superior height of the battlements, ships put out to harass the workers, and the rapidly increasing depth made the work more difficult and required much larger amounts of material.

Alexander's answer to the harassment was to built a pair of towers over the mole and place engines on them. These would keep the defenders' heads down, discourage boats from coming too near, and slow the shooting rate of the enemy artillery by making the crews duck for cover. Finding that the Macedonian towers were protected with green hides, so that ordinary incendiary missiles did no harm, the Tyrians prepared a special fire ship. They took a horse transport, filled it below decks with dry wood, both as fuel and to increase its buoyancy in case it was damaged below the waterline by Macedonian attack. Two tall masts were installed in the bows, each fitted with double yards hung with cauldrons of inflammable liquids. High walls were then built around the deck edges to protect the crew from missiles and retain stacks of yet more inflammables including sulphur and pitch. Finally, the stern was ballasted to reduce the draught at the bows as much as possible.

Waiting for a strong favourable wind, not so much for propulsion as to make flames stream fiercely in the right direction, the fire ship was towed towards the towers by two triremes. On getting near, the skeleton crew ignited the cargo, and swam to safety. The triremes, towing with separate cables so as to make a V with the fireship at the point, increased to racing speed, then sheered away as it struck the mole already burning fiercely. The towers were quickly burning, and the triremes lay off and shot at intending fire fighters. As the towers were abandoned by their crew, large number of Tyrians swarmed on to the mole to destroy its palisade and any engines not caught in the conflagration.

When Alexander finally drove them off, he set about widening the mole at its seaward end, both to accommodate more towers and to reduce their vulnerability to such attack. He also decided it was about time he got himself a navy, and set off to Sidon with the hypaspists and Agrianians. When he arrived, he found that he already had one. The kings of Arados and Byblos had arrived back with their squadrons, and the Sidonian squadron without its king. The 50 Sidonian warships and the other two squadrons gave him a total of 80 ships. These were then joined by a token three from Lykia, ten from the independent island republic of Rhodes which had decided to take his side, and finally by the Cyprus fleet of 120 ships. There was also a token Macedonian contribution of one 50-oar despatch boat! This fleet of 213½ warships gave Alexander complete naval superiority in the eastern Mediterranean.

While the fleet was being refitted and prepared for action, Alexander took some of the cavalry, the hypaspists, the Agrianians and the archers, and went off on a side trip into the hills, where tribesmen had been interfering with his wood cutters. Having made examples of a few groups who tried to fight, he received the submissions of the rest and returned after ten days to find the navy ready, plus 4,000 newly arrived Greek mercenaries from the Peloponnesos. Putting these and his hypaspists on board as marines to supplement the normal fighting crews, he sailed for Tyre.

The Tyrians may have had 80 warships, most of them triremes, but at least three quadriremes and quinquiremes, and had decided to fight a sea battle when Alexander brought up his ships. However, they were shaken to find that most of the Persian fleet had gone over to him, and retired into the harbour, leaving several triremes blocking the entrance with their bows. Alexander's fleet had a proportion of larger ships too, and these sank three of the defending triremes in bow-to-bow ramming before the remainder pulled back inside. It was not safe to follow them, as these would have exposed the attackers' more vulnerable sides. The fleet instead beached by the base of the mole. The Cypriots were on the northern side facing the main harbour, the Phoenicians on the southern facing a subsidiary harbour and near to Alexander's headquarters tent. Each was to find squadrons to blockade the harbour entrances as well as support the siege works.

By this time, talented engineers had been collected from all over Cyprus and Phoenicia, the damage caused to the mole by the fire raid and an ensuing spring gale repaired, and large numbers of engines were being constructed. Some of these were to be mounted on the mole, others on some of the transports and older warships.

Tyrian counter-measures had been concentrated on the part of the defences facing the mole, trusting to the ships for protection elsewhere. The wall had been built up and strengthened at this point, then supplemented with wooden towers like Alexander's own. Now that the Tyrian ships were blockaded inside the harbours, the weaker walls in other places were exposed to battery from Alexander's ships. However, these were discouraged from approaching by fire missiles and heaps of stones cast into the sea as underwater obstructions. When Alexander's ships tried to remove these stones, they were attacked by Tyrian ships sallying out on brief raids before the blockaders could react. When this was prevented by picketing with small craft converted into a sort of monitor with catapults and overhead cover for the crew, the Tyrians responded by sending swimmers to cut anchor cables, until these were replaced by chains.

The attacking ships now being able to come right up to the walls, the Tyrians decided to try a larger sortie to attack the Cypriot contingent while it was unprepared. They stretched sails in front of the harbour entrances to prevent the blockaders seeing what was happening inside, then waited for an opportunity. This did not come for some time, but finally the attackers relaxed their vigilance, thinking the Tyrian fleet had shot its bolt. One day, while the besieging ships had withdrawn for the mid-day meal, a picked force of the best Tyrian ships sneaked out from the harbour in single file and headed for the beached Cypriots. The seven triremes and three larger ships taking part rowed gently and quietly at first without calling the stroke, then speeded up and deployed when they saw they had been spotted. Heading straight in towards the beach, they caught some ships unmanned, some only partly manned, so that no effective resistance was made. The quinquiremes serving as the flagships of the three Cypriot kings were rammed and sunk. The triremes then cruised down the shore cutting the bow anchor cables of the stern-beached ships, so that they were tumbled about on the beach by the waves and damaged. For the next half hour, the Tyrians had a wonderful time throwing fire into half-helpless ships as the Cypriots tried to defend them.

As it happened, Alexander had not taken as long as usual over lunch that day, but had gone to visit the Phoenician squadrons. When the news of the attack on the ships on the other side of the mole reached him, he took his quinquiremes and the first five triremes manned and began to row right around the island to take the raiding party in the rear. The other Phoenician ships were to put out and lie off the southern harbour's entrance as they were manned, to block any sally from there. The Tyrians on the city wall saw what he was doing almost as soon as he started, and messengers ran to signal the ships to recall them. It was hard to attract the raiders' attention, but at last the point was got across, and they rowed desperately for safety. Alexander had something like three-quarter of an hour's rowing to do before he reached the entrance of the northern harbour, and did not catch all the raiders. However, he got most, one quinquireme and one quadrireme being taken at the very entrance. The crews managed to swim to safety.

The besieged could not hope to be allowed to repeat their trick, and the attacking ships were now being brought right up to the wall to batter it. The engines on the mole had little success against the strong wall they were facing, and neither did the ships against the northern wall. The southern wall was a different proposition, and was quickly shaken and partly brought down. Alexander ordered an immediate assault with the troops at hand, but withdrew them as soon as it was clear that the defenders were prepared.

He now waited three days for a flat calm, then launched a full-scale attack. This was not apparently on the existing breach which might be expected to be booby-trapped, but against a similar stretch of wall near by. First came a brisk battery with engines to bring down a good length of wall. These ships were then withdrawn and replaced by two others, each carrying ramps. One of these was manned by the hypaspists, the other by Koinos' unit of phalangites. As well as the main assault, other ships were to close the walls in many places around the whole circuit, cheering and shooting, to keep as many of the defenders pinned as possible. Two squadrons of triremes were to see if they could rush the harbour entrances while the defenders were distracted by events elsewhere.

The main assault was immediately successful. The defenders gave way, the Macedonians expanded along the wall until they held several interval towers and the curtain between, then descended into the city. Both harbour assaults also succeeded. The defenders fell back from their walls into the city and made a brief stand ending in rout and massacre.

Something like 8,000 Tyrians were said to have died during the siege. A further 2,000 were crucified along the shore in retaliation for the murder of the envoys and the slaughter of prisoners by dropping them from the walls. All the remaining 30,000 inhabitants were enslaved, except for those few who had trusted Alexander's promise of amnesty for those seeking sanctuary in the temple of Melkarth. Alexander had lost 20 men in the assault and 400 during the whole of the siege. He now arranged not only to install a garrison, but to open the city for colonists.

It was now late July and the siege of Tyre had lasted seven months. Events elsewhere had not stood still. Some of the fugitives from Issos had fled into Kappadokia, combined with the locals, and launched a series of dangerous attacks during the winter which might well have broken Alexander's communications with home. They had been defeated in three brilliant battles by Antigonos 'One Eye'. Many of the survivors had fled into exile. A few held out in the hills. The new Macedonian fleet had started work on eliminating the remaining pockets of Persian resistance in the islands linking Asia Minor and Greece and along the southern coast of Asia Minor. Trouble was brewing among the Spartans, but they had let the best moment slip, and might now think better of it. Daraios had not managed to raise a new army yet, but had increased his offer.

He now proposed that Alexander should marry his daughter, receive 10,000 talents, and have the River Euphrates as his border. Parmenion said that if he were Alexander, he would accept. Alexander said that if he were Parmenion, so would he! The formal reply to Daraios was a repeat of the previous one, except for the addition that as Daraios' daughter was already in Alexander's possession he did not really need Daraios' permission to marry her, should he choose to do so. On receiving this reply, Daraios realised that he now had no other recourse than battle, however poor his chances in that, and started with a heavy heart to call up his troops.

Alexander continued south towards Egypt, the remaining coastal towns submitting to him until he reached Gaza. Gaza was the last city before the desert bordering the satrapy to the south, and a very old and rich one. It stood on a tell, a huge mound built up of domestic debris slowly accumulated over many centuries. The approaches other than along the main road were protected by soft sand, and the three and a half miles between city and sea were obstructed by many salt water lagoons and pools. Gaza was a famous centre for the Arabian spice trade, and could afford to pay for its own defence. Batis, its eunuch governor, had hired a garrison of Arab mercenaries, brought in ample supplies, and was prepared to stand attack.

The main problem for the attackers was the height of the mound. Both battering stone-throwers and anti-personnel catapults had to operate with a flat trajectory, yet could not fire from the slopes of the tell without risk of tipping over. The answer was to build a further mound and mount the artillery on it, so that they could shoot on the level. Work was accordingly started on building a counter-mound around the city. It soon became apparent just how much work this would involve, and attention was concentrated on a section facing the south wall, this looking weakest.

On the day the attack was to be made, Alexander was sacrificing to the gods when a hawk passing over the altar dropped an object on him. Arrian says it was a stone but, knowing our local birds, I have my doubts! This was certainly an omen of the most significant kind, and Aristandros, Alexander's resident seer, was called upon to interpret it. He answered that the gods promised the city would fall, but that Alexander should be careful that day. Knowing Alexander, this was a pretty safe sort of prophecy to make, as he had already succeeded in two very difficult sieges and was apt to expose himself freely. Aristandros' success was, in fact, to be spectacular, making his reputation for life.

Alexander tried hard to be a good boy, and remained for some time watching from the artillery position. However, when a strong sally was made by the garrison to try and set fire to the engines under cover of missiles from the walls, he flung himself into battle at the head of the hypaspists and succeeded in stabilising the situation. However, while doing so, he was hit by a catapult bolt that penetrated both shield and armour to wound him badly in the shoulder. It was almost unheard of to survive a catapult hit, but luckily Alexander managed it. He was necessarily out of action for some time, but took comfort from the thought that, as one part of the prophecy had come true, the other part could be expected to as well.

He now sent for his heavier siege engines to be brought round from Tyre by sea, and in the meantime put the army back to work on his mounds. These were now to surround the entire city, and were to be 250 feet high and 500 paces wide. The engines arrived and were set to work. Simultaneously, he mined into the sides of the tell, driving tunnels under the walls, then firing the props to collapse the tunnels and shake the walls above.

The walls subsided into heaps of rubble over wide stretches, and three successive assaults were made after artillery preparation to clear the defenders from the breaches. Both Arab mercenaries and citizens fought fanatically in spite of huge losses from the engines, but the Macedonians first gained a footing, then spread out to tear down the gates and let in reinforcements. Even this did not end the resistance. The male population fought to the last man, and had to be routed out and exterminated one by one. The women and children were enslaved. The city was repopulated from the surrounding tribes, who thought of this as a promotion, and its defences reconstructed sufficiently for Alexander to use it as a fortified supply base for his advance into Egypt.

It is worth considering at this point what the result would have been if Alexander had died as a result of the risks he had taken along the way. As I see it, there were two possible legitimate heirs. Alexander's half-witted brother might have been acceptable with Parmenion as regent, but Parmenion would not have lived for ever, and he would have been unlikely to survive long alone or produce a credible heir. The young king of Epiros was married to Alexander's sister, and seems to have been reasonably competent, but was an awfully long way from the army. His Epirot birth would have been against him, but a later king of his country managed to get accepted. A possibly acceptable outsider would have been Ptolemaios, known as son of Lagos, but rumoured to have been a bastard of Philip's. He was present with the army as one of Alexander's close comrades and later made himself king of Egypt, but at this point was probably not prominent enough to get much support. The strongest candidate must have been Parmenion, whether he particularly liked it or not. He was a well-born nobleman, present with the army, a leading and successful general for many years, and had several grown sons and relations commanding important units. At home, Olympias would probably have had a screaming fit, but could expect less sympathy from Antipatros, who controlled the home army, than he would have for his old comrade in arms. In any case, whether as king or regent, Parmenion would have inherited control of the army in Asia.

If Alexander had been cut down at Granikos instead of being saved by Kleitos, the war against Persia would probably have petered out, providing his death had not resulted in the loss of the battle, as it well might, in which case the Persian cavalry pursuit and fleet might have utterly destroyed the expedition. If he had died of fever or poison at Tarsos, Issos would probably still have been fought, with reasonable chance of success. If he had died at or before Issos instead of being wounded, Parmenion would certainly on our evidence have accepted the Halys frontier, or if at Gaza, the Euphrates. It would then have been up to Parmenion's sons to initiate the next phase of expansion when they took over.

The degree of risk that Alexander was apt to take is illustrated by the casualties among the officers of the units which habitually accompanied him. So far, four hypaspist and three archer commanders had been killed in his presence. Of course, if he had not led from the front in the way he did, his troops would certainly not have performed so well.

The army now continued its march towards Egypt, arriving at the strong border fortress of Pelusion seven days after leaving Gaza. The fleet coasted along in company, arriving slightly before them. Alexander now learned that he was not to fight for this rich possession. Sabakes, the satrap of Egypt, had died at Issos. His deputy and successor Mazaces, having learned of the defeat of Issos and Daraios' shameful flight, seeing Cyprus and Phoenicia and their fleets under Alexander's control, and having had all his best troops called away to take part in the lost battle, accepted the inevitable and was prepared to hand the country over.

Alexander put his own garrison into Pelusion, marched up the eastern bank of the River Nile as far as the city of Memphis, met the fleet, embarked his picked troops, and sailed down the western branch of the river to the sea. Here he founded the famous city of Alexandria-in-Egypt.

He now had news from home by ship. The last of the Persian holdings in Asia Minor and the islands had fallen, although Pharnabazos and one of Alexander's Greek mercenary leaders who had gone over to him were still at large. He also heard of the fate of the 8,000 Greek mercenaries who had escaped in ships to Egypt after Issos. Finding themselves treated with caution and suspicion there as both enemies of Alexander and deserters from Daraios, they had accepted proposals from Agis of Sparta to aid him in an invasion of Crete, where they had already captured most of the cities. As usual when great powers fell out, piracy was on the increase and needed putting down.

Alexander now travelled west along the African coast to receive the submission of the Kyrenians, then cut south across the desert to visit the famous oracle of Ammon at the Siwa oasis. He next headed directly back to Memphis by a desert caravan route some 300 miles long. He found more seaborne reinforcements waiting for him in the shape of 500 Thracian cavalry and 400 Greek mercenary infantry. He now made arrangements for administering Egypt, and it was probably at this time that he was installed as pharaoh.

He divided Egypt into an upper and lower province, as under both the Persian and the native Egyptian regimes. Each province was put under an Egyptian with the title of nomarch, but there was to be no overall satrap. Greek mercenary garrisons were left at Memphis and Pelusion, and a small naval squadron was to be based at Alexandria. Garrisons and fleet were to be commanded by Macedonians, and Macedonian governors were also named for Kyrene and Arabia, although the latter had little joy from his charges, who were not inclined to take orders and could always disappear into the desert if he tried to enforce them.

The rich and ancient country of Egypt was a long thin one, basically a narrow fertile strip on each side of the Nile. Agriculture depended crucially on the regularity and quality of the annual floods caused by mountain snow melting in central Africa, and this encouraged the development of a powerful priesthood, headed by the god-king or pharaoh. The last native pharaoh had been Nektanebo II, who had led a brief revolt against Persian rule 12 years earlier, then slipped away and disappeared among the savage peoples of Nubia beyond the

Nile cataracts to the south. He was expected to return, rather like King Arthur, and a popular rumour made Alexander into his son. Apparently he had visited Macedonia disguised as a god and imposed on Olympias' credulity. Well, she doesn't seem to have been very bright.

Whatever the doubts about Alexander's royal Egyptian birth, he had one very impressive qualification for pharaoh. He was beating the living daylights out of the heartily disliked Persian former exploiters. Alexander played up by paying due deference to Egyptian religion, and by building extensions to two of the most ancient temples and dedicating these to the good examples of two extremely respectable long-dead pharaohs. Being pharaoh meant that he could get away with a very minimum of garrisons, saving his strength for the coming decisive fight with Daraios.

Before he could concentrate on Daraios, there was some tidying up to do. The Samaritans had submitted earlier, but then killed their governor. This had to be punished, which delighted their Jewish neighbours and largely reconciled them to Alexander's rule. He now heard that Agis had returned from his successes in Crete, bringing his 8,000 mercenaries with him, and that the Spartan assembly, drunk with success, had voted for war with Macedonia and her allies. They might have been encouraged in this by the way that Antipatros had been weakening himself to send reinforcements to Alexander but, with naval superiority now in Alexander's hands, they were facing long odds. Alexander despatched 100 warships to recover Crete and generally assist Sparta's Peloponnesian neighbours. Lastly, an Athenian embassy pleaded again for the freedom of their prisoners. This time it was granted, but Alexander still retained his 20 Athenian ships as hostages against Athens allying with Sparta.

It was now May. Alexander would spend this month and the next two in retraining his men for field warfare instead of the siege work they had had since Issos; then he would at last march into the heart of the Persian empire and challenge Daraios to battle.

Chapter 11

The thrust into the heartland: the Gaugamela campaign, 331 BC

Alexander now made final administrative adjustments to strengthen his base organisation before moving against Daraios. He started by sacking Arimmas from his post as satrap of Syria and replacing him. Arimmas had been set to gather supplies for the new campaign and, instead of finding ways around difficulties, had taken refuge in them as excuses for failure. He also made the gesture of appointing Harpalos as his chief finance officer. Harpalos was a boyhood friend exiled by Philip for helping Alexander's intrigue. As a cripple, he could not fight and so had been given a financial post in Asia Minor. Here he had been suborned by a Persian agent, and had fled to Greece, presumably accompanied by some of the army's funds. Alexander had forgiven him and called him back, and was now giving him even larger scope for his activities.

Supplies would be important, because the army's route would initially lead it for 300 miles across semi-desert terrain to Thapsakos. Hephaistion was sent ahead with an advance force to construct two bridges over the great River Euphrates at that place, while Alexander completed his supplies. Alexander may also have been hoping that 15,000 men now on their way from Antipatros would reach him in time to join in but, as it happens, they were to miss both his impending battle and those against the Spartans at home. There were two possible routes from Thapsakos onwards. One was south down the Euphrates to Babylon. This route lay through fertile country, easing supply, but was intersected as it neared Babylon by large numbers of irrigation canals, some offering considerable obstacles if defended. The alternative was to follow the river north to the foothills of Armenia, and then march along them to the upper reaches of the area's other great river, the Tigris. This gradually converged on the Euphrates, the two rivers being separated by only a few miles at Babylon.

Daraios and his army were gathered at Babylon. While he cannot have rated his army's chances against Alexander's too highly, having lost all his good infantry, he must have thought that the more open country for his cavalry and his intended use of scythed chariots at least gave him a chance. If he retired further, he would lose the rich heartlands of his empire. Without their resources to support it, his giant army would melt away, reducing him at best to a guerrilla campaign in the more inaccessible parts. This had little to recommend it, as by now he was becoming nervously aware that Alexander would not be deterred by terrain or weather and would keep pressing relentlessly after him. In any case, the empire would be just as much Alexander's if its most valuable parts were supinely surrendered to him as if Daraios had fought and lost. No, it had to be battle.

His next problem was which way Alexander would come. Alexander had so far tended to use the shortest and most direct route to battle, refusing to be swayed by difficulties, and counting on the speed of his march to catch his opponents off-balance. He was therefore almost certain to use the shorter route down the Euphrates. Determined not to be caught on the hop this time, Daraios sent a force up-river to Thapsakos to hold the crossing there as long as they could, send him warning, and fall back before the Macedonian advance, wasting the country so as to cause them supply difficulties and weaken them before the battle. This force consisted of the remaining 2,000 hoplites, possibly mounted for this occasion, plus 3,000 or 4,000 cavalrymen. It was commanded by Mazaios, an able man who had been overall satrap of Kilikia, Phoenicia and Syria until the greater part of those territories had been lost.

Hephaistion arrived at Thapsakos to find Mazaios on the far bank. He constructed his pontoon bridges, but did not attempt to throw them over the river while the far bank was occupied. On Alexander's arrival, Mazaios could no longer count on making good his bank against such heavy superiority and so marched off to the south to complete his mission. In view of the length of time that Greeks of both sides were facing each other across the river here, it has been suggested by one modern author that Hephaistion and Mazaios may have found the opportunity to communicate on matters which Daraios would not have approved. Mazaios was to command a wing in the coming battle which apparently threw up a possible opportunity to win it, and he was later given an important post by Alexander. It still seems to me a little unlikely. Mazaios was considered an honest man, and there are plenty of other explanations for his wing's actions, from Daraios' orders to sheer confusion caused by dust and noise. At any rate, he was to fight hard enough to make tough old Parmenion call for help.

Unfortunately for Persian assumptions, Alexander now took the northern route. Daraios was some time finding this out and, by the time he had finally got his unwieldy army on the move and marching up the Tigris, Alexander was through Armenia and had crossed that river, although apparently with some delay from the strong current due to a seasonal spate. As soon as Daraios had realised what was happening, he sent 1,000 cavalry ahead to forestall Alexander at the Tigris crossings, but he was already three days further on when they ran into him. They tried to start burning off the grazing and crops, but were attacked by Alexander with the Paionians and two ila of companions. They withdrew rapidly, but a few were caught, the prisoners confirming that Daraios was coming up as fast as he could, probably not very fast, with the main army. Alexander encamped for four days to rest his men, then learned from scouts that Daraios and his army had camped within a day's march, around the village of Gaugamela. He left his baggage and non-combatants in the camp, and marched off by night to try and surprise the enemy camp at dawn.

The two armies were about seven and a half miles apart. There were delays during the night march through the hills, and at dawn the Macedonians had only covered half the distance, and were crossing the last ridge before the Persian position. Daraios had also had scouts out. The Macedonian advance had been reported to him, and his army was already drawn up in battle order on the plain below. Alexander deployed into battle order and summoned his subordinates for a council of war. Parmenion advised that there was now nothing to be gained by an immediate attack. Up to this point, the Persians had made use of obstacles and stood defensively behind them. The plain looked bare enough from where they now were, but it would be a good idea to check. Alexander accepted this advice, and ordered the army to encamp, but in battle order. He himself took the companions and light infantry, and rode out on reconnaissance. He found that, so far from the ground between the armies being obstructed, what natural obstacles there were had been levelled. This immediately raised the suspicion that chariots were to be used.

He returned to his temporary camp and sacrificed to Pan, the god who could induce a blind fear, and who had been credited with the Persian defeat by the Greeks at Marathon long before. The polyglot nature of the present Persian army of course made it a prime target for the god to try his panic out on, should he so wish! It may also have been a precaution against his own troops being demoralised by the huge number of Persian camp fires they would shortly see glowing in the dark. However, their morale was probably reasonably good. There had been an eclipse at the beginning of the month, and the obvious interpretation of this, even without Alexander pointing it out, was that the mighty Persian empire was about to disappear. The Persian seers had probably tried to push an alternative explanation, but the troops cannot have found this wholly convincing.

As Alexander returned to his tent, he was met by a delegation of senior advisers who tried privately to convince him that he should launch a night attack. He is said to have replied, 'Alexander does not steal his victories.' He probably then went on to say, 'Make sure you have that written down for our propaganda after the battle. Now, I'll tell you the real reasons.' He certainly had not worried about stealing victory when he had marched to attack the previous night! There were, in fact, good reasons to wait for daylight. His experiences of the previous night had shown him the danger of confusion, the Persians could now be expected to be guarding against the possibility and, in case Daraios should get away, he did not want him to have any excuses. Alexander now worked alone at revising his battle plan into the small hours, then sank into a deep sleep. After his apparent lack of concern was commented on by his pages when they woke him next day, he made the point that he might well have worried if, instead of accepting battle, Daraios had declined it and retreated wasting the land behind him. As it was, Daraios was doing what he wanted, and it would be silly to worry about that. The Persians were in no such happy state. They had been kept in arms all night in expectation of a Macedonian attack, and were not only short of sleep but had had plenty of time to find things to worry about.

Daraios is said to have collected together nearly 250,000 men. However, as at Issos, only a fifth or so of these were troops of any quality, the rest being incompetent, unenthusiastic or even disaffected peasant spearmen. His right wing consisted of 5,000 heavy cavalry from Media, Parthia, Assyria and Babylonia. In front of these on the extreme right were 3,000 Armenian and Kappadokian extra heavy cavalry on armoured horses. Those a little further to the left were preceded by 50 scythed chariots. The heavy cavalry were joined on their left by 2,000 Skythian horse archers and 4,000 other light cavalry armed with javelins. These had the task of maintaining contact with the centre. The centre consisted of Daraios in his chariot surrounded by 1,000 horse guards, with 1,000 foot guards on their left. On either side of the guards there were two 1,000-strong units of Greek mercenary hoplites. In front of them were 15 elephants, flanked on each side by two more units of 25 scythed chariots each. Next to the left-hand unit of hoplites came 1,000 Indian cavalry, 1,000 Karian javelinmen and 1,000 Mardian archers. We now come to the left wing. On the right of this were 1,000 javelin light cavalry; then 1,000 heavy cavalry from around Susa; a mixed force of Persian cavalry supported by light infantry totalling 6,000; 1,000 javelin light cavalry; 1,000 Skythian horse archers; and 8,000 Baktrian heavy cavalry on the extreme left. In front of the mixed Persians was the main unit of 100 scythed chariots. In front of the Baktrians were 1,000 Baktrian and 2,000 Massagetic extra heavy cavalry. Behind all these good troops stood great masses of poor-quality infantry. The left wing was under the overall command of Bessos, the satrap of Baktria, the right under Mazaios. From the Persian troop distribution, it seems likely that the plan was to hold in the centre, block an expected Macedonian main attack on the left, and to sweep round and envelop on the right. The probable quality of the infantry masses behind is confirmed by their apparently being alloted no active role and merely left as spectators.

Alexander's strength totalled 7,000 cavalry and 40,000 infantry, so if only good troops are considered was more or less equal to that of the Persians. The right flank of his main line was formed by the companion cavalry, currently some 2,100 strong. Next came the 3,000 hypaspists, then the 15,000 phalangites. There was to be a new departure here. The six taxeis of phalangites were to advance in echelon, leading from the right, and each had in addition split into two as the drill manuals allowed, the rear eight of their 16 ranks leaving a large gap between themselves and those in front. This meant that the rear part could charge forward against any enemy penetrating behind the troops in front, or could turn about if any outflanking enemy should get behind them. On the left of the phalangites were 400 allied Greek cavalry, then 2,000 Thessalian cavalry. In front of the companion cavalry were 1,000 archers and 1,000 Agrianian and 1,000 Thracian light javelinmen. In front of the light infantry were the 600 prodromoi and 300 Paionian light cavalry and, in front of these, 600 Greek mercenary cavalry. Behind the companions as a flank guard were 6,700 Greek mercenary peltasts. Stationed as a similar guard behind the army's left flank were 700 allied and mercenary Greek cavalry, 300 Thracian light cavalry and 5,500 Thracian peltasts. This leaves about 7,800 of the Greek allied and mercenary infantry to account for. As Alexander as far as we can tell had not employed his 7,000 Greek allied hoplites in the previous two battles, but had kept them guarding his baggage, he may have done the same here. Alternatively, they might have been used to provide or reinforce the second line to the phalanx. I personally prefer the first explanation. As usual, Alexander commanded the right-hand half of the army, Parmenion the left, the split being between the third and fourth taxeis of the phalangites. This contrasted with the Persian threefold split.

Daraios' plan was a good one against an ordinary general, but against Alexander had what was to be a fatal flaw. It did not credit him with any subtlety. Good plans in war take into account all the enemy's options, consider the probability of them being adopted, and then guard against them. Great plans decide what the enemy is likely to do, then exploit his own actions to his ruin. Daraios expected a straightforward frontal attack with Alexander charging on the right, the phalanx trying to keep up, and Parmenion guarding on the left but prepared to exploit opportunities. That was very nearly what hap-

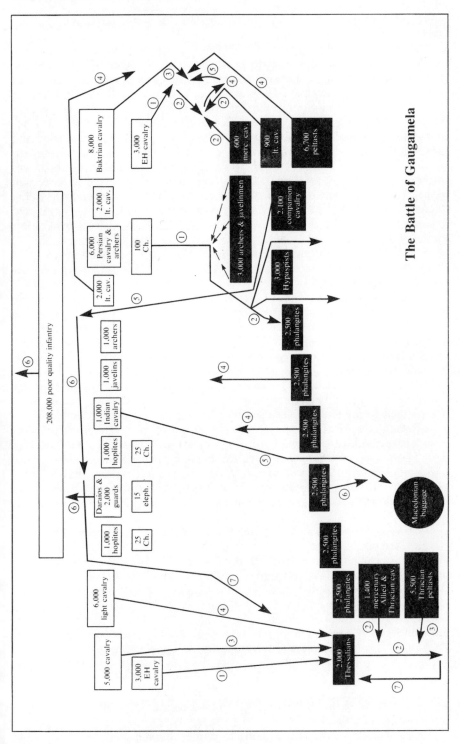

The Battle of Gaugamela

pened, but the nicely calculated and unobvious difference was enough to ruin him.

The first unpleasant surprise for Daraios was that, instead of advancing straight ahead in line, the Macedonians were not only echeloned back to the left, but were heading somewhat to the Persian right. The first meant that the Macedonian left would be far more difficult to envelop, the second that the Macedonian right might pass out of the terrain specially cleared for the chariots. Daraios therefore ordered Bessos to send troops to block further movement in that direction. Bessos accordingly despatched the Baktrian and Massagetic extra heavy cavalry from in front of his wing on a swing to the left. In order to comply, these had to expose their flank temporarily, which was promptly charged by the Greek mercenary cavalry leading the Macedonian right. The extra heavies had to turn hurriedly and counter-charge. Being heavier, they drove the Greeks back, only to be struck in their turn and disordered by the prodromoi and Paionians. The extra heavies broke, but rallied when the main body of Baktrians came to their aid. A standing mêlée ensued, with the Macedonians getting slightly the worst of it, but not enough to make them fall back. More of the Persian cavalry were now sent around the left to try and get at their flank.

Meanwhile, the main body of scythed chariots charged the companion cavalry, but most were intercepted by the light infantry and destroyed. A few managed to reach the cavalry, who dodged out of the way and these were later finished off by the hypaspists. Some others which had flinched away from the light infantry's showers of javelins hit the right-hand phalanx unit and did considerable damage before being destroyed.

All the Persian left flank cavalry was now engaged in a struggle with the Macedonian light and mercenary cavalry, who were reinforced by the mercenary peltasts to their rear. These would have been at a considerable disadvantage if charged by the opposing cavalry but, now that the cavalry had expended their charge and were jammed at close quarters, they could make themselves felt. Their intervention pushed back the Persian cavalry a little, allowing the prodromoi to disengage and reform for another charge. It must have been a shock for the Persian horsemen to find themselves attacked by infantry, as these would previously have been concealed by the dust and by the cavalry in front of them.

By now, instead of cancelling out the companions, the Persian left flank cavalry had not only got itself completely tied down by subsidiary opponents, leaving the companions unmarked, but had also denuded the point where it joined the centre by taking troops from there for flanking moves. Like a bolt from the blue, Alexander now led the companions in a whirlwind charge straight at the weakened point. Simultaneously, the extreme right and therefore most advanced taxis of phalangites contacted the enemy just to the left of the weak spot. Alexander penetrated easily, angled to the left, and charged into the rear of the units forming the Persian centre. Daraios was just preparing to loose the elephants and chariots protecting his front in a charge at the approaching second unit of phalangites, but it was too late. He was now involved in a desperate mêlée, losing his chariot driver, it is said, to a spear flung by Alexander himself. He dropped his weapons, whipped up the horses and managed to burst clear to his right rear.

Almost simultaneously, the rallied prodromoi charged again, their intervention turned the scale, and the whole of the Persian left crumpled and broke. Seeing their left wing, their centre, and Daraios in flight, the infantry masses in rear decided to make the most of their start and set off at their best speed towards the horizon discarding weapons and equipment like confetti in a paper chase.

Alexander rallied his men, prepared to set off in pursuit, but had to abandon his intention in the light of a message from Parmenion. We know much less detail of what had happened on the Macedonian left, except that the Thessalians had held their own and were beginning to push their opponents back when help arrived. Presumably the sequence was much like that on the right, with units being flung in as the battle swayed this way and that, and the savage Thracian infantry taking a major part. However, the Persian advantage in numbers and weight was much greater than on the other flank, and historians have been mildly surprised that they achieved so little. One possible reason might be that Mazaios had been got at earlier, and was not trying very hard, but this does not seem to me to be in character. The Armenian and Kappadokian extra heavy cavalry may have been reluctant to fight against the ruler who now controlled their homelands, but it is at least equally plausible that they would fight desperately in an attempt to free them. A more likely explanation is that the skirmishing light cavalry tactics of the Thessalians made it a long tiresome job to get rid of them.

The emergency Alexander was now called to was, in fact, not on the opposite wing but nearer to the centre, and it was already over. A gap had opened between two of the taxeis of phalangites, and Daraios had sent some of his bodyguards and the Indian contingent through it in an attempt to rescue the royal family from Alexander's camp. This thrust achieved initial surprise, as the defenders of the camp did not expect an attack through the doubled phalanx. However, they soon recovered and the attackers were then squeezed against them by the second half of the phalanx charging to the rear. Many were killed and the rest fled.

Alexander now arrived in the rear of the Thessalian's opponents, which caused the most deadly fighting of the day, as these strove to break through the companions and get away. Finally, those who could had done so. Alexander pursued until dusk and then halted to rest horses and men. Parmenion and the Thessalians continued, and captured the Persian camp with the baggage train, and the surviving chariots and elephants. Alexander set off again at midnight, and pushed on hard for Daraios' base town of Arbela. He reached there next morning after a 75-mile pursuit. Daraios had only stopped long enough to obtain fresh horses and was now out of reach, but he lost his spear, bow and chariot for the second time, plus his treasury. He had left the main Babylon road and cut over the high passes of the Kurdish mountains towards Ekbatana, accompanied by his 2,000 Greek hoplites, the remains of his bodyguard, and rather less than 8,000 of the Baktrian cavalry.

About a third of the Persian army had been killed, mainly in the pursuit, rather more captured, and the remainder scattered beyond immediate recall. Alexander's losses are not known, but the companions had over 60 killed, probably at least four times as many wounded, and had lost nearly half of their horses. Even if the horses were replaced by those captured, this was a temporary loss rate of 15 per cent of the troops actively engaged.

Chapter 12

The great pursuit: mopping up in Babylonia, Persis and Media, 331 BC to 330 BC

Daraios had fled eastward into Media because he expected Alexander to go south to Babylon, the centre of empire, and indeed he did so. The satrapy was situated in the plain between the two great rivers, Euphrates and Tigris. In spite of very low rainfall, it was considered the most fertile corn land in the known world, a fact made possible only by very extensive irrigation from the rivers by canal and shadouf. This irrigation system took a great deal of hard work to maintain, and largely fell out of use during the Arab conquests of the 6th century AD. The constant struggle to keep the system working led, as in Egypt, to the development of a powerful central government which could command the great resources of labour needed. This necessary concentration on civil engineering had led to the Babylonian state falling first to the Assyrians, then to the Persians, primarily military powers, but memories of former greatness kept the inhabitants always ready to rebel. Much of the best land had been split into estates for the great Persian nobles, and the irrigation scheme was starting to sag a little. However, horse breeding had expanded, and there were said to be 800 stallions and 16,000 brood mares at stud.

Alexander continued moving south by easy routes through Babylonia until he came to the city itself, where he was greeted by a procession of civic dignitaries bringing its submission. Babylon, unlike most cities of the era, which could be often little more than walled villages, was a city in the modern sense. Its outer walls, just high enough to discourage casual raiders, were approximately 37 miles long, and enclosed a dense pattern of villages and cornfields. The main wall was something else again, ten miles long, 45 feet high with towers rising to twice that height every 150 feet, and wide enough for two four-horse chariots to pass on the rampart walk except where it was narrowed by the towers. The whole area inside this wall was packed with buildings. Further towards the centre there was another wall of the same height but thinner.

The city's interior was divided by a rectangular grid of streets. The Euphrates flowed through the middle, crossed by several fine bridges. The public buildings included impressive temples and palaces, the famous hanging gardens, and the ruins of the 450-foot high zikoras of Marduk, more widely known as the Tower of Babel. The latter had been successfully completed in spite of the communication difficulties mentioned in the Bible. However, maintenance had been neglected as a result of rebellions against Xerxes and their aftermath, and the decay was now too far gone to be arrested. The main construction material for the city and its defences was brick, frequently coloured and glazed to produce grandiose decorations such as the well-known low relief lions, bulls and dragons. The riverside was lined with wharves, which included the terminal for one rather unusual form of river transport. The Euphrates was too fast for easy upstream travel, so a more usual mode was to float downstream to the city in a hide boat, which in addition to its cargo carried a tied-up donkey, or several depending on size. On reaching the destination, the cargo and the boat's wooden frame were sold, there being no local wood apart from palm which is unsuitable for construction, the hide covering folded and packed on the donkeys, and the crew walked home.

Here, Alexander gratified the locals by promising to help in the rebuilding of both the zikoras and the Persian-vandalised temple of Marduk, and recognising the privileges of the priesthood who ran the local administration. He restored the city's status as a satrapal capital, of which it had been deprived by Xerxes for persistent revolt, and appointed a new satrap. This was Mazaios, who shortly before had been commanding the Persian right wing at Gaugamela. This may have been a reward for not fighting too hard, but is more likely to have been in recognition of his role in arranging a peaceful surrender of the city. However, as was becoming usual, Alexander separated the military and civil roles which had been combined by Persian satraps, and appointed a Macedonian to command the satrapal forces. At the same time, he appointed Mithrines, the Persian who had surrendered Sardis to him after Granikos, as satrap of Armenia. A great deal of bullion had been found in the treasury, and some of this was now coined to bring the troops' pay up to date and give them a spree before the next part of the march.

While Alexander and the army had been marching to Babylon, a herald had been sent on east to Susa. He now returned with the satrap's son bringing an offer of surrender. The army had now had five weeks' rest, and could do with a march to pull it together, so Alexander set off in late November towards Susa. On the way, he met reinforcements marching down the royal road, 11,000 Macedonians and Greeks, including a complete taxis of phalangites, plus 4,000 Thracians. He now took the opportunity to divide all the ilai of companion cavalry into two sub-units for increased control.

Susa was the administrative capital of the empire, chosen originally because of its central position and its lack of important previous associations. Like several later capitals chosen on similar grounds, it did not have the best climate in the world. It was said that in mid-summer lizards died of heat-stroke while trying to cross the road. However, the palaces were magnificent, and the central treasuries of the empire even more, to the tune of 50,000 talents. Alexander reappointed the current satrap Abulites, but gave him the usual Macedonian military colleague. He also appointed Menes as overall satrap of Syria, Kilikia and Phoenicia, and sent him on his way with 3,000 talents, of which as much as proved necessary was to be sent to aid Antipatros against Sparta, and a pair of famous statues looted by Xerxes from Athens which Alexander wished to return. The Spartan war was, in fact, already over although Alexander had not yet heard this. Antipatros had marched to the Peloponnesos earlier in the autumn with 40,000 Macedonians and allies. Agis had met him with a much inferior force, to be crushingly defeated and killed.

Up to now, Alexander and his army had been having it fairly easy since the battle. Babylon, which had the defences and resources to delay him, had instead welcomed him as a liberator. Susa, which might have had the will to

CHORASMIANS

ARMENIA
● Artaxata

DAHAE SKYTH

CASPIAN SEA

L Matianos

CADUSIA

✕● Gaugamela

● Zadrakarta

HYRKANIA

Caspian
Gates pass ● Hekatompylos

●
Arbela

MEDIA

PARTHIA

R Tigris

ASSYRIA

● Ekbatana

● Babylon

BABYLONIA

Susa ●

SUSIANA

KARMAN

R Euphrates

● Parsagardae

● Karn

● Persepolis

ARABIA

PERSIS

Alexander's
Eastern
campaigns

PERSIAN GULF

AR

withstand an alien invader, had known that it could not do so, being totally unwalled, so had given in gracefully. As the army now marched out to the east, they were heading into very different conditions. The route now led through the territory of the Uxians. Some of the Uxians lived in the plains, had paid tribute to the Persians, and were now prepared to submit on the same terms to Alexander. However, those who lived in the hills had on the contrary always exacted blackmail from Persian kings to let them cross their territory without harassment and Alexander was not prepared to pay. He took the 3,000 hypaspists and another 8,000 mobile troops, and was guided by Susians over a difficult and little-known pass into the heart of the Uxian land. He attacked their villages, killing many of the inhabitants and driving the rest up into the hills, and captured much loot. He then marched hard for the main pass where most of the Uxian warriors were awaiting the approach of the rest of the Macedonian army. Alexander sent Krateros up into the hills above the pass with a strong force of light troops, then led the rest of his men down the road. The surprised warriors immediately took to their heels up into the hills, only to meet the blocking force and suffer severely. The tribe now submitted, and were granted their lands back in return for an annual tribute of 100 horses, 500 pack animals and 30,000 sheep.

Three days further on, Alexander came to a fork in the road. The eastern fork was the shortest route to Persepolis, but was through difficult mountain-ous territory. Alexander elected to take the companion cavalry, prodromoi, hypaspists, phalangites, Agrianians and archers that way, leaving Parmenion with the rest of the army to escort the baggage train by the other fork on a longer but easier route. Alexander's party was naturally the first to arrive at the defile called the Persian Gates, which he found defended by Ariobarzanes, the satrap of Persis, with 40,000 infantry and 700 cavalry. The road led up to a high mountain pass through a narrow ravine, blocked at its highest point by a hastily constructed dry stone wall. When Alexander assaulted this next day, he found that it sheltered not only archers, slingers and javelinmen, but artillery which had been brought out from Persepolis. He found the defences very difficult to attack effectively, suffered badly from missiles and from boulders dropped from the walls of the ravine, and finally had to pull back and encamp.

That night, leaving Krateros in charge of the camp with two taxeis of phalangites, some of the archers and 500 cavalry, with orders to assault frontally on receipt of a signal, Alexander took the rest of his force with rations for three days over a subsidiary pass, higher still and barely practical for mules, let alone horses. Coming back down into the main pass, he took the hypaspists, one taxis of phalangites, the Agrianians, the remaining archers, the royal ila and one other ila of companion cavalry, and turned back along it to take the defenders in the rear. The rest of the outflanking force was to march in the opposite direction and bridge the River Araxes. The Persians holding the pass had picquets out along other side paths to their rear. Two of these were rushed and destroyed, the other chased away from the defending camp into the hills. Ariobarzanes' men therefore had no warning before they were attacked from both front and rear. They had no chance, and sought to escape up the sides of the pass, but Ptolemaios had been detached with 3,000 men to forestall them. Ariobarzanes and a few horsemen got away, but most of the other defenders perished.

Alexander now marched as fast as he could for Persepolis before further resistance could be organised. The bridge was ready when he reached it, and he immediately crossed and marched on, joined by the bridging detachment. The governor of the city sent out his submission, and Alexander marched in, to be joined a few days later by Parmenion's force. Persepolis was the ceremonial capital of the Persian empire, just as Susa was its administrative capital. It now had a unique fate in store for it. No less than 120,000 talents were removed from the treasury, then the place was given up to sack and the palace deliberately burned to the ground. There are many reasons quoted for the burning, ranging from revenge for similar burnings in Greece during Xerxes' expedition, to a drunken prank at the suggestion of a dancing girl. It is worth bearing in mind that no better symbol of the empire now being under new non-Persian management could have been found, and that the news must have sent shudders down the spine of all Persians still resisting.

Before marching on in search of Daraios, Alexander made a few quick side excursions to bring local communities and nomad tribes under control. None was expecting him in the depths of winter, and they submitted on promise of fair treatment. Just what sort of treatment would be accepted as fair was an awkward question. Under Persian rule, Persis, the original homeland, had been untaxed. This could not continue, but friction might well result. A partial answer was found in the appointment of a Persian called Phrasaortes as satrap. He was the son of Rheomithras, who had fallen fighting against Alexander at Granikos, and could expect more latitude than most from the diehards when he started organising his administration. Another side expedition to Parsagardae netted 6,000 talents which had allegedly been in store there since the days of Kyros I.

In May, with the grass springing up to feed his horses, Alexander set out north to look for Daraios. The Macedonian capture of Susiana and Persis had outflanked Daraios' Median refuge from the south, leaving him the choice of fighting again where he stood, or fleeing east towards Parthia and Baktria. He hung on until the Macedonian advance north started, dithered for a while, decided to move north a little to give battle at the Caspian Gates defile with the aid of fresh Skythian and Kadusian troops, found out that the new troops had declined to budge, then made a last-minute escape to the east. I say last-minute, but in fact he left Ekbatana eight days before Alexander's arrival, taking with him 7,000 talents, 3,000 cavalry and 6,000 infantry including 1,500 remaining hoplites.

Up till then, Alexander had thought he might need his army again, but he now concluded that Daraios had neither the nerve nor resources to do him any further harm. He thus sent the Thessalian cavalry and the Greek allies home, paying them off in full, and with a 2,000-talent bonus to be divided among them. Once the news of that spread at home, he would have no difficulty getting fresh recruits! However, any who wanted to stay behind as mercenaries were welcomed. The various Persian treasures were to be escorted to Ekbatana by Parmenion and concentrated there under the charge of Harpalos, guarded by 6,000 of the phalangites with a few cavalry and light troops. Parmenion was then to take the mercenary and Thracian infantry, plus any cavalry not with Harpalos and Alexander, along the southern coast of the Caspian Sea to bring that area firmly under control and ruin any further chance Daraios might have had of recruiting its Kardusian troops. Alexander himself took the prodromoi, the companion cavalry, some of the mercenary cavalry, those phalangites not guarding the treasure, the archers and the Agrianians, and force-marched after Daraios. He had a lot of straggling and lost many horses, but made up time and reached the Caspian Gates only one day behind. However, his men and beasts could go no further, so he waited and rested them there for five days. He now learned that many of Daraios' men had, in fact, deserted him in his flight. Some of these came in and surrendered, but others made individually for their homes. Alexander appointed a Persian named Oxodates as satrap of Media, thinking that as he had been found imprisoned at Susa he must at least not favour the man who put him there, then went on. One day's march on the other side of the defile, the cultivated land came to an end, and he halted again to collect supplies before venturing further.

He now had two visitors from Daraios' camp, and learned that Daraios had been overthrown by a belated *coup d'état* organised by Bessos, the satrap of Baktria. On hearing this, Alexander did not wait for the return of his foragers, but pressed on in immediate pursuit with the companions, prodromoi, hypaspists and the light infantry, taking only the men's weapons and two days' rations. He travelled all night and till noon next day, rested a few hours, then marched again through the night to reach the Persian camp at dawn. He found only a few stragglers, who told him that Bessos had been proclaimed king in Daraios' place. Artabazos and his sons, and the Greek mercenaries, had not consented to this, but had been unable to prevent it. They had now separated from Bessos and his party, who were heading for Baktria with Daraios prisoner in a closed cart. The rebels had decided to use Daraios as a bargaining counter with Alexander if he caught up but, if they were not pursued further, to raise a new army from Baktria and its neighbours and try again. Alexander determined to keep pressing them, although his men and horses were now very tired. He travelled all the night and next day till noon, arriving at a village where Bessos had spent the previous night. The inhabitants here told him of a short cut, and he pushed on again. Seeing that the infantry could not be expected to keep up any longer, he dismounted 500 of his cavalry and gave their horses to selected infantrymen. He covered 50 miles that night, coming up with Bessos at dawn. Most of the Baktrians fled immediately, the others resisting only a short time before joining them. Bessos stabbed Daraios before abandoning his cart, and fled with only 600 horsemen still under control. Daraios was still alive when found by Macedonian troops, but he died before Alexander got to him.

So passed a king, who in Arrian's words, was weak and incapable in warfare, but in other respects had shown no great faults, although this may have been because the constant disasters he endured at Alexander's hands left him no time to indulge them. He was about 50 years old. Alexander had him buried honourably in a royal tomb, and prepared to revenge him on his betrayers, lest murdering kings should become a habit.

Chapter 13

An empire under new management: Baktrian and Skythian campaigns, 330 BC to 327 BC

Alexander now returned at a more leisurely rate to the Caspian Gates, picking up the men left behind on the way, then marched north. This brought him into Hyrkania, a rich and pleasant land adjoining that of the Kadusians to the south of the Caspian Sea. This was partly to subdue the inhabitants and partly because Daraios' mercenaries had headed that way. He split his army into three columns. He pushed on by the shortest and roughest route with most of the Macedonian and light troops, detached two taxeis of phalangites with some archers and cavalry to subdue the tribes which might otherwise be tempted to interfere with the march of his columns, and sent the mercenaries and most of the cavalry to escort the baggage by an easier but longer road.

By the time these three columns and various other detached forces had rejoined him at the city of Zadrakarta, the capital of Hyrkania, Alexander had acquired a prime collection of Persian nobles, mostly men who had remained loyal to Daraios and now preferred to serve his conqueror rather than his treacherous murderer. Alexander accepted their services gladly. The former Persian empire had to be administered, or the various parts would throw up local warlords who would need to be conquered all over again. Even if sufficient capable Macedonians could be provided without drastically weakening the army, they would be unfamiliar with the languages and local circumstances. If the former governors and their staffs could be trusted to rule in Alexander's interests rather than their own, this would be at least a temporary solution. Among those who now joined him were Phrataphernes, the satrap of Hyrkania and Parthia; Autophradates, the governor of the Tapurians; the ancient but spry Artabazos and his competent sons Kophen, Ariobarzanes and Arsames; and the cavalry general Nabarzanes. Some of these were restored to their former provinces and others joined the companions, where a scattering of their compatriots were already serving. The consideration with which the noble Persians were treated was sufficiently pronounced to produce Macedonian grumbles on the lines of 'Who won this war?'

Daraios' 1,500 surviving Greek mercenaries finally surrendered. They were lectured severely on the wickedness of Greeks fighting against the Greek cause, but tacitly praised for their loyalty to their employer in bad times. Those enlisted before the start of the war were now told they could go free, but were offered employment at Alexander's generous rates of pay. Those enlisted since were told that they must continue to serve and that they would be punished by receiving their old Persian rate of pay, not Alexander's higher rate! Their former general was retained in command.

Alexander now took to wearing the Persian royal diadem, a ribbon which was worn as a hat band or brow band. As a further sign that he now regarded himself as ruler over the Persians as well as Macedonia, he enlisted whole units of local troops for the first time. These were light cavalry armed with javelins and called hippakontistai. He now heard that Bessos was calling himself king and wearing royal insignia, so, after a total of 15 days' rest at Zadrakarta, he set out for Baktria. There could not be two kings in the empire.

There were two possible routes the army could take, the obvious one being more or less due east, initially through hill country, then through arid steppe with a part-way rest at the oasis of Merv, known to its inhabitants as the navel of the universe, but likened by travellers to another part of the anatomy. This route led through Parthia to Sousia on the border of Aria. Here, the satrap, Satibarzanes, submitted to him, and was reinstated with the usual associated Macedonian military commander. The march continued across Aria and on into Margiana, where Alexander was overtaken by bad news. Satibarzanes had revolted, killed his Macedonian colleague and his guard of 40 native light horse, was raising troops, and intended to follow up Alexander and operate against his rear to assist Bessos. This was the first time one of Alexander's Persian subordinates had let him down. Satibarzanes may have been provoked by the Macedonian or just overwhelmingly tempted by that tiny guard. In either case, he was now across Alexander's rear communications and had to be dealt with swiftly.

Alexander had had a comb out of baggage at Sousia, setting a good example by burning his own surplus possessions and wagons, and transferring as much as possible from wagon to pack transport. This had been intended to ease his crossing of the semi-desert of Margiana, but now speeded his march back to deal with Aria. Not content with this increase in mobility, he took the companion cavalry, the new Asiatic light cavalry, the Agrianians and archers, and two taxeis of phalangites, and left the rest to follow on while he force-marched a phenomenal 75 miles in two days. Satibarzanes, surprised by the speed of his approach, fled south-west into Arachosia with a few mounted supporters. Most of the rebel army dispersed, a few tried to hold a wooded hill but were winkled out by fire and massacred, and the satrapal capital of Artakoana was besieged. The main body of Alexander's army came up under Krateros, siege towers were built and put into use, and the city fell. The guilty among the inhabitants were executed or enslaved, and the city was then refounded as an Alexandria with new walls and a garrison of Macedonian veterans, to become in time the modern city of Herat. Much time had been lost and autumn was now well advanced, making the direct desert route to Baktria a little risky, especially as Satibarzanes would have to be left undisturbed somewhere to the south of it. Alexander therefore decided to kill two birds with one stone by pursuing Satibarzanes south, then taking the southern detour into Baktria. Somewhat surprisingly, the new satrap appointed for Aria was a Persian, although one of the sons of the honest old Artabazos, Arsames.

The army was now joined by 6,000 troops from the west, some of them reinforcements from home, and some troops detached earlier, including the Greek mercenary cavalry and the minority of Thessalians who had remained behind as volunteers when the main allied contingent went home. It marched south into Zarangia, where the satrap Barsaintes fled at its approach, being an associate of Bessos in Daraios' murder and having been warned by what had happened to the last attempt at resistance. However, he did not flee to Bessos, whom he possibly knew too well to have confidence in, but far to the east. He was later to be handed back suitably wrapped in chains by the Indian ruler he finally took refuge with, and was executed. The army settled down to rest for nine days around the satrapal capital of Prophthasia.

Alexander's main immediate danger was not from the enemy, but from plotters inside his own staff. A group of Macedonians had conspired to kill him, but one of them had not managed to keep his mouth shut, and neither had the man he confided in, who took the story to Philotas, senior general of the cavalry and son of Parmenion. As the hour for the attempt approached and no arrests had been made, the informer, getting desperate, approached Alexander himself through one of his pages. The man who was the next link in the chain killed himself before he could be arrested, leaving only the informer's memory of what he had been told as evidence of who was concerned. The only clear evidence was that Philotas had suppressed the news of the plot, so at the very least had connived at Alexander's murder. It is also possible that he instigated the plot, but this is unlikely, as his obvious ploy would then have been to arrange a convenient accident for an unwelcome informant.

Philotas was arrested along with the others named, tried, and executed by a firing squad with javelins. Some of the sources suggest that he had been accused of plotting while the army was in Egypt, but that Alexander had not given credence to this. Nothing very conclusive as to the origins of the plot emerged at the trial. However, if Alexander had been killed, Philotas as senior officer with one half of the army and with his father controlling the other half would, to say the least, have been extremely influential when the choice of a successor was made. Alexandros the Lynkestian, of semi-royal blood and son-in-law of Antipatros the commander of the home army, might well have been the choice. He had been arrested for treason in Asia Minor and had accompanied the army under guard. He was now belatedly tried and executed, showing that Alexander had made the connection.

An even worse danger now loomed. The father of the executed general was back in Ekbatana on the line of communications with approximately half the army under his direct command, including four taxeis of phalangites, the mercenary infantry and the Thracians. He had been ordered to bring these up to the Caspian area to join Alexander there, but for some reason had not done so, possibly because Ekbatana was not yet safe to leave. In any case, whether or not this behaviour implied guilty knowledge of a plot, he was fond of his son and a popular and competent commander. If he revolted to seek revenge, it could be very dodgy. In fact, no chances were taken. Men were despatched on racing camels which, although slower than a horse in the short term, could cover great distances faster. They bore orders from Alexander to Parmenion's subordinates for his immediate murder, which went without a hitch. This may have been necessary. It was certainly illegal under Macedonian law, not to say ungrateful for past services. Alexander was beginning to get a little quick on the draw, almost, his troops might think, like the oriental despot he had replaced. The situation would have been further complicated had Parmenion's second son Nikanor, who commanded the hypaspists and hence Alexander's body-guard, not died of disease shortly before. A group of Philotas' friends also came under suspicion. One fled, but it is pleasant to relate that the rest, although his brothers, were cleared and retained high rank, one later dying in battle. Suspicion was not yet equivalent to execution in all cases. The final upshot was the replacement of Philotas as overall commander of the companion cavalry by two men, Hephaistion and Kleitos. Presumably such an influential unit could not be safely trusted to a single man, even such close friends as they.

Kleitos had recently arrived bringing 6,000 phalangites from Parmenion's former force. They may have had somewhat of a shock to find how many Persians there now were in high places with Alexander and how many Persian customs had been introduced to make life more pleasant for the staff. Those present with Alexander the whole time had experienced these changes gradually and had become accustomed to them. The horror of the newcomers probably struck some of them as exaggerated and created further potential friction.

The combined army turned east and headed into the more fertile satrapy of Arachosia. Here a Macedonian became satrap, possibly to quiet grumbles, and was left 4,000 men. Alexandria-in-Arachosia, his capital, is now the modern city of Kandahar. This city would have made good winter quarters, but Alexander had no intention of wasting time resting while Bessos increased his power. Even the news that Satibarzanes had emerged from his hills after being strengthened with reinforcements from Bessos and was threatening Artakoana, now Alexandria-in-Aria, did not delay him. 6,000 troops were detached to clear the lines of communication under Artabazos assisted by two Macedonians, and Alexander pushed on with the remaining 32,000 or so.

The detached force found Satibarzanes with 2,000 rebels and crushed them in a fierce fight, Satibarzanes himself being killed in personal combat with one of Artabazos' Macedonian assistants. Either not expecting Alexander to push into the great mountain range now known as the Hindu Kush in November or unable to persuade his troops to move at that time of year, Bessos failed to guard the passes. Alexander finally halted for a three-month winter rest at Kapisa, the satrapal capital of Gandaria. This he renamed Alexandria-in-the-Caucasus, but could find few spare Greeks or Macedonians to garrison it and had to rely on natives. The exact position is unknown, but it may be modern Jalalabad in Afghanistan, just north of the famous Khyber pass. A Persian called Proexes became satrap.

The army was on its way north again before the snow had melted in the passes. Two and a half weeks later it emerged into the plains of Baktria, having had a very difficult time and losing many animals for lack of forage. However, the bodies of these had at least supplemented the men's dwindling food supplies. Supply difficulties were not yet done with, as Bessos had ordered the country on his side of the mountains to be wasted. Bessos now had 8,000 Baktrian cavalry, the remaining Persian troops of Spitamenes and Oxyartes, Sogdian cavalry from the satrapy to his north and Dahae Skythian horse archers from beyond the northern borders of the empire. However, he lacked the nerve to use these, and instead fled 200 miles north into Sogdiana, burning the boats by which he had crossed the great Oxos river. His Baktrians saw no point in going with him, so deserted to their homes instead. Alexander took Aornos and Zariaspa, the two leading cities, against only token resistance. He left a Macedonian commander in the citadel of Aornos and appointed the elderly but much respected Artabazos as satrap.

He now set off to follow Bessos into Sogdiana beyond the Oxos. This river was a major obstacle. It was deep, three-quarters of a mile wide, swift-flowing, and the combination of the current and soft sandy bed made a piled bridge impractical, especially as timber was hard to come by in that area and would have to be fetched from a distance. A bridge of boats was equally impractical, the current, the destruction of boats by Bessos and the lack of timber all being against it. Alexander's solution was to collect together the armies' leather tents, sew them into bags, stuff these with dry chaff, and use them to raft his army across with only five days' delay. While engaged in crossing, he heard reports which caused him to suspect that Arsames, the satrap of Aria, was behaving suspiciously, and sent back a Macedonian called Stasanor to arrest him and take his place. This is one of several indications that Alexander maintained an intelligence network in the territories he controlled, although apparently not outside them. To give Stasanor some teeth, he sent back with him a number of Macedonians too old and unfit for future hard service and the now time-expired Thessalian volunteer cavalry. These would install Stasanor, and continue their march towards home to a prosperous retirement. Alexander probably grudged the loss of manpower, but consoled himself with the thought that homeward-bound veterans loaded with gold made excellent recruiting advertisements.

Once across the river, Alexander force-marched to where Bessos had last been heard of. On the way, he received messages from Spitamenes and Dataphernes, who were now convinced that Bessos was a dead loss and wished to write him off. He accordingly slowed the march of the main force to rest it, but sent Ptolemaios son of Lagos, the future king of Egypt, on ahead with three units of companion cavalry, the native hippakontistai, one of the three units of hypaspists, one taxis of phalangites, all the Agrianians and half the archers. This detached force covered ten normal days' march in four days and arrived at the village where Bessos and his ex-subordinates had spent the previous night. Apparently Spitamenes and Dataphernes had had partial second thoughts. They still wanted to throw Bessos to Alexander as a sop, but did not want to give themselves up. On the strength of information received, Ptolemaios pushed on with the cavalry alone and surrounded a village occupied by Bessos and a few of his men. These handed him over on promise of safe conduct. On Alexander's instructions, Bessos was brought before him naked and restrained by a wooden collar. He was questioned as to his reason for murdering Daraios, tried to share the blame, and was scourged while a herald proclaimed that this was for treasonably and impiously murdering his lord. One suspects that a grovelling apology might have got him off if this had been the real charge, but he had no chance of escape from the offence left unmentioned, that of assuming royal insignia. In Macedonian eyes, this made him a usurper against Alexander, who had replaced Daraios as king of Persia. He was sent back to Zariaspa to be condemned and executed in traditional Persian style by those ex-comrades who had chosen the winning horse in time.

Alexander now took advantage of the opportunity to replace the horses lost in the mountains or by forced-marches with the fine quality local animals. Some of the owners objected vigorously and attacked his foragers, then occupied the only conspicuous hill in the area to await the inevitable reprisal. The hill was extremely rugged and steep, the defenders possibly 30,000 strong. The first attack was thrown back with many wounded including Alexander who was shot through the leg. A renewed attack penetrated the hail of missiles and got to close quarters. The defenders were now in turn hampered by the terrain as they strove to escape, and only 8,000 are said to have got away.

The army moved on to the satrapal capital Marakanda, crude as yet, but later to become the fabulous Samarkand. Alexander could not walk or ride, so was carried in a litter by troops who disputed for the privilege. A garrison was installed, and the army moved on some 150 miles north-easterly to the northern boundary of the empire on the Jaxartes river. Here Alexander intended to build another city, to be known as Alexandria Eschata, or 'Alexandria-the-furthest'. This would provide an anchor point for defence against Skythian raiders from beyond the river and a base for attack across it if that should be needed. It was now mid-summer and scorching hot, although the very low humidity must have made the temperature easier to bear.

Before work on the new Alexandria could commence, rebellion broke out all over Sogdiana. The Sogdians had only submitted to the loosest possible control from the Persians and were in no mind to accept more from Alexander unless they were forced to. The requisitioning of horses and supplies had naturally been unpopular and the fate of the 22,000 that had perished as a result of earlier resistance must have caused resentment as well as fear. Religion was also a factor. Neither burial nor cremation were the customary way of disposing of the dead in Sogdiana and Baktria. They were instead exposed on platforms for the vultures, the birds being thought to free their souls as they removed the flesh from the bones. Alexander had banned this practice, thus putting the population's prospects of heaven in jeopardy. The last straw was when all the local rulers were invited to a conference and promptly assumed that this was a plot to deprive them of life or liberty rather than a genuine consultation. The small garrisons which had been left in the minor cities were promptly slain and the larger 1,000-man garrison at Marakanda besieged. Worse, the revolt began to spread to Baktria, the inhabitants of which considered they had not been defeated by Alexander but let down by Bessos. Natural leaders were available in the shape of Spitamenes and Bessos' other surviving ex-henchmen.

Alexander decided that the most urgent need was to provide a strategic barrage in the north to prevent the Skythian tribes across the Jaxartes joining in. He started by acting against the seven rebel cities in that area. He ordered ladders to be made and engines to be assembled, then advanced against the weakest, called Gaza, while Krateros marched to invest the largest and best defended, Kyropolis. Krateros was to construct lines of circumvallation to prevent the inhabitants being either relieved or helping the smaller towns and was to have the army's artillery with him so that it could be assembled and emplaced ready for Alexander's arrival with the rest of the army. Gaza had only a low mud brick wall, so was immediately stormed with scaling ladders after clearing away the defenders with concentrated archery, slinging and javelins. The adult males were slain, the rest of the inhabitants enslaved and the loot carried off. Alexander now immediately marched to the next town and took it in identical fashion the same day. Next day, he marched the infantry to a third which was similarly taken, but sent the cavalry on ahead to the next two, where they caught the inhabitants in the process of evacuation and slew most of them. He now joined Krateros at Kyropolis. This was more of a real city, situated on a mound, with higher walls, and manned by the majority of the local tribes. Alexander commenced battering it with his engines, but noticed that the river running through the town was unusually low. While most of the army was assaulting the breaches, he personally led a small party along the river bed inside the walls, and opened a gate to admit dismounted companions, hypaspists, archers and Agrianians. He was then counter-attacked fiercely and was wounded by a stone at the base of the neck, but forced back the defenders out of the market place. The distraction enabled the force attacking the breaches to get a foothold. About 8,000 of the inhabitants were killed immediately. Another 15,000 got into the citadel, but had to surrender a day later for lack of water for so many. The seventh city surrendered before it could be attacked.

News now came from the garrison at Marakanda that it needed help. Unfortunately, the Skythian tribes were massing just across the river, obviously ready for trouble, and Alexander dared not take his eyes off them for the moment. He instead sent three officers called Andromachos, Menedemas and Karanos with 60 companion cavalry, 800 Greek mercenary cavalry and 1,500 mercenary infantry. These officers were accompanied by a Lykian staff officer called Pharnuches who was an expert on the country and good at dealing with its inhabitants. It seems likely that Alexander told the others to act in accordance with this man's advice. If so, he probably thought the trouble at Marakanda could be sorted out by political means. Had he known that the attack on the garrison was being organised and directed by Spitamenes, he might well have taken it more seriously and sent a top-grade commander. However, several senior officers including Krateros had been wounded at Kyropolis, so he may have been short of good men to send.

Alexander now spent 20 days on building a really strong wall for the new Alexandria. He then garrisoned it with the usual unfit veteran Macedonians and Greeks and transplanted inhabitants from the towns he had recently taken and which were now to be destroyed to prevent them serving as a focus for further revolt. He then held the usual founding celebrations including athletics contests and military parades, hoping to impress the Skythians across the Jaxartes. These, however, remained markedly unimpressed, shouting rude comments and trying long shots with their bows, which in fact could not clear the river.

Alexander cared neither for being called names nor being shot at and grew wonderfully irritated. He got out his tents again and started to turn them into rafts. He also told Aristandros the sage to test the omens. These turned out to be unfavourable, which annoyed Alexander even more. A little later, the tests were repeated and Aristandros told Alexander again that there was danger. Alexander replied that it might be even more dangerous in the long run to be considered a joke by Skythians, and went ahead. He started by setting up his artillery along the bank and shooting at the Skythians. Shaken by the range and power of their missiles, the Skythians fell back, and Alexander immediately began the crossing, himself accompanying the first flight. This was of slingers and archers to force the horse archers back still further. The next ashore were cavalry, the horses presumably swimming behind the rafts, then the remainder of the cavalry and infantry with equal priority.

Once the army was ashore, he sent the prodromoi and a mercenary cavalry unit to charge the Skythians. These happily got out of their way and then rode around them in a circle shooting at them with their bows. Meanwhile, Alexander advanced with the rest of the cavalry and light troops. When close enough to be noticed he sent three units of companions and the hippakontistai to charge frontally in line with the light infantry in support, the other cavalry to charge in two columns on their flanks, one led by himself personally. Half the men in the Skythian circle, busy poor devils concentrating on their nice target in the centre, suddenly found themselves surrounded, their path to the sides cut off by the columns, to the rear by the chargers and their supports, and to the front by their infuriated former victims. About 1,000 of them were killed, 150 were captured and the rest of the army fled in terror. Alexander pursued them until they reached the safety of hills eight miles away, then turned back. Later, a messenger arrived from the Skythian king saying that it had not been an official army but only private raiders and expressing extreme regret for the unfortunate incident. So the omens were wrong? Not a bit of it. Alexander drank bad water during his pursuit and went down with what I suppose we can call 'Skythian tummy'. Nothing hinders a mounted pursuit so much as having to get off your horse at frequent intervals.

Meanwhile, the force detached to relieve Marakanda was in trouble. At Marakanda itself, Spitamenes had launched an assault but had been driven back by a sally from the garrison. On hearing the relief force was approaching, he broke off and retired, probably towards Baktria. On his way, he met up with 600 Skythian cavalry who had crossed the border east of Alexandria-the-furthest and knew nothing of the events around there. These agreed to join up with him, and he decided to wait for the pursuers and give battle. Pharnuches had been urging the necessity of pushing the pursuit hard and disposing of Spitamenes once and for all, and the others, confused as to his precise authority, had been letting him have his way. Now they were suddenly engaged by a fresh enemy. Neither the infantry nor the cavalry on their tired horses could get within reach of the elusive horse archers, who poured in a constant stream of arrows to wound men and lame horses. Pharnuches tried to hand over command to the military men, but these refused, saying in effect 'You got us into this, you get us out of it. Why should we lose our reputations trying to retrieve your botched-up battle?' They were to lose more than their reputations. The force withdrew towards a wooded valley by the nearby river, where they would be less exposed to the archery. The cavalry commander abandoned the infantry and tried to cross the river. The infantry, demoralised, broke ranks and rushed after them down the steep banks, and the Skythians closed in to shoot at point-blank range. About 40 cavalry and 300 infantry managed to cross and get away to rejoin Alexander. Most of the others took refuge on a small island, where all but a few were shot down. The survivors were taken prisoner, and butchered when the victors changed their minds.

When Alexander heard, he marched immediately with half the companions, the archers, the Agrianians and the hypaspists, covering 185 miles in three or four days. Spitamenes fled again. Alexander pursued, burying the detached force en route, and continued the pursuit as long as there was any hope of catching up. Failing to gain contact, he joined up with the main army and marched south to winter at Zariaspa.

The army's situation improved during the winter campaigning break. The first sign of this was when envoys started to arrive from the peoples to the north of the empire. First by a short head came the king of the Chorasinians with an escort of 1,500 armoured cavalry. He had suffered equally from Sarmatian tribes north of the Caspian and Black seas and from the Skythians on his other flank, and offered Alexander an alliance against both. Almost simultaneously, Skythian envoys arrived, alarmed at Alexander's successful raid across the river, and possibly also at the prospect of being squeezed by Macedonians and Chorasinians from two directions. They offered the king's daughter in marriage and promised strong action to curb raiding by individualist chieftains. Alexander declined the princess, but it was probably at this time that he arranged to take Skythian horse archers into his service, thus giving an alternative source of excitement and profit to the hot-heads who would otherwise have been tempted to raid into his lands. Pharasmanes, the Chorasinian, was accepted as an ally, therefore extending the Skythian peace to him as well, and Alexander promised to co-operate with him against the Sarmatians if this became necessary on his return westward. For the moment he had his hands full with the eastern provinces and possibly beyond them. With the two northern powers thus neatly balanced off, there was a real prospect of stability in the future. However, at the moment there were still large bands of Skythian raiders wandering about in Baktria and Sogdiana who must be chased out.

The other welcome arrivals were reinforcements from the west, mainly Greek mercenaries, and sufficient to almost double his army from a rump of 25,000 to nearly 47,000. Apart from freshly recruited troops, this contingent included the men who had been detached to escort treasure westward. It was accompanied by a number of competent officers previously left administering the west but now urgently needed with the army to replace losses, notably Alexander's friend and future admiral Niarchos. Less willing members of the trek included the arrested former satrap Arsames and a number of captured henchmen of Bessos, who was now brought out of his prison, his nose and ears sliced off in the traditional Persian punishment for high treason, and despatched to Ekbatana for formal execution before the assembled Persian and Median nobles.

When the campaigning season opened, Alexander used his new additional strength in a concerted attempt to finish off the Sogdian and Baktrian rebels. Part was left in Baktria under Polysperchon, Attalos, Gorgias and Meleager with orders to patrol vigorously to discourage further rebellion and to hunt down existing rebels and parties of raiders. The rest he took into Sogdiana in five columns. One he led personally, the others being commanded by Hephaistion, Ptolemaios, Perdikas and jointly by Koinos and Artabazos. These entered Sogdiana on a wide arc converging to meet at Marakanda and effectively ended resistance in the area they traversed. Hephaeston was now detached again to plant garrisons at strategic points, Koinos and Artabazos were sent to follow up a rumour that Spitamenes had been seen in Skythian territory, and Alexander with the rest of the army operated against the remaining rebels from Marakanda.

It was now high summer in that arid region, encouraging a large intake of liquids. The local water was heavily mineralised and unpleasant tasting, the wine full bodied and strong, and Macedonians were not greatly given to mixing the two. It was probably excessive consumption of alcohol that now led to a tragic brawl. Kleitos, who had saved Alexander's life at Granikos, disapproved of the consideration now being shown to Persians and was further upset by the prospect of being removed from his command of half the companion cavalry and left behind to control Baktria when the army moved on into India. Alexander was planning further changes in the organisation of the companions which would lead to the two senior positions losing their pre-eminence and the Baktrian post was, in fact, very important, but Kleitos chose to see the change as a slight. He provoked a drunken quarrel, was hustled outside, but returned with further insults and was slain with a spear flung by Alexander in an equally drunken rage. He was bitterly ashamed of the murder not only of a former friend but of a guest at his table, and refused food and drink for three days.

The rumour that Koinos and Artabazos had been sent chasing was out of date. Spitamenes had been in Skythia and recruited 600 volunteers, but was now in Baktria, capturing one of Alexander's small forts in a surprise attack. He then raided the outskirts of Zariaspa, gaining much booty. 80 mercenary cavalry in garrison at Zariaspa pursued and scattered the Skythians, regaining the loot, but were in turn ambushed and largely destroyed by 400 Skythian reinforcements. The combined Skythian force was then jumped by Krateros, lost 150 men, but fled faster than it could be pursued, leaving most of the plunder.

Wonder of wonders, Artabazos was now feeling his age, and was permitted by Alexander to resign his satrapy. This was transferred to a Macedonian named Amyntas. Alexander then took the main army into winter quarters at Nautika in the south of Sogdiana, but left Koinos with 400 companion cavalry, all the hippakontistai, two taxeis of phalangites and a force of hired Baktrians and Sogdians to watch the Skythian border. Koinos' force was next attacked by Spitamenes who had managed to recruit another 3,000 Skythian adventurers for a late raid into Sogdiana. The Macedonians won convincingly, killing 800 of the enemy for the loss of only 25 cavalry and 12 infantry. The Skythians, insisting on some profit, obtained it by plundering the baggage of Spitamenes' remaining Sogdian and Baktrian followers, most of whom promptly deserted to the Macedonians. Now hearing a rumour that Alexander was marching on them, the Skythians sent him Spitamenes' head to divert his wrath, then went home. Spitamenes' use of the hereditary Skythian enemy as allies probably played a great part in reconciling the Baktrians and Sogdians to Alexander's rule. Stuart use of Scots in English civil wars and its effect on their former English supporters provides a good parallel. The rest of the winter was occupied with administrative changes. Three satraps were replaced, one having died, the others being suspected of disloyalty. The replacements were the usual mixture of Macedonians and Persians.

In early spring, Alexander was up and about again before the snow had cleared. There were two last strongholds of Sogdian resistance to be dealt with to the east. Both of these were mountain fortresses. The first he came to was called the Rock of Sogdiana. He offered the defenders safe conduct if they came down and submitted, at which they laughed and told him to come back when he had found soldiers with wings. He immediately called for experienced mountaineers from amongst his men. Some 300 volunteers turned out and were equipped with iron tent pegs, axes and ropes. A reward was then offered for the first 12 men to the top, the first to get 12 talents, the second 11 and so on. Thirty men fell to their deaths but the remainder could be seen on a dominating crest next morning when Alexander's herald pointed out to the Sogdians that the army did indeed include men with wings. The defenders promptly surrendered.

Among those found there were the daughters of Oxyartes, one of the few remaining Persian hold-outs. Hearing of their capture, Oxyartes himself came in and submitted. He was shaken and gratified to hear that Alexander had fallen in love with his daughter Roxane and was about to marry her formally.

The second stronghold was called the Rock of Chorienes. This was surrounded on three sides by a precipice and on the other was separated from more high ground by a ravine, the bridge over which had been broken down. Alexander started to fill up the ravine with a wooden staging. The tribesmen laughed at first, then as the work progressed grew worried, submitted, and made their stored food available to the army.

There were still a few rebels on the loose, and Krateros was sent after them with 600 companion cavalry and four taxeis of phalangites. He defeated them in a bloody battle in which they lost 120 horsemen and 1,500 infantry. His task then accomplished, he marched to rejoin Alexander in Baktria, where the main army had gone. He caught up with them at Zariaspa, where the final preparations were being made for the invasion of India. A far-reaching reorganisation of the army was underway. Hephaistion had at last been formally appointed second-in-command; orders had been given for 30,000 local youths to be taught Greek and how to use Macedonian weapons; and discontent was bubbling again amongst the more conservative element of the army.

The focus of this discontent was an attempt to encourage Macedonians to greet Alexander with the Persian ritual royal salute already used by his Persian courtiers. If they did not do so, it weakened his position with the Persians. The most vocal objector was Kallisthenes, a minor philosopher and nephew of Aristotle who was accompanying the army as a historian. He was a pretty abject crawler and flatterer himself but his dislike of Persian customs seems to have got the better of him in this instance. One of his minor jobs was to teach the royal pages and, when they hatched a plot to murder Alexander, he was suspected of influencing them to that purpose. He was imprisoned, and we are told that he died of natural causes before trial, which may even be true. The plot failed, incidentally, because Alexander stayed up drinking all the crucial night, so was not available to be stabbed in his bed. A more influential cause may be imputed to the fact that several of the lads' fathers had recently been removed from their commands. The execution of the treacherous pages had little impact within the army, which was much too busy sorting itself out into its new form. Preparations finished and summer fast approaching, the army marched south to Alexandria-in-the-Caucasus, leaving 3,500 cavalry and 10,000 infantry behind to garrison Baktria and Sogdiana. Alexander replaced his original satrap as he was incompetent, and then set off again for India. He was now 29 years old and had never been defeated.

Chapter 14

Indian armies and Macedonian changes to meet them

The first Indian armies Alexander was to meet were those of the hill states of what was later to become Afghanistan and the North-West Frontier province. These probably differed little from the Baktrians in their dress. However, their mountainous territory precluded them from placing much reliance on cavalry, although every chief would have had at least a few mounted followers. The richest might even have had a number of war elephants, but opportunities to use these effectively were few, and Alexander in the event was not to meet the giant beasts in battle until he descended into the lowlands, although many fell into his hands after sieges. The tribes' main reliance was on infantrymen armed with javelins or bow, plus a small round shield and sword or long knife.

All the tribes were brave and fiercely independent, much given to blood feud among themselves and the raiding of weaker neighbours. If an exasperated lowland ruler came after them with a large army, they would seek to ambush it in defiles or, if it was too strong, scatter into the mountains or stand siege in their fortresses. In Victorian times, each village had its thick mud brick walls and watchtower and posed a difficult demolition problem even for explosives. Much the same may have applied then.

The armies of lowland India were a very different proposition. They were recruited from the warrior class of a highly stratified society and were organised for formal battle on level ground. The most prestigious arm was the elephantry, next the chariotry, then the cavalry, and lastly the infantry. Artillery was not yet known, although it was to be introduced later as a result of contact with Alexander's army.

The war elephants were not fitted with howdahs but had their fighting crews sitting astride like the driver. A famous coin shows Alexander challenging the Indian king Poros, who sits astride behind the driver, and like him threatens Alexander with javelins. The usual crew was probably a driver and two other men, one of whom might have sometimes carried a bow instead of javelins. Neither elephant nor crew had much in the way of protection. A sort of quilted mattress on the beast's back served both as a seat for its riders and as a defence against arrows and javelins, and its forehead might have had a padded leather protection mainly for use in pushing down defences in siege work.

The great strength of the elephant in war was its effect on horses. Ordinary infantrymen had a hearty dislike of being trampled on and were extremely reluctant to go close, but horses that were unused to elephants became frantic in their presence. This, incidentally, was not due to the smell. Horses do not in general care much about smells and do not have very sensitive noses. It is strange sights and sounds which frighten them, and a trumpeting and rampaging elephant is a more impressive sight and sound than most.

The elephant's weakness is that it is intelligent and does not like getting hurt. Resolute men might kill it with loss of blood from a multitude of relatively innocuous wounds or hamstring it with axes, accepting the risk of close proximity. It is most unlikely that a single thrust or missile would penetrate far enough to reach a vital area and achieve an immediate kill. Its wounds might at first madden it and make it an even more formidable opponent, but in the end they are far more likely to send it out of control to the rear, as potent a danger to its own side as to the enemy. This would obviously be more likely if the driver were killed. Later users of war elephants gave the driver a hammer and chisel with which to kill it if it endangered its own side but, along with elephant armour and howdahs loaded with fighting men, this lay many years in the future.

The elephant, being taller than other animals, gave its riders an advantage in missile range and made an excellent vantage point for a general to direct his army from. One special tactic taught to Indian cavalry aimed to counteract this height advantage by training the horses to proceed in a series of rearing leaps on their hind legs, this raising the rider to the same height as the elephant crew to strike at them with hand-to-hand weapons. The extra height did, of course, make the elephant a more prominent target which would have been an advantage to artillery engaging it. In theory, artillery, with its much greater killing power, should have been an ideal counter-weapon. In practice, it was rarely (if at all) there when it was wanted, elephants being considerably more mobile and thus able to avoid its vicinity.

The original Indian chariot was drawn by two horses and had a crew of three. One of these was a driver armed with javelins, who is usually described in modern books as standing on the pole between the horses. A more practical interpretation of the pictorial evidence is that he was mounted on one of the horses. The other two crew members were archers. This vehicle was slow and clumsy and had by Alexander's time been largely replaced by an even heavier variety. This had four horses side by side with two poles. Armed drivers either stood on the poles or more likely rode two outside horses. The body of the chariot contained the usual two archers plus two javelinmen to protect them with shields and fight at close quarters. Such vehicles were at a great disadvantage on soft ground, but had their advantages. They could charge down infantry, keep out of the way of elephants, fight hand-to-hand on relatively even terms with cavalry, and had considerably greater shooting effect than other nations' chariots. Chariots always had an advantage over horse archers in that they could carry more ammunition and thus afford to shoot faster.

Indian cavalry did not enjoy the same high status as other nations' cavalry and, though brave enough, were generally less efficient. The horses were kept too fat for real fitness, and the eccentric habit of dosing them with wine before battle was probably not conducive to obedience or quick manoeuvre. Trappings were ornate. The cavalrymen were unarmoured but bore a small, usually round, shield. They were armed with a pair of bamboo-shafted javelins and a sword, and had a whip fastened to the left wrist.

The infantry were mainly archers. These had an unusually long and powerful bow shooting exceptionally long and heavy arrows. These were sneered at by Alexander's archers, but had tremendous armour-penetrating power. Being so

Left to right *Indian cavalryman, Rajah and driver on elephant, and infantryman.*

powerful, they were hard to string, and had to be braced by the left foot. This has been interpreted a little strangely by some writers, who believe that the bow was braced so in shooting. A little thought would have shown that this would make an excellent way to shoot rabbits while underground! Some of our sources suggest that the Indian archers had difficulty stringing their bows during the forthcoming battle due to slippery ground underfoot. As we are also told that a firm sandy area was selected as the battlefield to favour the chariots, this may not be completely reliable.

The rest of the infantry carried a pair of javelins and a long narrow shield of hide stiffened with bamboo which had a round top and flat bottom. Both archers and javelinmen also carried a sword. This was long and especially wide-bladed, so was swung with both hands. It had considerable armour-defeating power, but tended to expose its wielder, who could not use his shield properly at the same time. Casualties were thus likely to be high on both sides.

Very few men had any armour at this time. A king might have a metal scale corslet and helmet and lesser notables cotton quilting, but lesser lights usually went naked to the waist or sometimes wore an open bolo waistcoat. Animal riders had a length of coloured cloth tied twice around the head or helmet as a fore-runner of the turban. Others went bare-headed. Metal jewellery was worn, especially ornate collars. The amount obviously depended on social status. The wear below the waist was a long kilt, invariably white for infantry, usually so for cavalry, but likely to be coloured brightly in the case of elephant and chariot riders. Except for the king, who wore built-up soles to increase his height above that of common men, all went barefooted. Moustaches were more likely to be worn by lower-class warriors than beards. Upper-class beards were often dyed a bright red, green or blue.

Most of our information on the Indian army of this period is derived from Greek and Macedonian contemporaries, a little from carvings, although these are much rarer than those of later times, but quite a lot comes from a single book. This is the *Arthashastra of Kautilya*. Kautilya was prime minister to Chandragupta, a minor Indian subordinate of Alexander who after his death established himself as an independent power and completed the Indian conquests that Alexander had not. Kautilya was a rather Machiavellian character and his book is on government rather than on war alone. I have been fortunate enough to have access to one of the rare English translations. Regrettably, the reader is not likely to achieve this, but if he does he should bear in mind that Chandragupta did not follow the methods of his predecessors but a mixture of theirs and Alexander's. Armour was more plentiful in his army than that of Poros and discipline probably higher.

If Alexander was to fight against a new kind of enemy, he was going to need a new kind of army to do it with. The main lesson from all his battles so far was the extreme value of his disciplined lancer cavalry and his most important need was to maximise its strength and efficiency. He had started his invasion of Asia Minor with eight ilai of companion lancers and four of prodromoi, about 1,800 heavy Macedonian lancers and 600 light. A reinforcement of 300 companions had joined him at Gordion, 500 more in Kilikia and another 500 at Susa, bringing the total of heavy lancers up to 3,100. Casualties in battle had probably accounted for about 100, leaving up to 3,000 to be divided among the eight ilai. The larger ilai had proved clumsy, so had been sub-divided for the first time into two lochoi. At the same time, the ilai had been grouped into two hipparchia commanded by Hephaistion and Kleitos. Reinforcements since had probably added about another 500 companions, and Alexander decided to draft the remaining prodromoi into their ranks, giving possibly 4,000 heavy cavalry. This further increase in the strength of the eight ilai to about 500 men each justifed renaming them as hipparchia. This would have been something of a demotion for Hephaistion had he not now been named vizier with special responsibility for Persian affairs and in effect second-in-command. Alexander had taken over Kleitos' command, so there was no replacement's feelings to consider. Alexander naturally continued to command the agema. One of the other hipparchs' name is unknown. The others were Hephaistion, Perdikas, Krateros, Koinos, another Kleitos known as 'White Kleitos' to distinguish him from the late lamented, and Demetrios.

Professor Tarn considered the prodromoi to have been Thracians and that they had been returned home. He also thought that since the hipparchia appeared at a later date to have 1,000 men each that they must always have done. He accounted for the increase by assuming that the balance of numbers was made up by incorporating separate ilia of Persians into each hipparchy alongside the original Macedonian ilai. Sadly, there is no evidence for this, although it is very probable that selected noble Persians had, in fact, been incorporated into the existing units as individuals. After the campaign, the companions for a while mustered only four hipparchia. This may have represented reforming after losses or possibly a new opinion on Alexander's part that 1,000 men was a better all-round unit. The question had been confused by the translation of Hephaistion's new title of vizier as chiliarch 'leader of 1,000'.

Alexander had always tended to use the prodromoi as charging cavalry and it may have been with relief that they donned captured corslets and relinquished their scouting role to others! This could now be taken over by other cavalry, first the hippakontistai, and then the Skythian horse archers, both probably 1,000-strong.

Although there seem to have been no separate units of Persians or Medes, there were now units of Arachosians, Baktrians, Parapamisdae and Sogdians, mainly light cavalry. These may have been enlisted as much to keep them out of trouble as for their military services, but their losses in the great battle that was to follow showed that they took their profession seriously. Later in the campaign, Alexander would acquire Indian war elephants, cavalry and infantry, but preferred not to commit these to battle against their fellow-countrymen.

The hypaspists and phalangites do not seem to have been changed at this time. It has been suggested by one modern writer that the latter abandoned their pikes for some other weapon, seeming to imply javelins. None of the three main sources confirm this and two of them specifically mention the use of pikes in the great battle, so it is hard to see why. Pikes were heavy objects to carry, and it may be that they were sometimes temporarily left with the baggage for long forced-marches against light opposition, the phalangites then depending either on their swords or on borrowed javelins. But there is no specific evidence for this, however plausible it may seem.

One change which was in prospect was the equipping of the close-fighting infantry with metal corslets instead of the spolas. Losses from archery had been fairly high, especially among the phalangites whose smaller shields and preoccupation with their two-handed weapons made them especially vulnerable. Alexander had ordered 25,000 corslets to be made and sent to the army, but these were not to arrive until the campaign was practically over.

The light infantry remained the 2,000 archers and 2,000 light javelinmen of old, backed up by mainly Thracian peltasts. Alexander does not seem to have recruited any of the excellent Asiatic archers and slingers now at his disposal. His reason for this was possibly that the correct answer to skirmishers was not to skirmish back at them but to get to close quarters as quickly as possible and chase them away. It is worth mentioning that Hannibal, the next general of history after Alexander to be labelled a 'Great Captain' by military historians, also of choice used relatively few missile infantry.

Alexander's artillery and engineers were now highly experienced and the same can probably be said for his baggage train. The artillery could get into action quickly, wooden siege towers could be assembled ready for action in two days or less, and a pontoon bridging train was permanently in being. He had even fetched large numbers of boatmen and shipwrights from the west and could have a fleet on any large body of water in a remarkably short time. One such fleet was destined to sail all the way back from India to Persia, opening up a permanent supply and trade route for the future.

Chapter 15

To the edge of the world: the campaigns in India, 327 BC to 326 BC

Alexander now set off again east towards India, sending ahead heralds to seek the submission of the Indian kingdoms in his path, notably that ruled from Taxila, which is now modern Rawalpindi. This was obtained, so Alexander split his army. Hephaistion took half the companion cavalry, all the mercenary cavalry and three taxeis of phalangites along the direct route with orders to secure its cities and the crossings over the Indus. He himself took the rest of the companions, the hippakontistai, and the remaining infantry on a swing to the north to subdue the fierce and fanatically independent tribesmen of what was to become the north-west frontier zone of British India.

He headed up the Choaspes, now the Kunar river, through difficult mountainous country. Hearing that the local tribesmen were fleeing to their strongholds or driving their flocks up into the mountains, he pushed on ahead with all the cavalry, the light infantry, and 800 of his heavier infantry mounted on spare horses carrying their normal infantry shields and weapons. Coming to the first stronghold, he drove its defenders inside, although he was slightly wounded in the shoulder by an arrow which penetrated his corslet. The Macedonians camped for the night, and assaulted at dawn. The first of two walls was easily taken, but a sufficient stand was made at the inner one to enable most of the inhabitants to flee from the far side of the stronghold into the mountains.

The next stronghold, cowed by the fate of the first, surrendered at discretion. It was made into a temporary base for Krateros, who had now come up with the main body. He was to pacify thoroughly the surrounding area. Alexander again went on ahead with the hypaspists, archers, Agrianians, two units of the phalangites, five of companion cavalry and half the horse archers. His advance nearly but not quite outstripped the news of his coming. The inhabitants of the next stronghold fled to the mountains, but were caught and harried severely. One of their many casualties was their leader, slain by Ptolemaios who had dismounted to pursue him up a steep slope on foot. The chieftain's immediate followers ran away, but others, enraged by his death, turned back and attacked, a fierce little action being fought until Alexander came up with reinforcements.

Alexander now came to a place called Nysa, which surrendered after a brief skirmish outside its walls. The inhabitants' religion had many features in common with one of Alexander's own favourite Greek cults. An alliance was made, a contingent provided for the army, and a small number of troops left behind in retirement. Nysa's situation made it a useful base for control of the area. Alexander's force was now joined there by that of Krateros, and the combined army took a short rest.

The army's route shortly descended into lower country. A little further on, an outlying hill spur approached it from the left, and advanced scouts reported that at night this was covered by an immense number of camp fires. Alexander made a close personal reconaissance and decided that this was only a ruse to increase the apparent numbers of the enemy. He devised a three-pronged attack. He himself with the main body would advance in the centre. Leonnatos was sent up on to the mountain flank with two units of Thracian and Agrianian light javelinmen respectively. Ptolemaios was sent around the opposite flank with half the cavalry, the archers, the rest of the Agrianians, one unit of hypaspists and possibly one of phalangites. Seeing their approach, the enemy, who in spite of Alexander's ideas on the subject really were 40,000 strong, were not impressed by the size of the Macedonian force and charged downhill to meet it on level ground. Leonnatos' light troops therefore found themselves with little to do. Ptolemaios moved against the tribesmen's other flank, but ran into a flank guard occupying high ground and had a harder fight than the rest of the army. He finally broke through in time to intercept fugitives from the other two forces. Most of the enemy were captured, together with some very impressive oxen that Alexander wanted to send back to improve the breed at home.

He now heard that the Assakenians were massing to meet him less than 20 miles further on with 30,000 infantry, 2,000 cavalry and 30 elephants. He immediately marched to meet them, but they lost their nerve at his approach and dispersed to defend their cities. The most important of these was Massaga, at the entrance to the Katgala pass. The ruler had imported 7,000 Indian mercenaries. These together with the inhabitants launched a surprise attack as Alexander was encamping before the city. He decided to lure them on, so retreated to a hill about a mile from the camp site. The Indians pursued at speed and in considerable disorder. They were catching up and their arrows had started to fall among the Macedonians when Alexander turned and counterattacked. He should probably have left it a little later, because most of his erstwhile pursuers managed to regain the city before he could catch them. As he chased them, an arrow from the walls wounded him slightly in the ankle.

Including the mercenaries, the city had a total garrison of some 38,000. It was protected on the east by a swift-flowing and steep-banked river and on the west and south by ravines. The upper part of its wall was constructed of timber-reinforced brick, the lower part of stone, and deep ditches had been laboriously cut into the rock to protect the north face. This wall construction was adequate against normal attacks, but not against Alexander's modern siege equipment. His artillery made a small breach on the first day, but the assaulting troops were driven back. The next day one of his siege towers had been assembled, and under the cover of its archers and the army's artillery, pioneers were filling up the ditch. By the third day, a tower could be pushed forward across the ditch. Its drawbridge fell on to the ramparts, the hypaspists charged across, and the bridge broke under their weight! Seeing this, the defenders resumed their shooting and a party sallied out to make the confusion worse. The Macedonians withdrew with their wounded, pulling back the tower, which, although now useless for assault until repaired, could still be a useful vantage point for archers to command the battlements. Next day, the Macedonians started to bring another tower up towards the wall. The sight of this and the death of their commander, struck down through his armour by a bolt from one of the besiegers' engines, led the inhabitants to seek terms, which were granted.

The city was to remain under its own rulers, but the remaining Indian mercenaries were to enlist with Alexander. The mercenaries agreed to do this, marched out of the city, and encamped on a hill near by. However, not wishing to fight against their own homelands, they tried to break out during the night and get away. Alexander was forewarned and destroyed them as they attempted to escape.

While besieging Massaga himself, Alexander had despatched two mounted forces to invest the other two main towns of Ora and Bazira and neutralise them until his attention could be turned in their direction. The inhabitants of Ora sallied out, but were easily driven back. Alexander now decided to deal with the most enterprising set of enemies first. He asked Koenos, commanding the force at Bazira, to join him with most of this troops, but to leave a garrison at some convenient strongpoint to watch the town. Seeing Koenos retreating, the inhabitants of Bazira now sallied out, only to be turned upon and chased back inside with the loss of nearly 600 men. Ora proved to be easy meat for Alexander, who took it immediately, together with the 30 elephants that had been left there. Hearing this, the defenders of Bazira abandoned their city and fled at night to Aornos.

While Alexander had been campaigning in the mountains, Hephaistion had made his way to the Indus, accepting the submission of the cities en route. However, one of these, Peucelaotis, had then revolted behind him. The force immediately turned back and captured it after a 30-day siege. This settled, Hephaistion had returned to the Indus and had built many small boats as well as two larger ones of 30 oars. Alexander now marched south through the Malakand pass to join him. After a brief inspection of the boats, and appointing Nikanor satrap of the newly conquered areas, he marched north again, this time up the Indus river to deal with Aornos.

The Rock of Aornos was a mystery for many years but was finally identified by Sir Aurel Stein in 1926 as the flat-topped 7,000-foot mountain of Pir-Sar. The summit was large enough to grow crops to feed its garrison and had trees and springs in plenty. To the north, it was cut off from an even higher but more rugged mountain by a steep ravine. The east was protected by a series of gorges descending to a great loop of the Indus, the west by sheer cliffs. To the south, the mountain split into three long fingers, each very difficult to climb. The fastness was now occupied by all the remaining dissidents of the region. If Alexander could take it, he would rid himself of much future trouble. It had never yet been taken.

Alexander started by turning the nearby city of Embolima, probably modern Gunangur, into a base. He left Krateros there with part of the army to collect supplies for a long siege. He then took 200 companion cavalry, 100 horse archers, the Agrianians, the archers and selected hypaspists and phalangites on a personal reconaissance. Alexander was lucky enough to fall in with friendly tribesmen who offered to guide a force to the top. He arranged for Ptolemaios to make the attempt with the light troops and hypaspists. He was to seize and fortify a foothold, then make a signal bonfire. Meanwhile, Alexander would return to the main force and start it moving up as fast as it could. Ptolemaios was led up a difficult narrow path to the top of one of the southern spurs, entrenched himself, then lit his fire.

Alexander saw the fire, but so did the defenders of Aornos. They managed to get between Ptolemaios and Alexander. Alexander could make no progress up the narrow path overlooked by his enemies and, seeing this, the tribesmen launched furious attacks against Ptolemaios to sweep him away before Alexander could break through to him. However, the cliff-top force managed to hold out till night fell, thanks mainly to their archery.

During the night, Alexander got an Indian messenger through to Ptolemaios with a written order to attack downhill as he attacked upwards. Even so, it took nearly all day before the whole of the track was firmly in Macedonian possession. It was so narrow that only small numbers could be employed at one time, although Alexander did his best by arranging for frequent reliefs of those doing the fighting as fresh troops struggled up from below. Once firmly at the top of the spur, an immediate attack was made along it towards Aornos proper, but this petered out when the way was found to be blocked by an 800-foot deep and more than 200-yard wide ravine.

The night was devoted to widening and improving the path and bringing up artillery. Next morning, rather than send his men down into the ravine to climb up the other side, Alexander commenced to fill it in. The main fill material used was the cut-down trees of the spur. A day later, the heap had progressed enough for slingers on it to join the artillery in keeping down unfriendly heads on the far side. However, the amount of fill became greater geometrically as the ravine's depth increased and it had to be fetched further, so it was another three days before even a minimum force could be got across. An initial attempt to get men across gained a small bridgehead, but a venture by a small élite force to push on further was defeated with loss and it had to be withdrawn. Two more days were now spent on improving the causeway and on the assembly of a siege tower. This demoralised the garrison, and on the second day they requested terms.

Alexander was warned that this was not a genuine request, but an attempt to cover an evacuation. At nightfall, he took 700 hypaspists close up to the causeway and, when the gleam of torches showed that an evacuation was indeed under way, led an immediate attack causing heavy losses to the fugitives, many of whom fell over cliffs in the dark.

Alexander now garrisoned Aornos and appointed Sisikotos, a Persian of known reliability, as commander. He then swept the surrounding area for dissident fugitives but, before returning down the Indus, he indulged in a successful elephant hunt which made useful additions to his stock of these massive animals.

At the place where Hephaistion was waiting with his boats, the Indus was extremely wide but slow-flowing. Once the reunited army had crossed it, they were met by Omphis, the heir to the king of Taxila who had recently died. A very unfortunate international incident nearly occurred as Omphis approached with his army in line of battle studded with elephants. For a moment Alexander thought he was being attacked and deployed likewise. Seeing the misunderstanding, Omphis raced up alone on his horse and explained through an interpreter that the army had merely been brought for decoration. He escorted Alexander's army to Taxila, and there presented Alexander with his kingdom, 30 or 56 elephants, 700 cavalrymen and 200 talents. He also made sure that Alexander knew that he had been supplying Hephaistion with free corn.

Alexander returned all this and added another 1,000 talents, plus presents of ornate robes, horses, horse harnesses and gold tableware. This generosity offended a number of the Macedonian leaders, but must have had an excellent propaganda effect on undecided Indian rulers. Omphis now changed his name to Taxiles, the traditional name of the rulers of Taxila.

Omphis' windfall produced one immediate result. Another king named Abisares promptly turned up and submitted. We are not told whether he was discontented not to receive identical gifts. However, one king was not impressed. This was Poros, the ruler of Paurava, a larger rival of Taxila on the other side of the Hydaspes river, now the Jhelum. On being invited to meet Alexander on that river with his tribute, he courteously replied that he was happy to attend the meeting, but would Alexander mind if he brought weapons instead? To that Alexander could have only one answer, and his army forthwith set off on the easy 100-mile march to the Hydaspes.

When Alexander reached the Hydaspes, possibly at modern Haranpur, he found Poros waiting on the other side with 285 elephants, 420 chariots, 5,000 cavalry, 30,000 good infantry and an unknown but impressive number of much poorer infantry. This was a relatively small force compared with some that the Macedonians had met previously, but very much stronger in chariots and elephants, and on the far side of a real river which made those crossed at Granikos and Issos look like mere streams. They had dealt with chariots before, but not in such numbers, and even though they were now well used to the sight of elephants, they had never, as far as we know, faced them in battle. The few at Gaugamela do not seem to have become engaged and those of the border princes had been captured in sieges. However, Alexander must certainly have been aware by now of the dislike felt for them by his horses. The river was fast-flowing, half-a-mile wide, and swollen by the spring thaw in the mountains which fed it.

Alexander had transported his flotilla overland from the Indus, the 30-oar boats being cut into three, the smaller ones into two, and had prepared his usual chaff-filled leather floats. The river was fordable in summer, but now made dangerous by the force of the spate even when not too deep. Horses especially offer a large side area to a strong current and I personally have found it necessary to cross Dartmoor rivers in flood well above lines of stepping stones lest the horse be forced down on them and turned over. The rocky bed of the Hydaspes may well have provided similar dangers. One favourable point was that there were small islands in places which might enable the river to be crossed in instalments. Alexander was not unduly discouraged, and let it be known that if necessary he was prepared to wait until winter when the river would be at its lowest. His men did not themselves expect an immediate crossing as the first rains foretelling the summer monsoon were already beginning to fall and the river could be expected to rise further.

Poros also had his problems. The rains had started; life in tents and in the open would shortly get pretty uncomfortable and unhealthy; he had a big army to supply; and work on the land had probably been disrupted. Two weeks of night alarms in which noisy Macedonian cavalry excursions sent his army uselessly up and down river to counter non-existent landings had done nothing to raise his morale or that of his men. The rising river and the sight of stacks of forage collected on the Macedonian bank for a long stay finally convinced him that he was being had, and he ceased responding to the nocturnal provocations.

It was going to be quite difficult enough to keep his troops in the field till winter without exasperating them in that way.

This, of course, was the result Alexander was trying to achieve. He had found a site 18 miles upstream which offered concealment for an army forming up to cross and where a convenient island split the crossing into two fairly narrow channels, and his boats and rafts were already hidden there. Krateros was left to hold the camp with one of the units of companion cavalry, the Arachotian and Parapamisadian cavalry, two taxeis of phalangites and all the 5,000 Indian allies. His orders were to force a crossing if Poros left with this whole army or with his elephants, but to maintain his position merely threatening a crossing as long as there were any elephants opposing him. He was to light extra fires at night to simulate the presence of the whole army and Alexander's tent was to be left behind with its guards and even an imitation Alexander. The main crossing was to be made by Alexander with the remaining units of companion cavalry, the Baktrian and Sogdianian cavalry, the Skythian horse archers, the hypaspists, two taxeis of phalangites, the Agrianians and the archers. The mercenary cavalry and infantry were to cross at an intermediate point as soon as the enemy were seen to be engaged with Alexander. This intermediate force probably included the hippakontistai and, since one of their commanders was present, probably those taxeis of phalangites not already accounted for.

Although he was no longer perambulating up and down the river bank in the dark in response to Alexander's movements, Poros had mounted scouts to watch all the likely crossing places. The crossing itself could not be started till dawn for safety's sake, and the boats were seen as they rounded the island. This speaks well of Poros' troops; usually the sentries which appear in history have been surprised asleep! They galloped off to rouse the army 18 miles downstream. Alexander initially had some trouble, for his landing place proved to be another island rather than mainland as he had supposed, but the extra crossing forced on him turned out to be just fordable in spite of the way the river had risen in response to the heavy rain that night.

Once on relatively dry land, Alexander led on with the cavalry, the horse archers scouting in front. The hypaspists and phalangites followed under the command of Seleukos, the future founder of the Seleucid empire, with the light infantry on their flanks. The delay imposed by the second crossing had enabled a quick reaction force to arrive from Poros' camp before all the troops were across and formed up. This consisted of 60 chariots commanded by Poros' son. However, it had not attacked, but waited instead for a further 60 chariots and 2,000 cavalry coming up behind, so lost an excellent opportunity. This force was now engaged by the horse archers closely supported by the other cavalry. The outnumbered Indian cavalry lost 400 men, and as many again scattered instead of returning to Poros with the tale of defeat. None of the chariots returned. Their heavy weight made them not very mobile at any time and the soft ground after the rain did not help. Deprived of the support of their cavalry, they were easy meat for the horse archers, who could both outshoot them and easily avoid their clumsy charges.

When the news reached Poros as he watched Krateros ostentatiously making preparations to cross, he decided to leave a minimum covering force and take the rest of the army to meet Alexander on a suitable battleground where the rest of his chariots could be of service. He accordingly led his remaining 4,000 cavalry, 300 chariots, 200 elephants and 30,000 good infantry to a hard level

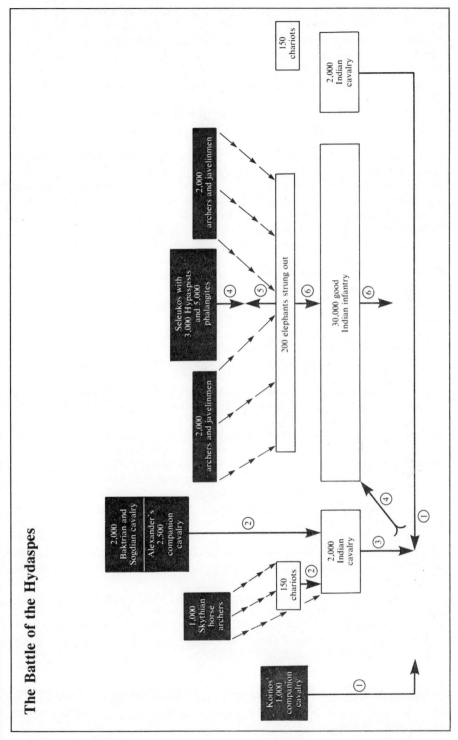

The Battle of the Hydaspes

sandy plain and deployed to wait. The poor-quality infantry left to guard against Krateros, now relatively few in number after desertions, had to be stiffened by 85 elephants. Poros drew up the main force with elephants spaced out at roughly 50-pace intervals. Deep blocks of infantry were drawn up behind the gaps in the line of elephants and more infantry continued the flanks beyond the elephants. The cavalry were evenly divided on the flanks of the infantry. The chariots were also evenly divided and placed in front of the cavalry, and Poros himself rode an elephant in the centre of the line.

When Alexander saw the Indian dispositions, he decided not to attack the centre where he would be up against the Indians' best weapon, their elephants, but to fight the main battle with and against the arm in which he had a marked superiority, the cavalry. To make the contest more uneven still, he decided to concentrate the whole of his cavalry against one of the enemy wings, the left. The attack would be opened by the Skythian horse archers, who were to attack frontally, dispose of the protective chariots which might otherwise blunt a Macedonian charge, then weaken and disorder the enemy cavalry, before fading off to the flanks to leave clear space for the charge. Meanwhile, Koinos was to move off to the right, beyond the extremity of the facing enemy left flank, and circle around to attack it in flank and rear with two units of companions, while Alexander with the others charged it in front. The infantry were to advance against the enemy centre but not to come within range until it was feeling the effects of the cavalry engagement.

Events went much according to plan, except that Poros, seeing Alexander's intentions, withdrew his right flank cavalry behind his centre and sent it to aid the left. The left flank had meanwhile been shaken by the shooting of the 1,000 Skythians, and Koinos' flank envelopment was becoming apparent. The reinforcing cavalry were forced to form front to the left rear to hold them off, and were still doing so when Alexander's charge sent the original left flank cavalry reeling into their helpers' backs. Koinos' charge now sent the whole mass back against the Indian infantry and elephants, disordering them.

The Macedonian infantry then closed, the light troops shooting at the elephants with their bows and javelins, and the phalangites, as two out of three of our sources specifically say, thrusting at them with their pikes. The elephants in turn charged into the Macedonian infantry, doing considerable damage to the phalangites, who could not take evasive action like the light infantry. The Indian infantry, who should have been shooting in support of the elephants, were too disordered to achieve very much. However, the charge of the elephants created a breathing space for the Indian cavalry, who now managed to get clear and charge again, but were once more forced back among the elephants.

The elephants were beginning to run out of steam and were no longer charging vigorously. Many of the drivers were dead, most of their beasts were wounded, and some were doing as much damage to their own side in their panic as they were to the enemy. Finally, they began backing away and refusing to charge, uttering that melancholy high-pitched hoot which is the elephant's notification that he is unhappy. We do not know when the mercenary force had joined the action, but by now it was certainly involved, as we hear from Curtius of Thracians attacking elephants with curved swords like falx, a word used in his day not only for the humble sickle but for the curved sword-axe of the closely related Dacians.

The Indians were by now nearly surrounded and in the end gave way and fled through the remaining gap. Krateros managed to get his fresh force across the river to take over the pursuit and this increased the Indian losses still further. All the surviving elephants were captured, none of the chariots escaped, and 3,000 cavalry and 20,000 infantry were dead. The Macedonian dead are said to have amounted to 20 companions, ten horse archers, about 200 other cavalry and 80 infantry. Taking the usual ratio of wounded to slain, this probably averages out to about five per cent out of action. For once, the companions had had an easier battle than the infantry, whose losses were nearly three times what they had been at Granikos.

Unlike Daraios, Poros had not led the way off the field but had been surrounded fighting gallantly while covering the retreat. When asked to surrender by Taxiles, he narrowly missed him with his last javelin, but was forced to give in when his elephant collapsed from wounds. When Alexander asked him how he thought he should be treated, he replied 'Like a king'. Alexander liked his style, and they were to become friends. He had certainly put up a far better fight than Alexander's previous opponents.

Alexander now reinstated Poros as king, confident that he was competent and would be loyal. Indeed, having lost most of his army, he had little choice as to the latter. Two new cities were then founded, Nikias, which means 'victory' at the battle site, and Bukephalos at the crossing site, in honour of his old horse who had finally expired as a result of being wounded in the battle against the chariots. Victory games were held, appropriate sacrifices made to the gods, and expeditions organised to neighbouring states beyond Poros' borders. These submitted without making trouble, and were added to Poros' realm until he was more powerful than he had been before the invasion.

The only resistance came from a city state called Sangala, possibly modern Lahore. The inhabitants had previously beaten off an attack by Poros and one of his most powerful neighbours and did not fancy submitting to Alexander only to be given to Poros. They called in their neighbours to help and, since they were too numerous for there to be room in the city, accommodated them in a triple-walled wagon laager outside. This was assaulted and the survivors driven into the city. The neighbours were now convinced that they were mistaken to get involved, and large numbers tried to sneak away on each of the next two nights, only to be caught by the cavalry. Poros now arrived with his elephants and 5,000 Indian troops to help. Alexander assembled his engines, then seeing how weak the brick walls were and how demoralised the defenders, changed his tactics to undermining the walls with light tools and hand weapons. The lack of effective response made him realise that he was still wasting time, so he ordered an immediate escalade with ladders. 17,000 Indians perished in the fighting and sacking and 70,000 became prisoners. The Macedonian losses were 100 killed, but 1,200 wounded. Arrian considered this an unusually high ratio of wounded to killed, but it may still imply that our ratio of four or five to one is rather low for pre-gunpowder warfare. Sangala was now razed, and the two cities which had assisted her, but now submitted, were put under Poros' rule.

Alexander intended to push on still further to the east. He was collecting all the elephants he could, having had ideas for improving their efficiency in war, and was expecting massive reinforcements from the west. Two weeks' march to the east would bring him to the upper reaches of the Ganges river. He could then march and sail east-south-east down that mighty river into the heart of the ancient empire of Magadha and its capital of Palimbothra. On the face of it, this would be a much worse proposition to fight than Poros had been. The empire boasted 3,000 elephants compared with Poros' under 300, 2,000 chariots, 20,000 cavalry and 200,000 infantry. However, it was potentially split wide open by internal divisions which could have been exploited. Its ruler was the son of a barber who had become the queen's lover and had been raised by her favour to a high position. He had then killed the king and ascended the throne as regent for the royal children, then stabilised his position by killing the children. The present king had all his father's unpopularity without apparently his political talent.

The problem now was the troops, who wanted to go home and live happily ever after on their loot and accumulated pay. Alexander made a speech setting out his future programme. If Arrian can be trusted, this was to conquer Palimbothra; travel down the Ganges to the sea; sail around India to the Persian Gulf; from there, around Africa to the Straits of Gibraltar; conquer Carthage; then home along the coast of Africa. This was not greeted with the usual cheers, but with stony silence. Koinos now put the opposite point of view on behalf of the men. This was roughly that Alexander should take the army straight home, then enlist a new one from yokels impressed by its riches to do any more conquering he had a mind to. This by way of contrast was greeted with considerable appreciation. Alexander dismissed the meeting without comment, and sulked in his tent for three days without speaking to anyone, probably hoping that the soldiers would change their minds and come weeping to him for forgiveness. They didn't. On the fourth day, he emerged and sacrificed to the gods for permission to continue. The omens were unfavourable. The soothsayers must have known that it would have been extremely unlucky for them personally to reach any other conclusion. Alexander now bowed to the inevitable and announced that he had personally decided that the army would go home. He was met by sustained cheers.

One last formality remained before starting back. This was to build 12 enormous altars to mark the eastern boundary of his empire. He also constructed a fake camp to discourage future trespassers. This was like any other cavalry camp except that huts, furniture, doorways, horse standings, weapon racks and mangers were all scaled to men of eight feet in height and proportionate horses!

Koinos never did get home to spend his loot. In fact, he died a few days after his speech, probably of natural causes. However, the coincidence probably did nothing to encourage future argument with the boss.

Chapter 16

An appointment in Babylon: the return west, 326 BC to 323 BC

Rather than return home the same way as he came, Alexander decided to end his eastern campaigns with a flourish by taking a new route and getting some fighting in on the way to remind his new subjects that it was dangerous to cross him. A large fleet had been constructed back on the Hydaspes and manned by Phoenician, Cyprian, Karian and Egyptian boatmen brought east for that purpose. The standard fighting craft was to be the 30-oared boat already experimented with. There were 80 of these, plus lighter craft for scouting, horse transports and a great mass of both purpose-built and impressed river craft making up a grand total little short of 2,000. Alexander intended to sail down the Hydaspes to its junction with the Indus, down that river to the sea, then finally along the coast westward to Persia.

On his march to join the fleet waiting behind on the Hydaspes, he fell in with the reinforcements he had been expecting. They included 5,000 Thracian horsemen, 7,000 infantry forwarded by Harpalos from Babylonia who were possibly Greeks no longer required there, and 25,000 metal corslets decorated with gold and silver inlay. Each of these had its implications. That such a large number of the Thracian robber nobles should arrive demonstrates equally that the pickings in the east were considered excellent and that there was no longer much scope for traditional rough sports under firm Macedonian rule at home. Henceforth, the Thracians would increasingly get their livelihood and excitement as mercenaries. The second implied that Harpalos was still loyal and the western provinces were quiet. The last shows that Alexander had realised the vulnerability of his pikemen to archery. From now on, phalangites would be clad in metal armour. The discarded spolas were piled in heaps and burned, possibly to keep them from the wrong hands, or possibly because they were worn out and insanitary.

On reaching the river, Alexander embarked the agema of the companions, all the hypaspists, the archers and the Agrianians on the boats. The main part of the army, with the 200 elephants it now included, was to march down the left bank under Hephaistion. A smaller force of infantry and cavalry was to proceed down the right bank under Krateros and a rearguard was to follow three days behind under Philippos. The Indian troops other than the elephant corps were to remain behind with Poros. The whole force moved downstream at the exceptionally gentle rate of five miles a day. By maintaining a land force on each bank and a squadron, Alexander had the option of moving the whole army against opposition from either bank.

The fleet made an impressive sight. The warships' sails had been dyed purple and their commanders had competed with each other to embellish them. All the boats kept in strict formation, and the calling of the strokes, and occasional rowing shanties when extra effort was called for, echoed between the banks where they were high. The inhabitants of the banks frequently took it for a religious procession, threw flowers into the water and danced and sung at its edge.

At first the rulers along the banks came in and submitted. However, further down lay the territory of the Mallians, openly hostile, and which had to be chastened if the Indus was to be a secure frontier for Alexander's empire. The situation was now complicated further by rapids at a confluence which damaged many of the warships, although not the more heavily built transports. After repairs, he split his forces in a different way. Nearchos was to take the fleet three days in advance and dominate the river. Hephaistion was to take a detachment five days in advance so that he could cut off any enemy fleeing from the rest of the army. If he moved fast enough, the tribesmen would not have time to concentrate sufficient force to do him harm. Alexander took a short cut through the desert with half the companion cavalry, the mounted archers, the hypaspists, one taxis of phalangites, the archers and the Agrianians. The main body including the elephants was to march downstream under Krateros, and Ptolemaios was to follow three days behind to intercept any enemy fleeing in that direction.

Alexander halted for the evening meal 12 miles on at the last waterhole, rested a few hours, filled every possible container with water, then marched on through the night. At dawn he was 50 miles away with his cavalry outside one of the Mallian cities. The Mallians were completely taken by surprise at being attacked from such an impossible direction. Many were killed and others fled into the city. Alexander waited for his infantry to come up, meanwhile cordoning off the city. When they arrived, he sent Perdikas with two units of companion cavalry and the Agrianians to surround the next city while he himself assaulted the first one. The tribesmen abandoned the circuit wall almost immediately. About 2,000 got to the citadel, but were overwhelmed and slaughtered in a fresh assault.

Perdikas found his city deserted by its inhabitants but pursued with his cavalry and killed many before the survivors took refuge in marshy terrain. Alexander fed and rested his men, and set out again at dusk, reaching a ford over the river Hydraotes. This is probably the modern Ravi, and the two cities may have been Kot Kamalia and Harapur. Most of the locals had already crossed in flight, but he slaughtered those he found there, and pressed on in pursuit of the others, killing as he rode. Most of the fugitives managed to seek refuge in a town which had been identified as modern Tulamba. Alexander left them to his infantry, who took the fortress at the first assault and enslaved the survivors.

Other Mallians had taken refuge in the neighbouring city of Aturi, which, however, was not a member of their own confederation. The inhabitants were driven from their brick walls by missiles, and these were then swiftly undermined, to be abandoned by their defenders who fled to the citadel. A few Macedonians who followed them inside were driven out again with heavy loss. Alexander ordered further undermining which brought down a tower and also breached a nearby wall. He then organised a combined assault on the two breaches and escalade with ladders. At first his men hung back, but were shamed into following when he attacked alone. The defenders, some 5,000 strong, declined to surrender and mostly died fighting.

Alexander now concentrated his detachments, rested them for a day, then led the army against the remaining Mallian cities. He found all those nearby to be deserted, so sent fresh detachments to beat the woods along the river banks for fugitives while he took the main body against the largest of the cities, to which many of the inhabitants of the others were said to have fled. They had indeed but, rather than try and hold it, they chose to cross the Hydraotes and defend its high banks. As soon as Alexander heard, he pushed on with the cavalry alone, crossed the river by a ford and sought to pin them in position with false charges until his infantry could come up. The Agrianians and archers were only a short way behind and so arrived quickly. Then the main body came into sight in the distance. The Mallians, now unnerved, broke and fled. Numbers were cut down, but most got into the most strongly fortified of their remaining cities, almost certainly modern Multan. Alexander made no immediate attempt to assault with his now utterly exhausted troops, but instead camped around the place.

Next day, he attacked it from two sides. The Mallians made no attempt to defend the circuit walls but withdrew to the citadel. Alexander forced his way in through a postern gate and made his way with only a few troops through the streets towards the citadel. The rest of his party had trouble filing through the narrow entrance which was all they had until the main gates were brought under control. The other assault was equally delayed by a shortage of ladders. Having got to the citadel, Alexander immediately organised an escalade with the troops available before the defenders could recover their nerve. Sensing reluctance on the part of the war-weary Macedonians, he again led the way up the first ladder to be planted and gained a foothold on the wall accompanied by two officers and a veteran NCO. Seeing this, the troops followed in a rush, and the ladder broke under their weight, leaving Alexander isolated and the prime target for archery from the dominating towers still in Mallian hands. He decided in a flash that he would be in no more danger if he leaped down from the wall on the enemy side, indeed might be a harder target, and that swift offensive action might break the enemy morale. He did so, accompanied by his three stalwarts, one of whom was shot as he jumped. They fought with their backs to the wall, killing several, until the enemy would not close but resumed shooting at them. One arrow penetrated Alexander's corslet to wound him dangerously in the lung.

As his two surviving followers tried to cover the wounded man with their shields, help came from outside. Some men tried to repair a broken ladder, others hammered pegs into cracks to climb up by, and yet others climbed on their comrades' shoulders. The first to get over leaped down to join Alexander's defenders, while others got control of a gate and let in their comrades. A grim massacre now ensued. The troops, almost hysterical about the danger they had subjected their beloved leader to, took their guilt out on the Mallians, leaving no living being to survive within the walls.

Alexander was carried back to the camp, where the barbed arrow was cut out. The sort of wound he had was almost invariably fatal, and none expected him to survive. However, his good health, physical toughness, luck and possibly his doctors pulled him through. To quiet apprehensions he let himself be seen on horseback, then walking a few paces, a demonstration which must have caused him agony as well as set back his eventual recovery. Then he had the gratification of receiving a Mallian delegation offering their submission.

The army and fleet now continued down river to the confluence with the Indus. Here another Alexandria was founded. Philippos was to have it as his satrapal headquarters with the Thracians as his garrison and was to build dockyards for a fleet to control the river frontier. Here Alexander was visited by Roxane's father and he made him satrap of the territories he hoped to conquer further down the river. He also despatched Krateros with the elephants and veterans to march overland through Arachotia to Susa and on west. Alexander had heard of an abortive revolt among the Greek mercenaries left in Baktria and probably considered that he could kill two birds with one stone, both giving his valuable elephants and worn-out soldiers an easier trip, and making a parade of force in a part of the empire he had not seen for some time.

He now started south again towards the state of a ruler called Musikanos, who was thinking of resistance but was frightened by Alexander's swift approach into meeting him with gifts instead. Further on, he took two cities by assault owned by a recalcitrant named Oxykanos, and then entered the domains of a King Sambos, where many cities submitted to him but one had to be taken by assault through an underground passage. Musikanos now revolted, was conquered by a side expedition, and was executed. Continuing south again, Sambos submitted, but this did not please the inhabitants of his capital who promptly revolted against him. They were lured out by an Agrianian raid, jumped by the rest of the army, and the weakened city then surrendered. Ptolemaios, among others, had been wounded by a poisoned arrow. Alexander personally took his treatment in hand and he recovered, whether by luck or judgement.

At last the fleet and army came to the city of Pattala at the head of the Indus delta, only to find that the inhabitants and ruler had fled. Alexander enticed them back, improved the city's fortifications, created new dockyards, and repaired his ships for the open sea. A first exploration down to the sea met with near disaster, Alexandria's Mediterranean sailors being totally unprepared either for the tidal ebb and flow which were unknown in their own sea or for the strong trade winds blowing constantly from the south, not from the north as all proper trade winds should! After repairs, it was decided that the fleet would not attempt to sail until the trades had died down in the autumn and been replaced with light land breezes suitable for a coasting voyage.

Having accumulated four months' supplies for the next stage of his journey, Alexander set out by land along the coast of Gedrosia, digging wells en route to provide water for the fleet which was to follow when the wind changed. This trip through the Gedrosian desert was to prove the most difficult and dangerous journey of his career. Although adequate supplies had been accumulated, the capacity of his transport to carry them through that terrain had been seriously overestimated. In addition, so many animals seriously overstrained the available water supplies; many died from exertion, or from lack of food and water; and many loads were lost. Rebellion broke out behind as soon as Alexander was well into the desert. The fleet was further delayed putting it down, and it may have disrupted supply arrangements even more. Both army and fleet were in distinctly poor condition when finally they were reunited on the far side.

The fleet was now reprovisioned and sent off to continue coasting to the mouth of the Tigris, then sail up the river. The army cut off inland to Persepolis, and on to Susa. Here Alexander found that the satrap had been taking advantage of his position, believing Alexander to be dead, as by rights after that lung wound he should have been. He was accordingly executed. The next event was a mass wedding, Alexander marrying both Daraios' elder daughter and the youngest daughter of the previous Persian king, and his senior officers marrying other daughters of the Persian nobility. He provided generous dowries for these women and for more than 10,000 other Persian girls'whom his soldiers had married during their adventures. As a further celebration, he paid off the debts of the whole army, at a cost to the treasury of 9,870 talents. A review was held of 30,000 Persian youths who had been trained during his absence in Macedonian military techniques and dressed and armed in Macedonian style. Also, the very best of the Asiatic cavalry which had served Alexander in India were incorporated into the units of the companion cavalry to fight in Macedonian style with lances instead of with Persian javelins. There were sufficient of these to justify organising an extra unit which, although mixed like the others, was given a Baktrian commander. These military innovations brought forth much grumbling from the Macedonians.

By this time, the fleet had arrived on the coast nearby. Alexander joined it, leaving Hephaistion to bring the army on by land. He sailed to the mouth of the Tigris which, unlike that of the Euphrates, was not blocked by a marshy delta, and then up the river removing various obstructions planted earlier by the Persians, who thought of the Tigris as an invasion route for enemies rather than as an avenue for trade. At its mouth he founded an Alexandria to serve as a counterpart to his naval base at the other end of the route on the Indus. This was to be one of his more successful foundations, greatly reducing the travel time to the east and vastly increasing trade.

He joined up with the army again at Opis. Here he announced that all over-aged and unfit veterans remaining with the army would be demobilised and sent home with an impressive discharge bonus. He must have thought that the army's recent performances in India showed that it was getting stale and cautious and that it would be all the better for a drastic pruning of dead wood. To his surprise and anger, he found that many of the veterans did not want to be discharged. They were no longer keen on fighting unless the odds were well on their side but neither did they want to return to the dull hard working life of a Macedonian farmer. They would rather remain in service and throw their weight around among these slavish Asiatics to whom Alexander was pandering. They adopted a policy of 'one out, all out'. To their horror, Alexander accepted this, and began making preparations for an all-Persian army. The strike collapsed in three days. About 10,000 Macedonians were now discharged to proceed home with Krateros, who was then to take over control at home. Antipatros was to come out east with sufficient recruits to replace them.

Rather than go straight to Babylon while the hot weather lasted, Alexander chose to pay a visit to the cooler Median hills. At Ekbatana, Alexander's life-long friend and trusted subordinate Hephaistion died. Alexander was at first inconsolable and ordered an extremely expensive funeral and monument, but then diverted himself with a punitive expedition against Kossian mountaineers, a term usually almost synonymous with bandit in the ancient world.

Alexander was now thoroughly sold on the advantages of sea power. He organised an expedition to the shores of the Caspian, where ships were to be built to explore that unknown sea. Timber from Lebanon and sails and cordage from Crete were to be taken to Babylon where a new fleet of 700 huge septiremes was to be built. These presumably would be taken by existing canals to the Tigris and down that river to the sea. The canal from the Mediterranean to the Red Sea which had long been completely silted up was to be re-opened, and Alexander's huge fleet of super-battleships would then be able to operate at relatively short notice anywhere between Gibraltar and the Indus, in time possibly further still.

His army was being scaled down. He had retained 2,000 Macedonian cavalry and 13,000 Macedonian infantry, and 10,000 replacements to augment these were to be brought out by Antipatros. He now had 10,000 Asiatics capable of serving as phalangites, plus 20,000 archers and slingers. His Asiatic cavalry had presumably been retained or, if not, could easily be summoned when required. Lastly, he had his 200-plus elephants. Up to this time, he had only used these for transport rather than fighting, but they were now organised as fighting units. Their Indian drivers were each accompanied by a Macedonian with his pike, an excellent weapon both for spearing a rival elephant's driver and for discouraging light troops from approaching to hamstring the beast. As the howdah was yet to be invented, the pikeman sat astride.

Who were these armaments to be used against? The only current opposition within the empire had been provided by Harpalos the treasurer who, in an attack of guilty conscience, had seized 5,000 talents, fled from Babylon and hired 6,000 mercenaries with ships to take them to Athens. The Athenians had admitted him, but later drove him out to Cyprus where he was knifed by a former friend. Macedonia was tranquil, and Alexander's mother had taken advantage of the death of the young king of Epiros on an expedition to Italy to seize control of his country. The fact that preparations were chiefly naval suggests a move to the west, and the fact that Alexander's ships were to be built at Babylon and not at Sidon or Tyre points strongly to Carthage. As you may remember, Persian attempts to move against Carthage had earlier foundered because the Phoenician sailors would not co-operate in an attack on their former colony. Alexander is known to have been hostile to the Carthaginians and to have had a particular dislike of their custom of burning babies as sacrifices. (Yes, I know modern apologists for the Carthaginians have cast doubts on the practice, but the archaeological evidence seems to me conclusive.) However, a preliminary expedition was to march against the Arabians to curb their robbing and get the new troops' hands in.

Alexander continued to Babylon. On the way he was met by a delegation of priests who asked him not to enter as the omens were bad. He seems to have suspected that their real motive was to hinder any enquiries into their financial affairs, and so disregarded the advice. The omens continued to be bad after his arrival. On one occasion the royal diadem blew from Alexander's head into the river and the sailor who rescued it put it on his own head as he swam back. On another, a stranger who had wandered into the palace was found sitting on Alexander's throne. Undeterred, Alexander kept working hard. He exercised the fleet, and tried out a new formation with archers and javelinmen occupying the centre ranks of a phalangite unit which, as it happened, was a failure, the missilemen being ineffective in that position and disturbing the pikemen's all-important cohesion. He oversaw the construction of docks for 1,000 ships, arranged for quinqueremes and quadriremes to be dismantled and brought overland to supplement present triremes and projected septiremes, and improved local irrigation schemes. After one of his boating trips, he became ill with a fever, worsened this by bathing and heavy drinking, fell into a coma, and died ten days later at the age of 32.

He left no obvious heir. Roxane was to give birth to a son shortly afterwards, but at that time the child's sex could not be foretold. When asked on his deathbed who was to succeed to his power, his voice was indistinct. Alexander may have said 'Krateros' but he was on the way to Macedonia, and the others chose to hear it as 'Kratistos – 'the strongest'. It was to take many years of warfare to find out who *he* was.

Chapter 17

Sequels and might-have-beens

Alexander had passed his seal ring to Perdikas, who had earlier succeeded to Hephaistion's job as chiliarch, roughly translatable as prime minister. He now urged in council that Roxane's unborn child should be accepted as Alexander's successor. This was not acceptable to the majority, and the final decision was that Alexander's idiot brother and Roxane's child, if male, should be joint kings; Perdikas was to continue in his post; and Krateros was to be regent over him.

Krateros was on his way back to Macedonia with the veterans. He would have been wise to return to Babylon and take possession of the heirs, but he had just heard that Athens had formed a league of Greek states and revolted, and that Antipatros was hard-pressed. He decided to carry on home, where his old gentlemen showed that even if not too spry at climbing Indian walls they could still sort out Athenians. The revolt was quickly settled.

Perdikas now started throwing his weight around and permitted Roxane to murder all Alexander's other wives and girl friends. Antipatros and Krateros did not like this and refused to take his orders; Ptolemaios quietly appropriated Egypt, with which he was quite content; and Antigonos-One Eye, who we have not heard of for some time, also took advantage of the situation. Perdikas resorted to force, sending his assistant Eumenes, a non-Macedonian Greek and lately Alexander's secretary, to fight Antigonos, while he himself fought Ptolemaios. Antigonos was then backed by Antipatros and Krateros, but Eumenes shook everybody by proving to be a superb soldier, and Krateros fell in battle against him. Perdikas manoeuvred against Ptolemaios until both armies got tired of it and tossed up to see which they should murder. Perdikas proved to be the unlucky one.

With both the regent and prime minister out of the way, Antipatros called a conference of leaders. Antipatros was appointed regent and took the heirs back to Macedonia. Antigonos became commander-in-chief and was commissioned to hunt down the outsider Eumenes. Eumenes made rings around Antigonos for a while before his army was bought out from under him and he paid the inevitable penalty. Ptolemaios retained Egypt and Seleukos kept the eastern provinces, where he was having trouble with one Chandragupta.

Chandragupta had been one of Alexander's Indian subordinates and acknowledged that he had learned a lot from the example. He now intrigued and fought himself into control of the Indian empire which the Macedonians had not let Alexander attempt, then started leaning on Poros and Seleukos. He disposed of Poros, and bought Seleukos' Indian provinces off him in exchange for an enormous number of elephants.

Antipatros now died and was replaced by Polyperchon, a respected, senior, but second-rate Macedonian general. Since he was not clever, he was probably picked for his honesty. None of the rulers accepted him, and even his second-in-command, Antipatros' son Kassandros, rebelled.

Kassandros drove Polyperchon out of Macedonia into Greece. Polyperchon brought Olympias in on his side from Epiros, and she murdered the half-witted half-king. This lost her public support, and Kassandros captured her in turn, handing her over to the relatives of her many victims for fast requital.

Antigonos and his son Demetrios were starting to look much too powerful in Asia Minor and Ptolemaios and Seleukos combined against them. The two affairs were now linked by the fact that Kassandros could not stand Demetrios, who had been a little too funny at his expense on some occasion. By this time Kassandros held Macedonia and southern Greece, Polyperchon was in control of Thessaly, Thrace was held by Lysimachos who was currently allied to Kassandros, and Ptolemaios had expanded into Syria. The new war started as Antigonos versus the rest, but he acquired Polyperchon as an ally and held his own. A truce from which Seleukos was excluded resulted. Antigonos, however, made little headway against him.

When hostilities broke out again in the west, Demetrios succeeded in driving Kassandros out of Greece, then defeated Ptolemaios in a great naval battle off Cyprus which left him with complete naval superiority. Antigonos tried to invade Egypt but failed. Kassandros now simplified the political situation by murdering Alexander's son, and the war ended with each leader proclaiming himself king of whatever he currently held.

With the last of Philip's dynasty dead, there was little chance of the empire being unified again. When the dust settled, it left Antigonos' descendants ruling Macedonia and Greece, those of Ptolemaios governing Egypt, those of Seleukos in Syria, an Iranian dynasty from Parthia east of them, and the descendants of Chandragupta in India.

When it comes to guessing what might have happened had Alexander recovered from his fever, history books are obviously little help. However, we can look to the greatest of modern historians for guidance. In his book, *Some Problems of Greek History,* published by Oxford University Press in 1969, Arnold Toynbee includes three essays, one on the role of the individual in history, another on what might have happened had Philip not been murdered when he was, and the third on what the result might have been of Alexander's recovery. These light-hearted but scholarly romps are thoroughly recommended as an antidote to Marxist historians and their concentration on great economic and social tendencies which produce inevitable results.

Briefly, Toynbee's alternate history starts with Alexander agreeing to obey his doctors. The Arabian expedition is successful and opens up the sea route from Babylon to Egypt. The canal is re-opened, and the capital of the empire becomes Alexandria-in-Egypt. Tyre is refounded, and Phoenician colonies are planted along the trade route to India at Kuwait, Bahrein, Kism, Aden, Tajurra Bay and Masawa. Among those to emigrate are the worshippers of an obscure god called Yahweh, who henceforth cease to be a nuisance to anyone.

Alexander now sails to Thrace which he pacifies, sends reinforcements to Antigonos in Kappadokia, and sends his mother to rule the island of Socotra for her health and his own peace. Antipatros dies and is replaced by Leonnatos. Kassandros is not employed and flees to Carthage. Ptolemaios is sent to Sicily and organises a confederation of cities similar to the league of Corinth. Agathokles of Syracuse joins Alexander's staff.

Carthage is attacked and conquered and a new Alexandria set up at Gibraltar. Alexander reads an account of Pytheas' recent explorations beyond the straits and makes him a large grant for follow-up work. Africa is circumnavigated.

Italy is next. Samnium has just beaten Rome in a war for which Rome seeks revenge and gets it as Alexander's ally. A league of Italian cities is set up which will restrict future Roman expansion. The Samnites are deported to India.

Alexander returns to India, completes his conquests, and imports Buddhist priests whose religion spreads fast through the empire. A new expedition is sent into what is now China. It finds the state of Chin busy conquering its neighbours, who unite with Alexander to crush it, and then form yet another league. The Phoenicians establish a sea route.

Alexander finally dies at the age of 69, but has been senile for some time and his son by Roxane has long taken over rule. Demetrios rebels in China and is put down. Hannibal son of Hamilcar discovers America in the reign of Alexander's great grandson. Two reigns later, the ruling descendant encourages Heron to invent a workable steamship.

The author dedicates his history to the current world ruler Alexander LXXXVI!

Chapter 18

Organising and running an Ancient wargames campaign: guidance for umpires

A wargames campaign needs an umpire, players to take the roles of important characters, people to play off battles on the table, a map, a list of characters and resources, sets of rules for the campaign moves and the resulting table-top battles, and means of communication.

The umpire
The umpire is almost certainly the instigator of the whole thing. He produces the map, keeps track of what is happening, produces the character and resources lists, writes the campaign rules and communicates with the players. He gets his enjoyment from being the only person involved who knows everything that is going on, seeing the various stratagems of the players develop, writing news for general consumption, and sometimes from fighting the battles.

There are two things he must not do, both of which are proved by repeated experience to be sure death to any campaign. One is that he must not control a character himself. The second is that he must not attempt to run the campaign democratically, obtaining player's opinions and votes on rule or organisational questions. This can be relied on to bog the whole thing down in delay and recrimination, and is, moreover, unrealistic. The real world declines to alter laws of nature to suit human preconceptions and a campaign umpire should run his own world the same way. If this leads to apparent injustice, well, that's good training for life. Heaven maintains a suggestion box but no complaints department.

Funnily enough, it is not necessary for the umpire to be strictly neutral between players, although he normally should be. Some characters, such as Alexander for instance, appear to have been luckier than most men, so can have the odds of any dice throw altered somewhat in their favour. The umpire can also reward or reprove players, as suggested under 'Role of the gods'.

What qualities does the perfect umpire need? He should have a deep interest in human nature, a well-developed sense of humour, at least a moderate knowledge of his period, be hard working, literate, hard to bully but easy to convince, and should have plenty of spare time! The best umpires are also very likeable people, this probably helping them survive the occasional wrath of the players.

Characters
These are divided into those played by people and those who are not, the latter

usually being called 'cardboard characters'. Of course, the other players do not necessarily know if a character is cardboard or not, and it is advisable for umpires occasionally to provide evidence intended to confuse this situation.

Players should, if possible, be picked to correspond psychologically with their characters. For example, an indecisive, defensively minded Alexander, a rash Parmenion, or a treacherous Hephaistion could have exceedingly strange effects on the course of the campaign. Players should be told the attributes of their characters and warned that seeking to act outside that framework may be penalised by the umpire in proportion to the gravity of the transgression. They may not, in fact, know when they are penalised as the usual penalty is to weight some dice throw against them.

The player to avoid or weed out ruthlessly if he sneaks in is the chap who cannot answer letters promptly. The first few times this occurs, it should be assumed that the character was ill, drunk or dallying, so that his troops either carried on what they were doing already or remained inactive. Against an active player this can have drastic consequences. If the behaviour persists, an obituary should appear deploring the character's death from natural causes, alcoholism or an outraged husband's sword. The character is then succeeded by his second-in-command and a new player recruited to control him. This method is preferable to having even an important character taken over by a fresh player. After all, Alexander might have died of his fever in Kilikia. The goal of the campaign is not to enforce a pre-ordained victory, but to enable players to compete freely in a historical context.

Cardboard characters must also have attributes. In some cases these will be partly known from history, but in others they will have to be decided by the umpire by throwing dice. Two different methods of doing so in detail are included in Tony Bath's book *Setting up a Wargames Campaign*, but you will be able to devise other methods for yourself. It is not necessary to establish attributes for every character at the start of the campaign. It can equally be done when events during the campaign first make it necessary to know a character's attitudes.

Characters' attributes should be treated as relative and potential, rather than fixed. For example, a tendency to treachery would be far more likely to become actual in an unreliable profession such as that of an Athenian politician than in a normally honourable one such as that of an Athenian serving as a mercenary. Such tendencies could also possibly be moderated by gratitude for services rendered, worsened by a desire for revenge or being short of money, or merely disappear through long disuse.

Attributes are usually used by the umpire to weight the score of a dice which he is throwing to find out how a cardboard character will act in a specific instance. For example, if dicing to see if a muleload of silver will induce the commander of a Persian fortress to open its gates, the umpire might decide that a six must be scored if the commander is an honest mercenary, politically opposed and paid up to date, while a two would suffice if he were a Persian, slighted by the king, demoralised by a recently lost battle, with a garrison nine months in arrears, and of marked treacherous tendencies. Most decisions affecting cardboard characters should be taken in this way, although occasionally the appropriate action may be so obvious as to obviate the need for dicing.

The sort of attributes worth enquiring into may include bravery, loyalty, greed, racial prejudice, ambition, energy and honesty and their lack. Some campaign umpires also take into account looks, relatives, personal fighting skills, charisma, health and age. This is largely a matter of the particular campaign and the umpire's approach.

The campaign map

The umpire obviously needs a master map on which he can follow the movements of the various forces. This need not be in great detail, so long as distances are shown to scale, the main areas of difficult terrain indicated, and important cities marked. The sort of detail shown in the maps in this book, including only those cities which are capitals of provinces or otherwise strategically important, and only those rivers which are major obstacles, is usually sufficient. However, if you want to have fun researching and building up a more detailed picture, don't let me stop you!

The ideal map would be outline traced from a modern map of 1:5,000,000 scale, giving a total size of about four feet by two feet for the area Alexander fought over. The ancient cities and major topographical features should then be marked in, the whole thing watercolour-washed in appropriate shades if you want it to be pretty, then fastened to a piece of softboard from a DIY shop. Coloured map pins can then be stuck in to show the positions of armies after the last set of moves. There is no need to mark the map in squares or hexagons to show move distances. Real maps of the time did not have them and it's just as easy to measure distances straight on to the map when needed. Also, the practice of marking maps off in hexagons encourages the idea that armies can move anywhere. In practice, there were only a few practical routes for armies, and these were followed time and again.

The master map is for the umpire's use. The players must never be allowed to see it except possibly after the campaigning season has finished and before preparatory moves for the next season have started. They should instead have partial copies of their own. These should show the land occupied by the player himself in full detail, show neighbouring territory in less detail, and have only vague information at the best for more distant regions. The player can add more information as he gets it.

Lists of resources and characters

Basic lists for an Alexandrian campaign are given in a later chapter. Players are entitled to know their own resources, but not necessarily the true characters of their subordinates or the resources of their neighbours. If the umpire withholds some of the information on these grounds, it will not only make the campaign more realistic, but also encourage sales of this book, in my opinion two *very* good causes!

Campaign rules

Basic suggestions are made in a later chapter, but these must remain the prerogative of the umpire, who can at any time change a rule in order to get a more realistic result next time, although not to alter a decision already reached. He can also invent a rule off the cuff to cover a situation not previously foreseen. In my opinion, the player should have only the most limited knowledge of the mechanics of the rules, mainly confined to how far he can expect to move in average conditions. If he wishes shipping to be collected to ferry his army across a strait, he does not need to know that there are x ships to each 100 miles of coastline or how to work out the weather. Instead, he orders 'Let shipping be collected at Byzantion'. The umpire then does the necessary, and writes back 'Ten large and five small ships arrived at Byzantion from north by May 1, but unfavourable winds have prevented any arriving from south. Despatch boat sent to Kyklades to find others has not reported back. Rumours that Persian squadron recently left Halikarnassos. Do you wish to start crossing with ships presently available or wait?' This means that the decisions the player has to make are those which a real general would have to.

Battles

Umpires usually like to fight the battles resulting from campaign moves themselves, pressing local friends into service to act as opponents. Indeed, many campaigns start off as a mere excuse for the umpire's battles, although he usually quickly develops other interests. If the character players live locally, they can always fight their own battles. However, a more common approach these days is for the umpire to have two separate crews of players, one for the campaign, the other for the battles.

If the umpire is fighting the table-top battles, he can obviously pick any set of rules he likes, or even write his own. If he wishes to compile his own, he will find quite enough information on weapons and tactics earlier in this book to let him make a good shot at it. He can even play it out as a board game, although that is not for me. In my opinion, board-gaming techniques, although adequate for the strategic sphere, are much less so in the tactical. Besides which, a well-painted metal figure is much prettier than a square of cardboard.

If other people are doing the fighting, it is likely that they will wish to use the rules published by Wargames Research Group which for the last ten years have been the international standard set. As the co-author, it would ill-become me to tell you how good they are, but I will say that their reaction test feature makes them especially suited to campaign battles. This is a provision by which the troops themselves can over-ride their commander's intentions in response to a locally favourable or disheartening tactical situation. However, the perfect set of rules has yet to be written, ánd it might turn out to be yours. We, of course, hope it will be our own next set!

The same arguments that I used to justify the character player being ignorant of the campaign rules apply with equal force to the battle rules. All he needs to do is plan dispositions and write orders as if he were a real general. If the set of rules used are reasonably accurate, all he then has to worry about is the possibility that the other side has better dispositions and orders.

I apologise to any readers who were expecting to find a set of battle rules included. The cruel fact is that even if copyright permitted their duplication, the 50 pages they occupy would just not have fitted in.

Communication

There are three types of communication. The first is between the umpire and an individual player. The player sends in orders at regular intervals, and in return receives a sitrep (situation report) telling him the latest position of his troops, what has happened to them, any information he would have gained on enemy troops and plans, and possibly asking for special decisions.

The second is communication between player and player. Ideally, all such communications should go through the umpire so that he knows what is going on and can enforce transmission delays. Sanctions he can apply include not acting immediately on orders deriving from information that has not passed through him, and in treating such information as unfounded rumour. This means that if it is untrue, the gods will take no action against the fabricator.

The third is communication between the umpire and all the players. This usually takes the form of a campaign newspaper such as Tony Bath's *Shadizar Herald* and Bruce Douglas' *News of the Known World*. These are a favourite part of the two campaigns in question, supplying much genuine and some misleading information and a great deal of amusement. Their primary function is to keep the interest of those whose areas are currently quiet by telling them what is happening elsewhere. The *Herald* at various times printed a fair amount of quite good epic poetry, to the chagrin of the well-known player that the verses were directed at by one of his rivals, and one memorable headline from the *News* was 'Hunnic plans are seldom simple. All good plans are simple. Not all simple plans are good'! I especially liked the story of the chieftain, who hearing a prominent and respected assassin was passing through, invited him in to make an offer – then found he already had a contract.

But surely there were no such things as newspapers in Alexander's time? Well, no, but there were equivalents. Travellers got free drinks at inns in return for news of foreign parts, and merchants kept their foreign trading partners informed. You could think of the equivalent as *News from the Merchants' Bar* or *Gossip from the Marketplace* taken down in writing by a ruler's scribe for his master's information.

The role of the gods

One problem in producing a realistic historical simulation is that the characters in real life held beliefs which we do not hold today. The degree to which the ancients actually believed in their gods is not entirely certain, but the evidence available suggests that some took them very seriously and sceptics found it safer to at least pay lip service. On the whole, the level of religious belief was probably higher than today, but this did not lead to intolerance, except of atheists. Followers of one set of gods were usually prepared to equate them with those of a foreign set, so that for example the Greek Zeus was considered the same as the Roman Jupiter and the Egyptian Ammon.

All the religions had one senior god to whom the others acted as assistants, advisors, friends and relations. His equivalent in an ancient wargames campaign is naturally the umpire. During this era, the gods were not expected to manifest themselves by personal appearances, raining fire on disobedient cities, feeding multitudes in the wilderness, parting the waves or striking sinners dead with lightning bolts, although the latter may recommend itself as an occasional means of removing poor correspondents or players with the temerity to invent gunpowder or other technological innovations. Instead, they were believed to operate through portents, oracles, omens, prophetic dreams or visitations of ill-luck upon oath-breakers. All these are within a campaign umpire's competence.

The reason we include such provisions is that contemporary people did believe in such happenings and were influenced by them. If a modern player is to behave as though he believes, he must be given some incentive to do so, and this is the simplest way. The umpire must, of course, not let things get out of hand, and be equally prepared to penalise excessive superstition as irreligion, for example by delaying a march until after the completion of a religious festival.

Oracles

The most important oracles in this era were those of Delphi in Phokis, Delos in the Kyklades, Cumae in Italy, Dodona in Epiros, and Ammon at Siwa in Egypt. Requests from a character for an oracle should be accompanied by a gift to the shrine and a failure in generosity may provoke the umpire to withhold or slant the prophecy. Prophecies may also be slanted according to the interests of the shrine, bribes from third parties such as the Persian king, or the chance of a thwarted enquirer utilising armed force.

Prophecies from Delphi, Delos or Cumae must have the following characteristics: 1) they must contain genuine good advice to the best of the umpire's ability; 2) they must be capable of being misunderstood by the enquirer; 3) they must be obscure in language and allusion; and 4) they must be short. They will be communicated only to the enquirer and to such players as offer bribes. The enquirer can decide to publicise them if he wishes, for example to improve army morale. They become public when fulfilled.

Ammon and Dodona operate differently. They remain secret to the enquirer and are invalidated by disclosure, although hints or rumours may be acceptable. The only answers are yes or no. The enquirer must come personally to the shrine and is allowed two questions. The questions answered are those asked, which are not necessarily those the enquirer meant to ask! The priests of Ammon are likely to be prejudiced against Persia, so unresponsive to Persian bribes.

Portents

The umpire should maintain a list of portents, which can include such things as thunderbolts, temple fires, birth of freak animals, lightning strikes, red rain caused by African dust in the upper atmosphere, unseasonable snow, earthquakes, large hail stones, lights in the sky, comets, partial eclipses, tidal waves, volcanic eruptions, plagues and locusts. These should be called up sparingly by dice throwing. Two out of three should be genuinely random, the third employed by the umpire as a warning of trouble or danger in a given area.

Omens

It was the custom for an army's priests to consult omens before engaging in battle or starting a day's march. The usual method was to examine the liver of a sacrificial animal, but other omens could include the flight of birds or the feeding habits of sacred chickens. The amount of respect for such omens among commanders varied. Some are suspected by modern historians of fixing suitable omens for the courses they wished to persuade their men to. Others insisted on abiding by them even though this looked like, and later proved to be, tactical suicide. A general who wished to disregard an omen was normally followed by his men, but their morale would be reduced unless he thought of a way apparently to twist it in his favour. The well known story of William the Conqueror falling on his face on Pevensey beach has its precedents.

The umpire should not test for omens on every occasion possible, but only when requested by the player or when the situation or timing appears crucial. The test is made by throwing a dice. If the character has previously behaved in an over-superstitious way, two is deducted from the score. If the tactical situation is considered to be favourable or unfavourable, a further one or two can be added or deducted. If the score is now two or less, the omens are unfavourable and the player must be informed.

Prophetic dreams
The umpire can provide a limited number of prophetic dreams. These should be obscure and hard to interpret, and should not be more than a quarter of the dreams reported to players. They should be limited to players who are acting morally by ancient standards and retain the umpire's good will, and should never exceed one per campaigning season.

Irreligious behaviour
A player who acts in an irreligious manner by professing doubts about the gods, ignoring omens, breaking promises or looting shrines should be penalised by having his political support or troops' morale downgraded. Really serious offences against contemporary morality such as temple robbing or breaking a solemn treaty made at a shrine too quickly can be further penalised by bad luck. One convenient way is to use two dice for random decisions affecting the player and count the least favourable.

The umpire has room for discretion. For example, he may decide that moral strictures should not be enforced too harshly against folk such as Afghan hillmen or radical Greek politicians who know no better, or he may employ lesser sanctions against associates than against principals.

Another form of irreligious behaviour consists of annoying the gods in their umpire manifestation by arguing back or being slow to reply to letters. A player who behaves in such a way may find himself treated as a whited sepulchre even if he sacrifices and endows temples with the best!

The favour of the gods
It might be argued that these procedures enable the umpire to play favourites. However, every campaign umpire, no matter how honest, is always accused of playing favourites whatever the rules. It seems players find it hard to admit that their orders could have been inappropriate, their plans ill-conceived, their dice unlucky or their opponents more clever. Let them then strive to win the favour of the gods for themselves by getting into the spirit of their role, with quick, clear and concise orders, and with gems of political or strategic cunning that tickle his fancy!

Chapter 19

Taking part in an Ancient wargames campaign: the rules players work to

Just as the last chapter was intended primarily for the umpire, this one is aimed at the players and, although short, should give them all the information they need to control a character, except for the fact-files on the various states which are found in the next chapter.

Periodical sitreps

Each player will periodically be given a situation report telling him the latest position of any of his troops who are moving, the results of any fighting, his current immediately available financial resources, a warning of any unusual expenditure which may be required during the next campaigning period, and such information private to him as reports from his scouts or spies, the weather and forage situations in his vicinity, the apparent morale of his troops, and answers to specific queries he has put to the umpire. This sitrep should rarely exceed half a page of A4 paper and will usually be much shorter.

The news sheet

This will be sent to players at the same time as the periodical sitrep and is the same for all participants. It represents the 'grapevine' of gossip carried by merchants and other travellers. As the primary function of gossip is entertainment, the news is likely to be that of general interest, garbled, exaggerated or even fictitious. Some items may have been provided by players as a public relations exercise or to deceive potential enemies, so may be reported with a little editorial scepticism. The news sheet is the main source of information on what is happening elsewhere in the campaign and is always popular, so may build up to several pages in length as the campaign develops.

Orders

Each sitrep must be replied to as soon as possible, as the campaign cannot move on to the next stage until every player's wishes have been attended to. Failure to reply promptly will often cause troops to remain idle instead of reacting to other player's moves, being rationalised by the umpire as sickness or some other preoccupation of the character. Repeated failures will have to result in the player being written out of the campaign.

The news and orders cycle

Experience shows that the time taken to receive and process players' orders and to prepare the next sitreps and news sheet averages about a month. It is therefore convenient to have the period of campaign time they deal with also to equal a month. This provides an automatic reminder of time of year and so on. As few of us are familiar with the Greek months, a good compromise is to settle on 13 lunar months, each of exactly four weeks, merely numbering them I to XIII and the days 1 to 28. Since the ancient campaigning season seldom started before the growth of the first spring grass to feed the horses and transport animals, months I to III will usually be spent mainly in financial and political affairs, so may be combined into one sitrep.

Special sitreps and orders

As a lot can happen in a month, the umpire may have to refer back to a player where timing is important. For example, if the move ordered by the player for month V results in scouts sighting an enemy force on the 3rd of V, the umpire will write back with the information and ask for battle dispositions and orders. He will then probably have to come back to the player again with the result and ask for decisions on exploitation. However, anything that can conveniently be fitted into the usual cyclical reports should be.

Maps and moves

Each player will be provided with a small map showing his own territory. This will probably be supplemented with further maps traced from parts of the umpire's master map as he moves into new areas.

The rate at which movement takes place across the map will vary according to the number and type of troops involved, the difficulty of the terrain, the weather, nationality and the energy of the character in charge. Forced marches will concentrate a given amount of movement into less days but, as extra compensatory rest days must be taken, will not increase the total monthly move. They are also likely to lead to loss of men and animals through straggling and exhaustion.

Although the actual distances covered must be at the umpire's discretion, the following distances per day can be taken as a guide to daylight movement in good weather. At least one day in ten must normally be a rest day. Bad conditions will naturally affect the slower troops and transport columns more.

	miles
A previously prepared relay chain of mounted messengers in friendly country	50
A single mounted messenger, if for only one day	50
An entirely mounted army force-marching up to three days	40
A combined mounted and picked lighter infantry force force-marching up to two days	30
A Skythian light cavalry force	30
Other entirely mounted forces	20
A mainly European force of mixed cavalry and infantry	15
A European mixed force including baggage and siege train	10
An Asiatic army	10
Ships	60

Finance and supply

Troops are expected to feed themselves from their pay, buying food from sutlers with the army. Their pay is split into two parts, ration allowance and salary. Ration allowance is due at the start of each month and will automatically be paid on your behalf by the umpire so long as you have any cash left. Failure to pay it means instant mutiny, desertion and probably the general's murder. Salary is in theory due at the end of each month and will be paid only when you order this. Troops will usually stand being in arrears of salary, so long as they are paid up to date by the end of the campaigning season. Troops are normally paid only ten months a year, taking the other two as unpaid leave. Remember to arrange for your garrisons to go on leave in two halves.

Rates of pay can be varied. A heavy demand for mercenaries will put up the cost, and peace or bad harvests bring it down. Higher pay rates will improve troop morale and loyalty. Bearing these factors in mind, the following are the likely average wage costs per month for 1,000 land troops or a warship crew, allowing for officers' pay.

	Talents ration allowance	*Talents salary*
Cavalry	4·0	4·5
Hoplites	2·0	3·0
Regular peltasts	2·0	2·0
Light or irregular infantry	2·0	1·0
Trireme	0·35	0·2
Quinquereme	0·65	0·5

Other costs, such as those of fortifications, ship building or siege equipment, must be requested from the umpire.

The normal taxes and financial reserves at the start of the game are specified in the next chapter. Reducing taxes will normally improve a player's political support so long as this is not too obviously a short-term ploy. Conversely, increasing taxes will create political opposition, possibly rebellion, add to the cost of collection, and reduce future prosperity.

A bad harvest will enhance the bad effects of excessive taxation.

Scouting and spying

The umpire will normally assume an army to have scouts a few miles in front of it, except when force-marching. Longer-range reconaissance must be specified by the player, who must send a minimum of 200 men and lay down the direction they are to follow.

Spies must be paid for and given specific instructions. The player risks them turning out to be conspicuous, incompetent, gullible, unable to count above ten, or double agents. He may also invent and specify measures to be taken to detect any spies in his own camp.

Battle

Battles will often be fought out on the table-top by the umpire or his assistants, so will be largely outside the campaign player's control. However, there is nothing to stop him telling the umpire in advance if he has any favourite tactics in given circumstances. These can then be incorporated when appropriate.

Other characters

How many of these are controlled by players, and how many are 'cardboard' characters controlled through the umpire by chance devices such as dice, will obviously depend on the number of volunteers available. A player may not know who the other players are. All communications with other characters should in any case go through the umpire.

Chapter 20

A gazetteer of states and provinces for an Alexandrian wargames campaign

While much of the following information is reasonably authentic or at least conforms with known information, even more than usual is plain guesswork. However, it is certainly consistent enough to allow a reasonable campaign.

The incomes quoted are in attic talents of silver and represent the cash available for maintaining an army or navy, or for bribery. Income may vary ten per cent or more depending on the local harvest, and may be reduced by as much as 50 per cent when a province has been repeatedly ravaged by armies. Cash reserves include not only bullion and coin, but quickly realisable property. Unless otherwise stated, they are assumed to be located at the national and provincial capitals, and will fall into enemy hands if these are captured. If reserves are spent on a large scale, this will have an inflationary effect which is best simulated by cutting all real incomes and remaining reserves by one per cent for each 5,000 talents net withdrawal from reserves totalled over all countries. Greek states may also find it possible to borrow from bankers. The arbitrary limit set is one year's income, and the minimum interest rate for a moderate risk is five per cent per month. States can also borrow from each other at whatever terms the players agree.

The troop totals quoted represent those men the government can muster at short notice and who are of appreciable fighting value. Persians and other easterners can hire any quantity desired of very poor-quality infantry at standard irregular rates, but they are unlikely to be worth the expense. Any state can also hire western mercenaries, but there are a finite number of these to be competed for. All cities and towns are assumed to be defended by their inhabitants. In most cases, the oldest eighth of the soldiers was retained for home defence. Each year, a fortieth of the theoretical strength is added as recruits, a fortieth of the actual strength is added to the veterans, and a twelfth of the veterans die of old age. Mercenaries usually retire instead of becoming veterans, and are either lost to the army or can be transformed into military colonists. Mercenary recruiting is doubled in poor harvests. Troops start paid to date and rationed for a month.

Ships are expensive, but can be laid up when not required, taking one month to get back into service. They can be built only in places where timber and skilled shipbuilders are both available. Rhodes, Cyprus and Phoenicia have both; Greece and Egypt have shipyards; Macedonia and India have timber. Most ships available at the start are triremes, but one-tenth are pentekonters or smaller, and another tenth can be quadriremes or quinqueremes.

State	Income	Reserve	Ships	Troops	Rulers	Capital
Macedonia	500	132	10	2,600 companions 600 prodromoi 3,000 hypaspists 25,000 phalangites	Alexander as king	Pella
Thessalia	175	70	5	4,000 cavalry 20,000 hoplites	Alexander as elected leader	Larisa
Chalkidike	100	50	10	2,000 hoplites	Incorporated into Macedonia	Olynthos
Thrace	500	100	20	6,000 cavalry 10,000 peltasts 2,000 javelins 1,000 hoplites	Incorporated into Macedonia, but kings still rule inland tribes with Alexander as suzerain	Philippoi
Epiros	80	50	5	20,000 peltasts 2,000 cavalry 2,000 archers	Alexander of Epiros	Dodona
Agrianes	30	25	0	5,000 javelins	Langaros, ally of Macedonia	
Paionia	30	25	0	1,500 cavalry	Alexander as suzerain	
Dardanoi	60	50	0	10,000 peltasts	Kleitos the Illyrian	
Adiaioi	10	25	0	5,000 peltasts	Glaukias the Illyrian	
Autariatai	10	25	0	5,000 peltasts	Kleitos as suzerain	
Triballoi	60	25	0	10,000 peltasts	Syrmos	
Kelts	60	25	0	20,000 peltasts	Brennos	
Danube Skyths	30	25	0	5,000 h/archers		
Thebes	175	150	0	12,000 hoplites 2,000 cavalry	Oligarchy	
Boeotians	25	25	0	4,000 hoplites	Reluctantly subject to Thebes	
Phokis	50	0	0	2,000 hoplites	Democracy	Delphi
Aitolia	30	10	5	2,000 javelins	Democracy	Naupaktos
Akarnania	30	10	5	2,000 javelins	Democracy	
Athens	400	50	60	10,000 hoplites 1,000 cavalry	Democracy	
Corinth	100	100	10	5,000 hoplites	Democracy	
Achaia	40	10	0	2,000 javelins	Democracy	

Region				Forces	Notes	Cities
Arkadia	100	100	15	8,000 hoplites 2,000 cavalry	Anti-Spartan alliance of cities	Megalopolis
Lakonika	200	50	10	5,000 very good hoplites 500 cavalry	King Agis and an oligarchy	Sparta
Euboia	100	50	10	2,000 hoplites	Divided into pro- and anti-Athenian blocks	
Kyklades	80	40	15	0	Alliance of islands	Delos
Crete	30	50	5	2,000 archers	Theocracy plus bandit chietains	
Rhodes	175	100	30	2,000 hoplites 1,000 slingers	Democracy	Rhodes
Ionian Islands	200	50	10	0	Spithridates (Satrap)	Mytilene
Bithynia	167	50	10	1,000 cavalry	Arsites (S)	Daskylion
Mysia and Lydia	450	500	10	2,000 cavalry	Also Spithridates	Sardes
Karia, Lykia and Pamphylia	320	50	10	1,000 cavalry 3,000 javelins	Orontobates (S)	Halikarnassos
Pisidia and Phrygia	200	50	0	1,000 cavalry 5,000 peltasts	Atizues (S)	Kelenai
Kilikia	650	50	20	1,000 cavalry 1,000 javelins	Arsames (S)	Tarsos
Kappadokia	200	50	0	2,000 EH/cavalry 5,000 cavalry 5,000 peltasts	Mithrobuzanes	Mazaka
Paphlagonia and Pontos	100	25	0	5,000 L/cavalry	Also Atizues	Sinope
Armenia	520	50	0	3,000 EH/cavalry 2,000 L/cavalry 20,000 cavalry 5,000 archers	Orontes (S)	Artaxata
Cyprus	155	150	120	0	Daraios suzerain of kings: Pnytagoras of Salamis (Anti-Persian) Androkles of Paphos Pasikrates of Kition	
Phoenicia	300	100	0	1,000 cavalry 2,000 archers	Mazaios (S) over 5 local kings:	Damascus

State	Income	Reserve	Ships	Troops	Rulers	Capital
Phoenicia *continued*		25	40	0	Gerostratos	Arados
		25	40	0	Enylos	Byblos
		50	50	0	Straton	Sidon
		50	80	0	Azemikos	Tyre
		50	0	0	Batis	Gaza
Egypt and Kyrene	910	800	10	1,000 archers 2,000 cavalry 2,000 archers	Sabakes (S)	Memphis
Arabia	100	25	0	5,000 cavalry 5,000 camelry 5,000 archers	Several independent chieftains	
Assyria and Babylonia	1,300	500	0	1,000 cavalry 20,000 peltasts 200 chariots	Bupares (S)	Babylon
Susiana	390	65,000	0	2,000 cavalry 15 elephants	King Daraios Oxathres (S)	Susa
Media	585	500	0	3,000 cavalry 20,000 peltasts	Atropates (S)	Ekbatana
Persia	0	126,000	0	4,000 cavalry 20,000 peltasts 4,000 archers	Ariobarzanes (S)	Persepolis
Kadusia, Kolchis and Hyrkania	910	50	0	1,000 cavalry 5,000 peltasts	Autophradates (S)	Zadrakarta
Karmania	780	50	0	2,000 L/cavalry	Satrap not known	Karmana
Parthia	80	25	0	2,000 cavalry	Phrataphernes (S)	Hekatompylos
Margiana	70	25	0	1,000 L/cavalry	Satrap not known	Merv
Aria	80	25	0	1,000 L/cavalry	Satibarzanes (S)	Artakoana
Drangiana	70	25	0	1,000 L/cavalry	Barsaentes (S)	Prophthasia
Arachosia	80	25	0	1,000 L/cavalry	Also Barsaentes	Kandacha
Gedrosia	520	25	0	1,000 L/cavalry	Satrap not known	Pura
Gandara	70	25	0	5,000 archers	Proexes (S)	Kapisa
Baktria	467	50	0	1,000 EH/cavalry 8,000 cavalry	Bessos (S)	Zariaspa

Province				Forces	Ruler / notes	Capital
Sogdia	80	25	0	1,000 L/cavalry; 3,000 archers	Oxyartes (S)	Marakanda
Massagetae	150	100	0	2,000 EH/cavalry; 5,000 H/archers	In theory acknowledge Daraios in practice hardly their own king	
Dahae	100	50	0	5,000 H/archers	As Massagetae	
Chorasmia	80	100	0	2,000 cavalry; 4,000 archers	King Pharasmanes. In theory accepts Daraios as suzerain	
Sarmatae	150	100	0	2,00 EH/cavalry; 4,000 H/archers	Independent tribes	
Peukala	60	100	0	30 elephants; 2,000 cavalry; 30,000 infantry	Astes	
Taxila	30	200	0	30 elephants; 1,000 cavalry; 4,000 infantry	Omphis	
Paurava	87	300	0	285 elephants; 420 chariots; 5,000 cavalry; 30,000 infantry	Poros	
Sangala	30	200	0	20,000 infantry	Sangalos	
Mallia	100	200	0	900 chariots; 10,000 cavalry; 80,000 infantry	Sudrakatos leads league of several cities	
Minagara	30	100	0	1,000 chariots; 300 cavalry; 20,000 infantry	Musikanos	
Sindomana	100	100	0	500 chariots; 6,000 cavalry; 60,000 infantry	Sambos	
Patala	30	100	0	20,000 infantry	Soeris	
Magadha	1,000	500	0	3,000 elephants; 2,000 chariots; 20,000 cavalry; 200,000 infantry	Ksandrames	Palimbothra

If a ruler's name is not given it is because it is not known and it is impossible to make a reasonable guess. If no capital is stated, this is either because the capital of a city state is naturally the name city, or because nomads have no capital.

The following numbers of European mercenaries are available for hire at the start of the game.

Hoplites up to Spartan		Archers	5,000
standard	30,000	Slingers	2,000
Lower-quality hoplites	20,000	Javelinmen	5,000
Peltasts	15,000	Heavy cavalry	2,000

The following collections of names will do for generals on detached service in addition to the rulers already listed.

Macedonian: Parmenion, Antipatros, Kleitos, Krateros, Hephaistion, Koinos, Antigonos, Ptolemaios, Perdikas, Seleukos, Polysperchon, Niarchos, Eumenes, Leonnatos.

Persian: Rheomithres, Petines, Niphates, Mithridates, Rhoesaces, Arbuphales, Pharnaces, Mithrines, Sisines, Autophradates, Pharnabazos, Datames, Bubakes, Artabazos, Kophen, Arismas, Oxathres, Spitamenes.

Mercenary: Memnon, Omares, Hegistratos, Lykomedes, Thymondas, Amyntas, Aristomenes, Bianor, Chares, Pantalion, Ombrion the Cretan, Klearchos, Aeschylos, Ephippos.

Bibliography

Contemporary histories of Alexander's campaigns were written by Kallistenes, Ptolemaios son of Lagos, Aristobolos, Niarchos and Onesikritos. None of these survive, but several other ancient texts based on them do. These are all available in translation in the Loeb Classical Library series published in England by William Heinemann Ltd, and in America by Harvard University Press. They are currently in print and can be bought at bookshops or obtained from any medium or large public library. They are:

Arrian: *History of Alexander and Indica* Two volumes (Also in Penguin, but without Greek).
Curtius, Quintus: *History of Alexander* Two volumes.
Plutarch: *The Parallel Lives* Alexander.
Siculus, Diodorus: *History* Book 17.
Other Loeb books useful for background are:
Aeneas Tacticus, Asclepiodotus and Onasander (Tactical manuals bound together).
Frontinus: *Stratagems*.
Herodotos. Four volumes.

All modern works are based on these, sometimes with a few extra facts added from other sources, from personal visits to sites, or more rarely from archaeology. The authors cited occasionally have useful insights. However, many of them have a distressing tendency to go beyond the evidence, and so should be treated with caution. Do not trust them implicitly (or trust me for that matter). Go to the Loeb books and decide for yourself if the evidence warrants their opinions. The opinions differ anyway, and so they cannot all be right. The most important modern histories are:

Burn, A. R.: *Alexander and the Hellenistic Empire* (English University Press, 1947).
Green, P.: *Alexander the Great* (Weidenfeld & Nicolson, 1970).
Lane Fox, R.: *Alexander the Great* (Allen Lane and Longman, 1973).
Tarn, W.: *Alexander the Great* (Cambridge University Press, 1948).

All but the first, which is unfortunately the hardest to get hold of, are at their weakest when dealing with the armies and fighting. Tarn, in particular, should be disregarded in those respects unless you can also read the articles by Brunt and Griffith in the *Journal of Hellenistic Studies*, 1963.

The best history of Philip is:

Ellis, J. R.: *Philip II and Macedonian Imperialism* (Thames and Hudson, 1976).

Useful modern works on the army side are:

Bar-Kochva, B.: *The Seleucid Army* (Cambridge University Press, 1976).

Greenhalgh, P. A. L.: *Early Greek Warfare* (Cambridge University Press, 1973).

Griffith, G. T.: *The Mercenaries of the Hellenistic World* (Cambridge University Press, 1935).

Marsden, E. W.: *The Campaign of Gaugamela* (Liverpool University Press, 1964); and *Greek and Roman Artillery* (Clarendon Press, 1969).

Parke, H. W.: *Greek Mercenary Soldiers* (Clarendon Press, 1933).

Scullard, H. H.: *The Elephant in the Greek and Roman World* (Thames and Hudson, 1974).

Snodgrass, A. M.: *Arms and Armour of the Greeks* (Thames and Hudson, 1967).

Last, but I hope not least, the following can be obtained from the Wargames Research Group at 75 Ardingly Drive, Goring by Sea, Sussex:

Ancient and Medieval Wargames Rules 3000 BC to 1490 AD.

Barker, P.: *Armies of the Macedonian and Punic Wars.*

Bath, T.: *Setting up a Wargames Campaign.*

Nelson, R.:*Naval Wargames Rules for Fleet Action 1000 BC to 500 AD. Armies of the Greek and Persian Wars* and *Warfleets of Antiquity.*

Basic information for the beginner can be found in:

Barker, P.: *Airfix Magazine Guide 9: Ancient Wargaming* (Patrick Stephens Ltd, 1975).